MORLEY COLLEGE

A 125th anniversary portrait

MORLEY COLLEGE

A 125th anniversary portrait

GENERAL EDITOR: **JANET SACKS**

THIRD MILLENNIUM
PUBLISHING, LONDON

Morley College: A 125th anniversary portrait
© 2015 Morley College and Third Millennium,
an imprint of Profile Books Ltd

First published in 2015 by Third Millennium,
an imprint of Profile Books Ltd
3 Holford Yard
Bevin Way
London
WC1X 9HD
United Kingdom

www.tmiltd.com
www.profilebooks.com

ISBN 978 1 908990 36 5

Edited by Janet Sacks
Designed by Helen Swansbourne
Production by Debbie Wayment
Reprographics by Studio Fasoli, Italy
Printing by Gorenjski tisk, Slovenia

Front cover: *The Rebuilding of Morley College*
by Kathleen Allen, 1957

Inside cover: A tap dance class at Morley pays tribute
to Charlie Chaplin. Chaplin lived very locally to the
College and performed in the music halls of south
London before moving to Hollywood to find fame and
fortune. However, that did not include Lambeth's
'people's palace': the College's founder, Emma Cons,
rejected his application to perform at Morley's home,
the Old Vic, for the want of a self-addressed envelope!

CONTENTS

PREFACE

Jonathan Miller giving a Penny
Lecture on 20 September 2012

WHEN I WORKED for Laurence Olivier at the Old
Vic theatre 40 years ago, I was unaware of the
fact that Emma Cons, the philanthropic
founder of what we now know as Morley College, leased
this theatre as a location for providing affordable entertainment and education for the local community within
the Waterloo district. This egalitarian enterprise was
generously supported by Samuel Morley, after whom this
admirable institution is now named. In its many years,
the College has been staffed by a succession of outstanding artists, musicians and visionary teachers, many of
whom are mentioned in this book. So that now, 125 years
after this remarkable educational establishment was
inaugurated, it is generally recognised as one of the most
valuable resources in London for public education, both
formal and informal, for young and old alike.

What the College provides is an astonishing range of
disciplines and instructions, the variety of which could
scarcely have been anticipated when Emma Cons
initiated it so many years ago. But then Morley has
always been in the forefront of what is happening, and
has constantly moved with the times.

And here am I at the age of 80, excited by the prospect
of engaging myself in one and maybe several of the art
classes which are on offer. Apart from the skills which I
hope to acquire, it will be a great pleasure to be engaged
in the social life for which this noble institution is so
widely appreciated. I wish Morley success for at least
another 125 years.

JONATHAN MILLER

FOREWORD

Learning for Life

FOR 125 YEARS, many thousands of students have enjoyed and benefited from the vast and wonderful array of courses at Morley. This volume hopes to provide a potent insight into the infinite variety of learning contained in the College's history. That history shows Morley's foundation to be part of the radical social reform movements of the 19th century which sought to tackle discrimination and inequality, including lack of education, poor health and housing. It was born of a vision of equality and most remarkable for the times – indeed a landmark in the history of the women's movement – was that Morley should be open not only for working men, but also for working women. This vision of equality has permeated the College's history in many different ways and continues to remind us of Morley's role in making learning accessible to all.

It is a history influenced by the imperatives of the age and often described in relation to the many distinguished figures who have shared their knowledge and skills in Morley's classrooms. However, it is also a history of the magic that takes place in every classroom, day and evening, between the people drawn to Morley as students and the many professional and experienced tutors whose major vocation is that of teacher.

What draws people to a college which promises skills and opportunities to try something new or just learn for the sheer pleasure of learning? For some, a qualification may be important, but most are motivated by something less tangible than formal qualifications and more appropriate to their individual circumstances and ambitions, which may change over time. Many are also motivated by the collective experience of learning, what the Quakers, the early founders of much adult education, called 'fellowship'. The practice of bringing together the interests and needs of the individual and the experience of collective learning depends on the ability of teacher and student to work together as partners in an 'atmosphere of fellowship', where the teacher builds on the motivations of each student and the common needs of the group to enable learning.

The success of this 'fellowship' depends on the skills of teachers: government initiatives, fashions, technological innovations come and go, and they bring new thinking about teaching and learning – with varying impact! However, it is undeniable that much of the outstanding teaching that takes place at Morley is down to the passion and subject expertise of teachers, high expectations, well-planned lessons and teachers' ability to provide inclusive practice to meet the individual and diverse needs of students. Whilst the infinite variety of what is offered at Morley responds and changes with the times, all depends on the magic of the interactions within the classroom. This does not happen by accident.

While it is impossible to cover everything that Morley offers, the pages that follow embrace teaching, learning, achievement, self-improvement, transformational experiences, spiritual fulfilment, social engagement – and also fun and enjoyment. Morley has been teaching for 125 years; our students have, throughout, been learning for life.

ELA PIOTROWSKA

MORLEY'S
STORY

buttress   blue and green   watcher tower   purple and gold   Spanglet   Salmon   comet

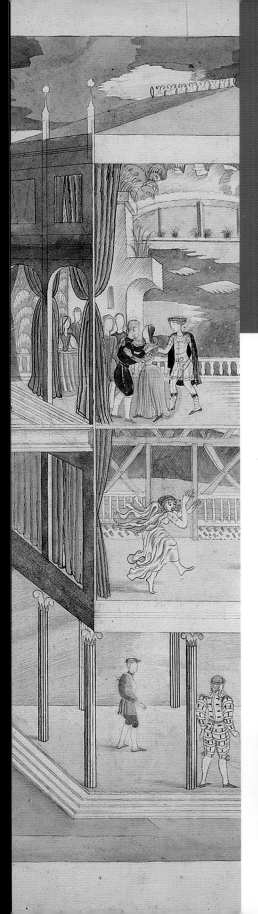

Morley's First 50 Years

DENIS RICHARDS, from *It Might Have Been Worse: Recollections 1941–1996,* chapter 7

T HE COLLEGE OF WHICH I HAD improbably become Principal was arguably the country's foremost centre of adult education. It had a remarkable history, stemming from the days when Emma Cons, artist turned social reformer, had taken a lease on the notorious 'Old Vic', the Royal Victoria Theatre in the Waterloo Road. Backed by the temperance movement she had transformed this, in 1880, into the Royal Victoria Coffee Hall. Banishing crude melodrama and suggestive variety from the stage, and strong drink and prostitutes from the

LEFT: Detail of a sketch by Eric Ravilious c.1930 for one of the murals in the Refreshment Room, all of which were destroyed during the Blitz

BELOW LEFT: The Royal Victoria Hall, late 19th century

BELOW: The original college entrance

saloons, she had set out to provide wholesome entertainment for the local working classes in teetotal
surroundings. Only on Saturday nights, however, had
the receipts from this purified fare ever exceeded the
expenses. It was to save money on artists' fees that Emma
Cons introduced, on the slacker nights, such economical
attractions as temperance meetings and 'penny popular
scientific lectures'.

The penny lectures, the first of which was on 'The
Telephone or how to talk to a man a hundred miles away',
were given unpaid by well-known scientists of the day.
They caught on among the more intelligent local clerks,
tradesmen and artisans, and soon led to a demand for
more regular instruction. In 1885 Emma Cons had
responded by providing evening classes in scientific
subjects in the spare dressing rooms – where she had
already started a 'working men's club' (canteen, games
room and reading room). Financial disaster still threatened, but was staved off by a small government grant for
successful examinees in the classes ('payment by results')
and by gifts from devoted supporters. Prominent among
these was Samuel Morley, Nottingham hosiery manufac-
turer, Liberal Cabinet minister, noted philanthropist, and
chairman of the Hall's governing committee.

Morley died in 1886. It was Emma Cons who cleverly
suggested that his memorial in London should take the
form of purchasing the freehold of the Vic and putting
the activities there on a permanent footing. An appeal to
the public brought in donations, and the newly consoli-
dated City Parochial Charities made a grant of £1,000 p.a.
Of this, £350 p.a. was specifically for the educational work,
which was to have its own separate part of the Vic
building. So, in 1889, came into being the Morley
Memorial College. It occupied the back end of the theatre
– its classrooms and social facilities, including a library
and gymnasium, being walled off from the auditorium
and running beneath, behind and above the stage. Its
foundation statutes defined its main object as 'the
advanced study by working men and women of subjects
not connected with any handicraft, trade, or profession'.
Uniquely for the time, it offered a liberal education to
working women as well as to men; and the presence of
social as well as educational facilities soon helped to
generate a strong collegiate spirit.

In the 20 years following its foundation, Morley College
developed a great range of evening classes, achieved

Gymnastics class
in 1895

financial stability on the basis of grants from the new
London County Council, and began to draw students from
a much wider area. Distinguished men and women
anxious to help their less fortunate brethren became
voluntary tutors, notable examples before the end of the
century being Graham Wallas, J. Holland Rose, P. Chalmers
Mitchell and G. Lowes Dickinson. In the first decade of the
new century, G. M. Trevelyan was to be found running a
History study group, Virginia Stephen (later to be Virginia
Woolf) an English literature circle, G. E. Moore a class in
Philosophy, and Ralph Vaughan Williams a class in the
History of Music. In the early 1920s, Bertrand Russell (who
for his second venture in matrimony married the
daughter of the College Council chairman) was offering a
class in Psychology, and Harold Laski and Hugh Dalton
classes in Economics. And from 1907 an original genius,
Gustav Holst, appointed on the recommendation of his
friend Vaughan Williams, was forging for the College an
outstanding reputation in music.

The advance of the College, only temporarily checked
during 1914–18, had been seriously threatened in the early
1920s by developments in the theatrical half of the
building. Emma Cons's redoubtable niece, Lilian Baylis, a
much less amiable character than her aunt, had
succeeded to the management of the theatre at the turn
of the century and had become passionately committed
to the cause of popular Shakespeare and opera. She
became determined to present them nightly at prices
that all could afford. In the Vic she was desperately

Graham Wallas

cramped for room, and she badly needed the College part of the building. Her chance came when the London County Council served notice on the Vic to improve and increase its dressing accommodation or else lose its theatrical licence. A struggle followed, with the College agreeing to move if the Vic paid for suitable premises elsewhere. The Vic of course had no money; but a theatrical impresario, (Sir) George Dance, turned up trumps and wrote a cheque for £30,000. With the help of the major part of this, the College moved in 1924 to an adapted and enlarged building half a mile away in the Westminster Bridge Road. It had originally been an 18th-century house, built on land leased from the Magdalene Hospital for Penitent Prostitutes. Later it had become a Yorkshire Society School and finally the Britannia Club for Soldiers and Sailors.

The opening of these new premises by the Prince of Wales in 1924 brought the College still more into the public eye. So too did the public lectures by eminent men and women and a notable series of murals completed in 1929. Following the success of Rex Whistler's light-hearted

murals in the Tate Gallery restaurant, their sponsor, Lord Duveen, had been persuaded to finance similar decorations at Morley. He paid three recent students of the Royal College of Art – Edward Bawden, Cyril Mahoney

MY PARENTS AND MORLEY

KATHERINE DARTON

Morley College was very important to my parents, Reginald and Marjorie, who met there. Although my mother had gone to a good school and on to further education, my father had left school at 14, so Morley was particularly important to him. The middle one of three children, he was born in 1905, and lost his mother in 1913; his father remarried and went on to have four more sons, and he had to leave school because the family needed him to go out to work. But he was highly intelligent and he really valued education: 'Morley College for Working Men and Women' was exactly what he needed.

I don't know when my parents each started going to Morley, but they met, probably in about 1930, in the Spanish class, where the teacher was called Peppi (who lived in Harrington Square – which they remembered giggling about because it was the name of a type of nappy), and they made life-long friends who became our unofficial 'aunties' when we were children, and came to stay –

which was when the reminiscences tended to happen. My father was a student rep and knew some of the staff quite well. They were also very keen members of the Rambling Club. London at that time was smoggy, with 'pea-soupers' in which people sometimes had literally to feel their way home; it must have been all the more wonderful to spend a day in the fresh air of the countryside.

My parents married the day the war started (3 September 1939, filling sand-bags while queuing for a special licence, they said) and, like many people, delayed starting a family until the end of the war. They lived in Streatham throughout the war, my father serving in the Civil Defence; he never spoke of

that part of his life, which must have been grim. In the early 1950s they made the life-changing decision to move to Suffolk, so their days at Morley must have ended with the end of the war. But they used to talk about Morley a lot – I knew about Emma Cons, Lilian Baylis, the College's beginnings with classes at the Old Vic, Mrs Hubback, the Edward Bawden murals in the refectory. They spoke of Gustav Holst and his daughter Imogen (who my sister and I met much later with Suffolk Youth Orchestra), and Michael Tippett. When, in the 1960s, my examiner for Grade 6 music exams was Priaulx Rainier, I was surprised that my parents knew of her and were able to tell me something about her – they must have met her at Morley where she was part of Tippett's circle.

Morley College enriched their lives so much, not just with the education it provided, but also with the friendships made, and the social life that developed as a result.

Terracotta frieze by George Tinworth showing Samuel Morley and students

and Eric Ravilious – the princely sum of a pound a day (or ten shillings half a day) to decorate Morley's bleak Refreshment Room and Concert Hall. The resulting works of art displayed remarkable qualities of design and wit and were hailed as inaugurating a new era in British mural painting. The opening by Stanley Baldwin . . . was widely reported, and Queen Mary quickly expressed a wish to see the new murals. She became interested in the College, and when a new and handsome addition – a classroom block, a library, and a chamber music room publicly subscribed in memory of Holst – was built in 1937 to the designs of Sir Edward Maufe, she readily agreed to perform the opening ceremony.

So matters stood, with a flourishing and increasingly beautiful College, and a student roll of 3,300, when war broke out in 1939. Hostilities brought a brief closure for the installation of black-out and other precautions, but in the absence of enemy action the classes and clubs were soon re-started, and the session ended successfully. Then, in September 1940, the German bombing of London began. Unable to hold classes at night, the College arranged to run weekend courses in daylight, beginning in mid-October. Meanwhile it took in some 250 local men,

women and children who had been bombed out of their homes in the first attacks. On the evening of October 15 1940 a parachute-mine descended directly on the concert hall. Fifty-seven of the shelterers lost their lives, another 50 were severely injured, and the entire fabric of the College, with the exception of the new steel-framed wing of 1937, collapsed like a house of cards.

Samuel Morley

BY 1883, EMMA CONS'S attempt to reinvigorate the insalubrious Royal Victoria Theatre, which she had reopened as the Royal Victoria Hall and Coffee Tavern on Boxing Day 1880, was seriously faltering. Her purpose had been clear: to improve the Waterloo neighbourhood by stopping the drinking and soliciting associated with the Vic and 'elevate the character' of the entertainment. Its variety acts, as described by one supporter, now comprised 'comic songs, clog-dancing, hornpipes, acrobatic performances, minstrelsy, performing animals, comic ballets, and such like – the ordinary entertainment at music-halls, but cleansed from objectionable matter'.

Samuel
Morley

That supporter was one Samuel Morley, a Nottingham-shire (and later a Bristol) MP, a successful businessman (his manufacture of woollen garments became the largest in the world), and a respected figure in the worlds of noncon-formism, philanthropy and politics. Such entertainment, together with the ballad concerts, temperance meetings, lantern lectures, opera excerpts sung in costume and accompanied by illustrative tableaux, and the newly formed Royal Victoria Choir (a precursor to the College's many and varied vocal ensembles), may have been 'improving', but did not pay the bills. As the struggle to balance the books reached its lowest ebb in 1883, Emma Cons wrote to Morley who, abroad and ill at the time, answered merely that he would enquire into things on his return. He remained true to his word and provided £1,000 towards buying the remainder of the theatre's lease from the Coffee Music Halls Company, removing the burden of rent and so enabling its good works to continue.

But he didn't stop there. As chairman of the Executive Committee, Morley assumed a leading role in the running of the theatre. Despite innumerable other interests, he still found time for small and thoughtful acts, such as sending holly from his estate in Kent to decorate the theatre at Christmas, and took a detailed interest in the Vic's development. In a speech at Grosvenor House, he spoke of the work at the Hall:

> I have been to the Royal Victoria Hall several times. I don't know that I have ever laughed so much as on these occasions. I believe in good hearty laughter, it tends to health. The great object of these attractive entertainments is to win people from the public-house … many must have been won to a better life by the kind of entertainments offered, including, as they do, admirable lectures, which are listened to with deepest interest by large audiences.

It is slightly ironic, given how much the Old Vic depended on aristocratic patronage in its early days, that Morley declined the offer of a peerage as he did not agree with the principle of a non-elected chamber.

Samuel Morley died in September 1886, but not before providing further financial assistance and helping develop one of the Hall's growing attractions, its lecture series, which he encouraged and often chaired, into the antecedent of today's College. When in September 1889 the College opened its doors, it was as the 'Samuel Morley Memorial College for Working Men and Women' in honour of its late benefactor.
NICK RAMPLEY

Morley's Manor

WHAT WERE THE social conditions in North Lambeth and North Southwark at the time of Morley College's foundation; if they were as bad as some commentators say, why did the College even survive, let alone thrive; and who were its first students?

Inner South London – by which is meant the area between Waterloo in the west and Rotherhithe in the east – was, in the 1880s, a challenging area in which to start an adult education college. While there was certainly a need among its disadvantaged residents, there was little evidence at the time of strong demand. The area can be characterised as hosting all the attributes essential to a city, but to which it never wants to draw attention: industry, trade, communi-cations, people, poverty, immigrants/incomers/new residents, the marginalised, antisocial and polluting activities, lawlessness and low-life entertainment.

This is amply confirmed by statistics, statement and anecdote. The population was significantly greater than that of today (20,000 or so people live in Waterloo today, against 86,000 in 1891) and the problem of space in which to live was compounded by a much higher pro-portion of land given over to industry. Public health statistics were correspondingly shocking: in St George's, Southwark, in the 1890s, one-fifth of children died before their first birthday. The sensational and influential pamphlet *The Bitter Cry of Outcast London*, published in 1883, described an area just off Borough High Street:

An engraving by Henry Rushbury of housebreakers in Lambeth, 1886

However, this bleak picture is not all it might seem. There were areas of relative affluence, such as the Georgian houses along Kennington Park Road, or well-built and well-managed developments such as the Trinity House estate near Great Dover Street. There were also examples of housing reform, such as the new model tenements of the 'five per cent philanthropists', the name given to institutional housing providers in the late 19th century that set out to provide housing of a better standard to that of most private landlords, but also wanted to make a commercial return on it (five per cent?). This they did, for instance, by charging higher rents, enforcing tenancy terms on prompt and full

Charles Booth's poverty map of 1891, covering Waterloo and showing areas of relative deprivation. Dark blue indicates the very poor and red, the middle class

There are . . . some 650 families, or 3250 people, living in 123 houses. The houses are largely occupied by costermongers, bird catchers, street singers, liberated convicts, thieves and prostitutes . . . Entering a doorway you go up six or seven steps into a long passage, so dark that you have to grope your way by the clammy dirt-encrusted wall . . . the walls are separated only by partitions of boards, some of which are an inch apart . . . In this room an old bed, on which are some evil-smelling rags, is, with the exception of a broken chair, the only article of furniture.

One of the surveyors working for Charles Booth's poverty survey of the late 1880s forthrightly said of Redcross Place, off Borough High Street: 'There is in this round a set of courts and small streets which for number, viciousness, poverty and crowding is unrivalled in anything I have hitherto seen in London.' This was against the background of an unregulated private housing market, where most people rented. A largely indifferent state at either national or local level had little inclination and few powers or resources to interfere in matters of welfare, housing, education or public health.

Prevalent industries were food processing – Sainsbury's, Oxo; brewing – Courage's and the hop trade; printing – HMSO; riverside wharves; engineering – the Rennies at Blackfriars Bridge; power generation; and further east in Bermondsey was the leather industry. A scattering of bone boilers and catgut makers added further colour. Work was mostly unskilled and casual.

Workers from Terry Bros, plaster of Paris manufacturers, Kennington, 1880

ABOVE: Crown tavern, Vine St, Waterloo, 1898; and TOP: Jonas Smith moulders, Waterloo 1898

payment, and not permitting subletting. Examples of these tenements are Peabody dwellings and Emma Cons's own scheme in Kennington.

The late 1880s and 1890s were a period of significant social and educational activity. Settlements, which were centres for social and educational work often set up by universities or schools, were established, such as Cambridge House on Camberwell Road (1889) and the Women's University Settlement in Nelson Square (better known as Blackfriars) of 1887. In 1890 there were 20 or so temperance lodges in the area; there were adult lectures being given at Lambeth Baths; public libraries were opening, such as St Saviour's in Southwark Bridge Road in 1894; Borough Polytechnic was established in 1892.

Crucially, Emma Cons's lectures came half a generation after the establishment of universal state education – the London School Board provided 15,000 places in the area in the first decade after 1870, producing a new generation, more literate, more numerate and possibly more curious than the one before.

The 1880s were also a time of change in employment, with an increase in clerical work and for this group, as well as skilled manual workers, came shorter and more predictable working hours. Both groups had some disposable income and leisure time. There had also been a recent and rapid growth in suburban housing, such as Brixton and Peckham, and Morley was as accessible from these places as it was from Waterloo or the Borough.

The College's Annual Reports are silent about where students lived, but they give a detailed analysis of their occupations, and this gives a clue as to students' social status and motivation, and allows us to assess if the College was enrolling students from the groups in society

that it hoped to attract. The largest group by a huge margin (always a factor of three over the next highest) were clerks. This was a title as unhelpfully vague, and probably representing the same pretension and aspiration, as the modern executive. It was a group whose excesses were satirised by George and Weedon Grossmith in *The Diary of a Nobody*. They were a new phenomenon in London: literate, numerate, ambitious, sometimes prosperous and with leisure time, and one that largely colonised the new suburbs: in 1901 Camberwell had more clerks than in any other area. The next most numerous occupations in the reports were skilled artisans: engineers and those associated with the printing trades. Gradually as the 1890s progressed, other groups appear, such as teachers and apprentices, and women, some identified by trade, such as dressmaker or servant, some as wives.

So Morley College in its fragile early days was one of a number of organisations working to better the lot of the working classes. What is exceptional is not that it was doing this, but firstly, that it was in the vanguard of such initiatives and was highly unusual in that it admitted women on an equal basis to men, and secondly, that it survived. Its survival was due in part to the energy and imagination of staff in providing an appealing curriculum which balanced educational and recreational activities, but also to Cons's ability to weather the College's regular financial crises. She did this by securing and retaining a generous grant from the City Parochial Charities fund, which in the early years was the single biggest income source by far, and also by her persistent and persuasive powers of raising funds from elsewhere.

LEN REILLY

Emma Cons

BORN IN 1838, Emma was one of the seven children of Frederick and Esther Cons. The family's fortunes changed when Frederick became ill, and it was necessary for the daughters to earn money. Emma trained as an artist, first at the Art School in Gower Street, and then at the Ladies' Co-operative Art Guild, set up to provide 'employment for ladies with artistic ability'. Here she met Octavia Hill, with whom she formed a close friendship.

Emma found work as an illuminator, where she attracted the attention of John Ruskin, who engaged her to restore some of his manuscripts. She discovered the delicate craft of engraving the backs of watches, and became a skilled engraver. Later, she became the first woman employed at James Powell & Sons' Whitefriars Glass factory, designing and restoring stained glass, including the restoration of some windows of the chapel of Merton College, Oxford.

In the late 1860s, Emma began to redirect her energies to what became her main passion: better housing for the poor. She and Octavia Hill assisted in a new project for housing in Paradise Place, Marylebone. Emma devoted an increasing amount of time to housing work, going further than Octavia in her concerns for improving her tenants' lot by organising concerts and trips to the country for them. In 1879, Emma persuaded some of her wealthy philanthropic contacts to invest in the building of a tenement to be called Surrey Lodge, at the junction of Lambeth and Kennington Roads. She chose to live on site so that she could intervene when necessary and come to her tenants' aid, not least that of wives seeking protection from drunken husbands returning from taverns and music halls. Ever practical, she was known never to be without a penknife and ball of string, and was not averse to undertaking odd jobs herself.

Emma's determination to fight alcohol abuse led her to take over the music hall in Waterloo, which became the Royal Victoria Hall and Coffee Tavern, run along temperance lines. She introduced science lectures for the local working people, and as their popularity grew, Emma started science classes in some of the disused dressing rooms; from these small beginnings came the Samuel Morley Memorial College for Working Men and Women. Although Emma's time was taken up with duties managing the Vic, she tried to slip into the College for a

few minutes every night, and remained the Honorary Secretary until her death.

Emma was known for practising strict economy, as reported by Edith Marvin, Secretary of the College in 1896. On a visit to Hever, Miss Marvin found herself cutting thistles with Emma, whilst learning much about Emma's work and outlook on life. The cottage at Chippens Bank, a small farm in Hever, Kent, belonged to her great friend Ethel Everest, and was Emma's weekend retreat. She and Ethel regularly entertained groups of students there. When Emma died in 1912, her ashes were scattered at Chippens Bank.

Lilian Baylis, her niece, said of her aunt, 'There were two great passions in her life – her love of beauty and her devotion to temperance.' Catherine Webb described Emma's photograph, which hung in the Common Room, as a completely satisfying picture of a charming yet vigorous elderly lady of the nineties. Her sweet face with its firm chin framed by the strings of the dainty

Chippens Bank, c.1906. Ethel Everest seated on left, Emma in centre

bonnet, and her neat workmanlike dress and coat, are so altogether becoming that no one can call it 'old fashioned'. She died in 1912, old in years but still young in heart and mind, never looking back, but always to the future, planning for the betterment of those for whom and with whom she worked so long and so successfully.

This same photograph now hangs outside the hall which bears her name.

The *Morley College Magazine* of June 1920 contained an appreciation of Emma by James S. Clough, who described her as 'A most enthusiastic and energetic worker on behalf of the students. She was strongly in favour of treating men and women on an absolute equality and always this principle of equality has been maintained.'
ELAINE ANDREWS

Eva Hubback

E va Hubback was born Eva Marion Spielman in 1886. She was educated at St Felix School in Southwold, Suffolk, and studied economics at Newnham College, Cambridge, where her wide circle of friends included Rupert Brooke. After gaining a first-class degree, she worked for the Care Committee of the London County Council [LCC] and became a Poor Law guardian. Eva married Francis William Hubback in 1911; their

Hampstead house 'Threeways', designed by Charles Cowles Voysey, remained Eva's home until her death. (After the main College building was destroyed in the Blitz, it was Voysey to whom the College turned to design its post-war replacement.) Bill died in France of wounds received in 1917, leaving Eva with three small children. She taught economics briefly at Newnham in 1916/17, before becoming parliamentary secretary for the National Union of Women's Suffrage Societies. Later, she became president of the National Union for Equal Citizenship, which successfully campaigned for reforms to the laws affecting the rights of women and children.

Eva became Principal of Morley College in 1927, and soon made her mark on the rather dreary building by bringing in comfortable chairs, curtains and better lighting, and also improved the appearance of the Programme of Classes and Annual Reports. Among her many innovations was the introduction of class secretaries and open days, the first of which, in 1929, attracted over 2,000 people. She also started the tradition of the Annual College Dinner in 1928. She formed the London Council for Voluntary Occupation during Unemployment with Alan Collingridge, a member of the College Council; from this came the South London Orchestra for unemployed musicians, conducted by the young Michael Tippett. Eva introduced new lecturers and lively personalities to the Council, including her friend, Amber Blanco White.

Eva Hubback in 1947

CENTRE: Eva Hubback's memorial table outside the library

BELOW LEFT: Sculpture by D. W. Rowles-Chapman commemorating Eva Hubback on the wall of the College, 1963

BELOW: The first Annual College Dinner, held in 1928

Eva was a formidable letter writer, and many of her letters still exist in the College archives. Her energy for fund-raising attracted the interest of Queen Mary, who made a donation to the 1937 extension. It was through Eva that exhibitions of paintings appeared on the walls of the extension, one of them by Julian Trevelyan, whose uncle, historian George Macaulay Trevelyan, had lectured at Morley in the early days.

Eva was always accessible to the students, as evidenced in this quote from the *Morley Magazine*: 'Mrs Hubback is an amazing woman in the variety of her interest. And yet she is never too busy to lend a willing, sympathetic ear to any student who approaches her with any question or problem. Indeed, she welcomes such personal contacts with her ever-present smile and with her head characteristically perched to one side.' Her energy was legendary, getting up early in the morning to deal with correspondence. H. A. L. in the *Morley Magazine* (Autumn 1948) notes: 'Mrs Hubback's amazing robustness, physical and mental, has a deceptively still quality about it, like the motion of a spinning-top . . . the revived and thriving Morley of today is, not least, a monument to the unswerving purpose and seasoned experience of its present Principal.' Another student recalled that he was finding it difficult to pay for his courses, and Eva said, 'Well, in the case of people like you, whom we know, we just ask them to pay half-a-crown.' She also found time to write a book, *The Population of Britain* in 1947, as well as several papers on education and citizenship. During 1946–8, she represented Kensington North on the London County Council.

The bombing of the College in 1940 was a huge shock but, characteristically, within a few weeks Eva had drawn up plans for the new Morley, including a large Refreshment Room, art studios, a photographic studio with dark rooms, and a Common Room with two open fires to welcome the student and visitor. Sadly Eva's health had been impaired by constant hard work and she died unexpectedly in 1949, without seeing Morley rise from the ruins. A memorial fund was formed and the money (around £2,000) paid for a lectern, still used outside the Holst Room, a table near the Library, a sculpture on the outside wall, created in 1963 by D. Rowles-Chapman, and finally a history of the College, written by her successor Denis Richards in 1958.

ELAINE ANDREWS

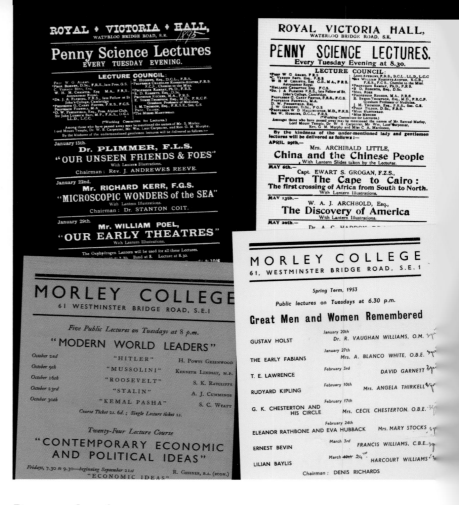

Penny Lectures

BY SUMMER 1882, the programme of 'improving' entertainments at the Royal Victoria Hall and Coffee Tavern (aka the Old Vic theatre) included talks with 'dissolving views', as lantern lectures were known. The success of these prompted Emma Cons to write to the scientific journal *Nature*, appealing to scientists to come and address her audiences. The idea of making the wonders of modern scientific developments accessible to all was not new, but there was little of the sort being held in London at the time and Emma's appeal drew a response from several distinguished scientists.

And so it was that in the autumn of 1882, William Lant Carpenter spoke to the Vic's rather mixed audience on the subject of 'The Telephone or how talk to a man a hundred miles away'. He was followed by his father, the distinguished physician and zoologist Dr W. B. Carpenter, the microscopist Dr William Dallinger, the astronomer Norman Lockyer, founder and editor of *Nature*, and others. From autumn 1883, the science lectures became the Vic's

MORLEY COLLEGE
61, WESTMINSTER BRIDGE ROAD, S.E. 1

Summer Term, 1952

Poets Reading

Poets reading and commenting on their own verse

At 6.30 p.m. on

Tuesday, May 6th	EDITH SITWELL
Tuesday, May 13th	LOUIS MacNEICE
Tuesday, May 20th	KATHLEEN RAINE
Wednesday, May 28th	JOHN LEHMANN
Tuesday, June 3rd	STEPHEN SPENDER

MORLEY COLLEGE
61, WESTMINSTER BRIDGE ROAD, S.E. 1

1942-43

Five public lectures on Tuesdays at 6.30 p.m.

THE BALLET

October 6th
ORIGINS AND DEVELOPMENT — A. V. COTON

October 13th
THE SADLER'S WELLS BALLET — NINETTE DE VALOIS

October 20th
CHOREOGRAPHY — RUPERT DOONE
(with demonstrations by Mary Skeaping)

October 27th
THE BALLET JOOSS — KURT JOOSS

November 3rd
THE DIAGHILEFF RUSSIAN BALLET — LYDIA SOKOLOVA

MORLEY COLLEGE
61, WESTMINSTER BRIDGE ROAD, S.E. 1

Session 1944-45

Seven public lectures on Tuesdays at 6.30 p.m.

WRITERS ON WRITERS

September 19th
SAMUEL TAYLOR COLERIDGE — STEPHEN POTTER

September 26th
WILLIAM BLAKE — J. BRONOWSKI

October 3rd
ALFRED, LORD TENNYSON — THE HON. HAROLD NICOLSON

October 10th
JOHN KEATS — STEPHEN SPENDER

October 17th
THOMAS HARDY — EDMUND BLUNDEN

October 24th
JOHN DONNE — KATHLEEN RAINE

October 31st
JOHN MILTON

MORLEY COLLEGE
61 WESTMINSTER BRIDGE ROAD, S.E.I

Public Lectures, Autumn 1938

THE ARTS TO-DAY

Tuesdays at 8 p.m.

4th	POETRY	WALTER DE LA MARE
11th	DRAMA	HARCOURT WILLIAMS
18th	THE NOVEL	J. D. BERESFORD
25th	ARCHITECTURE	EDWARD MAUFE
1st	PAINTING	HERBERT READ
8th	SCULPTURE	ERIC GILL
15th	MUSIC	EDWIN EVANS
22nd	THE CINEMA	THOMAS BAIRD
	THE BALLET	ANTONY TUDOR

Morley College is proud to launch a revival of the

PENNY LECTURES

COME AND
BE INSPIRED

PENNY LECTURES HAVE COME BACK

regular Tuesday night attraction, early lectures including such topics as 'Light and Colour', 'Air and Ventilation', 'Ancient British Glaciers' and 'Yankee Humour'.

With encouraging reviews in the press, the fame of the science lectures gradually spread, the audience growing to 700 or 800 strong. Prices were kept low: threepence in the balcony, tuppence for the pit and – giving the events their popular moniker – a penny for the gallery.

It was in 1884, after another William Lant Carpenter lecture, this time on 'Electricity', that two clerks approached Emma to ask for more systematic teaching in the form of regular scientific classes in the evenings. Their modest enquiry led, five years on, to the establishment of the Morley Memorial College for Working Men and Women. Meanwhile the lectures continued into the new century as part of the theatre's spread of activities (with free entry for College students) and began to broaden their appeal with subjects ranging from geography, history and literature to social issues ('Consumption', 'Adult Suffrage') and matters of practical utility ('How to Make a Garden in London' and 'Care of Your Horse').

When the College moved out to its new premises in Westminster Bridge Road in 1924, the lectures were dropped by the Old Vic. Forty-two years' worth of lectures would have been no small achievement, but the Council of the College was soon to suggest that the College should take up the baton and in the 1926/7 session, public lectures were delivered, free of charge, by social and economic historian R. H. Tawney, the industrialist and economist Sir Josiah Stamp and Lord Thompson. A full programme of lectures followed in the 1928/9 session, some 800 attending the first, which was Sir Oliver Lodge's talk on 'The Moon'. The Morley College Public Lecture series were to run for more than a further 30 years, the list of speakers who graced the series reading as a veritable who's who.

Their spirit lives on in the numerous talks and conferences that are part of Morley's activities even now. The College was particularly honoured in recent years to welcome the writer, director and polymath Dr Jonathan Miller, following in his father's footsteps: Dr Emmanuel Miller, a pioneer of child psychology, had been a penny lecturer in the early 1930s! And in its 125th year, Morley's Penny Lectures maintain their eclectic nature with talks ranging from surgeon Roger Kneebone's 'The Theatre of the Theatre' to Shami Chakrabarti, director of Liberty, 'On Liberty'.

NICK RAMPLEY

Morley's Wartime

Morley in the Great War

W HEN MORLEY COLLEGE broke up for the summer in July 1914, no one could have predicted the enormous changes that would take place in the months ahead. The first impact on the College was the reduction in the number of men, but the number of women increased, so that the roll dropped only slightly. Pre-war the number of women enrolled was 49.4 per cent of the total, but by 1918 it had risen to 77.9 per cent.

Classes continued with a greater demand for French and decreasing numbers wanting to learn German. The clubs, particularly tennis, cricket, cycling, men's gymnastics and swimming, were disbanded as their members were absorbed into the conflict.

Rationing took effect, as was noted in the *Morley College Magazine* in 1917, advertising the Easter Soirée: 'Owing to the Government's restrictions on food, it will not be possible to provide the usual refreshments, but tea, coffee, and biscuits will be served during the evening. Those who take sugar in their tea and coffee are requested very kindly to bring some with them.' Another article mentioned visiting a butcher and sampling horsemeat. Air raids became another problem; the Old Vic Theatre was used as a shelter, as shown in this jokey 'Notice to the Music students' in December 1917: 'Singing will begin at 7.30, and will continue until we are turned out (Mr. Church please note this), unless there is an air raid, in which case the singing will continue until breakfast time if not interrupted by an "All clear" signal.'

Morley College Magazine began to print a Roll of Honour from December 1914, listing all those serving in the forces. This first list has just 29 names. The Annual Report of 1915/16 noted, 'Month by month, the College magazine gave a list of members known to have joined the forces.' In the final list of April–May 1920, there were over 220 names, 26 of whom had died. The College Council was also depleted by several members joining the services, including Richard H. Tawney, Fabian Ware and Captain Chettle. The latter two were sent to France in 1914, and later worked for the Commonwealth War Graves Commission.

ROLL OF HONOUR.

PRIVATE F. BALLAM (French Club and Class), Royal Fusiliers.
RIFLEMAN C. H. BRABHAM, Empire Battalion, No. 3671, No. 10 Platoon, Section 6, Queen Victoria Rifles (Harmony Class).
PRIVATE H. S. BROCK, 14692 Royal Field Artillery.
PRIVATE S. BRESSEY (Harmony Class), G Company, 15th County of London Battalion, 4th London Infantry Brigade, 2nd London Division.
PRIVATE W. H. CANDY (French Club and Class).
PRIVATE G. V. CLARK (French Class), at Malta.
PRIVATE N. COURTINE, R.A.M.C.
RIFLEMAN C. COLES (Teacher of Singing Class), Queen Victoria Rifles.
PRIVATE G. F. FLYNN (Shorthand Class).
PRIVATE E. GROSS (Gymnasium Class).
PRIVATE W. G. GUIVER (French Class).
CORPORAL LOEBER (Harmony and Singing Classes), 3rd Company, Post Office Rifles.
PRIVATE F. J. LUCAS (Economics Class), 15th Battalion County of London Regiment.
PRIVATE T. J. MAYFIELD (French Class), 151 Section A, 3rd London, City of London Field Ambulance.
PRIVATE J. MARTIN (Shorthand Class), Expeditionary Force.
PRIVATE A. C. MORRIS (Book-keeping Class), London Irish Rifles.
PRIVATE J. H. NEILL (Shorthand Class). Civil Service Rifles.
H. A. PARKER (Book-keeping and Violin Classes), D Company, Naval Volunteers, 1st Division.
PRIVATE P. J. PARKER (Book-keeping and Typewriting Classes), 1st City of London, Royal Fusiliers.
PRIVATE T. E. POLAND (Gymnastics Classes), 12th Battalion, County of London.
PRIVATE L. W. PYE (Violin Class).
PRIVATE C. H. ROBOTTOM (French Class and Club), 13th County of London. Joined at beginning of war and has gone to France.
F. RUSSELL (Violin Class), Royal Navy.
PRIVATE STYLES. Old Student.
PRIVATE J. A. TILBY (French Class), London Irish Rifles, St. Albans.
PRIVATE A. WATKINSON (French Club and Class), 24th County of London, The Queen's London Regiment.
PRIVATE G. E. WATKINSON (French Class and Club), London

From November 1914, the *Magazine* started to publish 'Letters from students on active service'. These gave away surprising details of where the men were and what was going on. One was from Trooper Joseph H. Searl, who found himself in Egypt with the Imperial Camel Corps and gave an amusing account of how he met his camel for the first time (see page 134).

Two of the music students, Sydney Bressey and Cecil Coles, kept in regular contact with the College's Director of Music, Gustav Holst. They both composed music whilst in the trenches, and Bressey's piece, 'When soft voices die', was often sung at College concerts. Cecil Coles was already a successful composer and sent new compositions back to Holst. Sadly both men were killed. Bressey was awarded a Military Medal, one of four students decorated. Holst wrote in the *Magazine*, 'Cecil Coles was writing a suite for small orchestra in the trenches. Luckily he sent me the first movement before the rest was destroyed, together with most of his papers, by a shell. We hope to produce it and thus pay our last tribute to our old friend in the manner that would have pleased him most.' As part of the College's commemoration of the outbreak of the First World War and celebration of its 125 years of musical heritage, the Morley Chamber Orchestra

TOP LEFT: Cecil Coles; and ABOVE: the first roll of Honour, December 1914

INSET: Coles's manuscript for 'Behind the Lines: suite for small orchestra', with a note by Holst

Works by Cecil Coles were performed by the Morley Chamber Orchestra in a concert marking the College's 125th anniversary

performed Coles's 'Cortège', (a work much used by Channel 4 as the theme music for its First World War series), and the premier of a new arrangement of his 'Sorrowful Dance'. Holst himself had been rejected for war service on account of his short-sightedness and a neuritic right arm, but continued to inspire the remaining students without a break until 1918, when he took a year's leave to work with the YMCA, organising music for the troops in Salonika.

Those students left behind took up first aid and home nursing courses with enthusiasm, and formed a Red Cross Detachment. They raised money for a bed in the Shapter-Robinson Ward at the Hanover Park VAD Hospital in Peckham by collecting silver paper and tinfoil, and by holding concerts. In June 1917, the wounded soldiers from the hospital were entertained at the College. Tea was followed by music and recitations, and supper was served before the guests left by a special tram-car chartered for the occasion. One student, Miss Violet Filer, was given a Red Cross Society War Medal for her support of the war effort, in particular the Hanover Park VAD Hospital. She was also awarded the Martineau Memorial Prize in 1916/17.

The College roll rose dramatically with the end of hostilities and in the year 1918/19 numbers reached 1,216, surpassing pre-war levels.

ELAINE ANDREWS

Bombshell!

The bomb fell on Tuesday, 15 October 1940. The war was just 13 months old, but already the 'phoney war' of 1939 had given way to the 'invasion summer' of 1940. Norway, Holland and France had fallen and Dunkirk was recent raw history; the Battle of Britain had been won (the Luftwaffe had abandoned its attacks on RAF airfields) and

instead, from August 1940, London was being bombed. What had begun as a terrifyingly novelty (after the first raids, Civil Defence workers complained about crowds coming to stare) had now become a grimly familiar daily routine.

In September 1940, Morley College had been redesignated as a rest centre; the Gymnasium and

Bomb damage, 1940

GOVERNMENT HOUSE,
BAHAMAS.

12th January, 1941

Dear Colonel Chettle,

Thank you for your letter of October 29th informing me that the older building of Morley College, which I inaugurated in December 1925, has been completely destroyed.

I regret that the College along with so many Institutions in London, has become a casualty - and the loss of life in this instance is appalling. I am interested to hear, however, that it is proposed to resume normal working in the Extension despite the disaster that has overtaken the College.

An extract from a letter from the Duke of Windsor, 1941

Refreshment Room, with windows shuttered and blacked out, had been strengthened with sandbags and converted into emergency dormitories which, by October, were home to the bombed-out and displaced of North Lambeth. Several large blocks of flats had been bombed and left uninhabitable, and over 250 tenants were packed into Morley. When the raids were on, some would decamp across Westminster Bridge Road to the security of Lambeth North underground station, but most took their chance with the more comfortable camp beds in the Gymnasium.

When the 1000kg HE bomb fell at 7.45pm, it was dark and the moon was already up. It was a night of heavy raids and elsewhere in Lambeth bombs would fall on Ethelred Street (11 dead), Hercules Road (4 dead), St Oswald's Place (2 dead), Tinworth House (3 dead), Kennington Road (2 dead) and on the public trench shelters in Kennington Park. But Morley would be the biggest 'incident' that night. The bomb sliced through the Prince of Wales Hall and shattered the main College building from one end to the other, throwing masonry, brickwork and reinforced concrete into the air, which then fell on and demolished houses in King Edward Walk. The local wardens heard 'a heavy thud proceeded by a terrific swishing noise' and initially could see nothing as a huge cloud of dust was blotting out the moon.

Some 195 people were sheltering in the College that night; in the basement the dead and injured were found crushed and trapped between the collapsed walls and floors of the upper rooms. Civil Defence teams from Lambeth and Southwark had to cut people from the debris with saws and St Thomas church hall opposite became a temporary first aid post. Most of the 54 hospital casualties and 57 dead were got out in the first two days

of digging, but it took three weeks before the last body, Ellen Harman, was retrieved on 4 November.

Back in 1939 on the declaration of war, Morley's Principal, Eva Hubback, had resisted the concerted attempts of the LCC, Lambeth Council and the Home Office to close down the College. Instead and rather defiantly, Morley maintained its clubs (folk dancing, chess, French, film and German – and its Pacifist Group); students could still play badminton in the Gymnasium or tennis at its Eltham sports ground; and the Monday public lectures covered art, biology and the 'Psychological Problems of Wartime'. Now, immediately after the bombing, there was renewed pressure to close, but Hubback still refused to concede. Instead some unused rooms were discovered at nearby Joanna Street School and on the Saturday after the bomb, the College reopened there with 164 students offering 21 classes. Boxing, theatre classes and a paperback lending library were also started for railway workers in the shelters under Waterloo station.

Into this chaos came Michael Tippett. He took up the post of Director of Music at the end of October 1940 just as the last of the bodies were being dug out. Three-quarters of Morley had disappeared along with Ravilious's and Bawden's murals and the College archives. The orchestral performance space, the Prince of Wales Hall, was destroyed – but then the Orchestra and the Choir had shrunk to a mere nine players and eight voices between them.

Morley's post-war main entrance

The one building that survived was the 1937 extension. By December a path had been cleared through the debris and on Saturday, 21 December, tea was served in the music room to the accompaniment of an orchestral 'entertainment'. However, this was just an interlude to the dark counterpoint of aerial bombardment as three weeks later the same space was serving as a temporary mortuary for the dead excavated from the homeless men's hostel opposite. The crowded three-storey building had collapsed, crushing its sleeping occupants between floors; it took eight weeks to retrieve the 71 bodies, which were then laid out beneath the pear wood resonator and the pale Italian pink walls and the summer-night blue ceiling 'with a suggestion of planets' of the Holst Music Room.

In March 1941 the College formally reopened in the extension building. Even in its desolation, Morley was still smiled upon and Hubback's and Tippett's networks of friends could be relied on to come up with something distinctive: lectures by Ninette de Valois on ballet and Ralph Vaughan Williams on opera drew enormous audiences. 'Life Goes On' and 'Morley College Carries On' were the jaunty headlines in the press.

In these incredibly difficult conditions, Tippett set about reviving overlooked English and European composers – Purcell's *Ode for St Cecilia's Day* was performed in November 1941 and a set of Monteverdi madrigals and Dowland songs in 1943 – while his protégé, Walter Bergmann, directed a concert of Telemann quartets and sonatas in 1942 – all works that were either unfashionable or unknown. The performance of Purcell's *Dido and Aeneas* that Tippett staged as a fund-raiser at the Arts Theatre in March 1942 best exemplifies the 'make-do-and-mend' spirit that informed such productions: the reduced Morley Choir was accompanied by a single piano and the female singers were in costumes made from dusters, towels and rags 'to save on coupons'. Nevertheless, it was a crowd-pleasing fusion of wartime austerity and cultural defiance that caught the eye of the national press.

Morley was a home for contemporary music as well. Walter Goehr conducted the UK premiere of Stravinsky's *Dumbarton Oaks* in the Holst Room in 1942, and Benjamin Britten and Peter Pears came to deliver the first performance of Tippett's *Boyhood's End*.

In the *Morley Magazine* of January 1940 the editor had written of Morley's role in perpetuating knowledge and

Michael Tippett and Walter Goehr

culture built up over centuries until 'the happy day when war lies once more behind us' and exhorting students, 'That culture is in danger – be sure to guard it well.' That it was the last College magazine for five years merely made those words more resonant, for the real achievement of Morley College during the war was in not waiting on that 'happy day', but rather in continuing to provide an extraordinary offering of education and culture for local Londoners under sometimes absurdly straitened circumstances. Under the tutelage of Tippett, Morley offered an ongoing performance space for Western European musical culture, regardless of its national origin.

JON NEWMAN

REHEARSING WITH GOEHR

ALISON COX

My parents met and got engaged when they both sang in the Morley Choir. My mother (Barbara Butcher) was a primary school teacher and she went to Morley from the mid-1940s onwards. My father (David Vassall Cox) was in a junior position at the BBC and he joined Morley later. He eventually became the External Services music organiser at the Beeb. My mother said that they were rehearsing one day with Walter Goehr conducting when Goehr received news that his wife and children had just safely arrived in the UK from Nazi Germany. The details escape me, but my mum said that she will never forget the look of sheer relief and joy on Walter's face as he heard the news. The family included his son, Alexander, who would teach at Morley himself as the 1950s turned into the 1960s, before a career as one of the country's most distinguished composers and professor of music at Cambridge University.

Morley Since the Second World War

The courtyard in 1958

Summer fete at the sports ground in Eltham, 1950s

ABOVE: The Queen Mother with Denis Richards at the opening of the new building, 1958

RIGHT: The Queen accepting a bouquet from the librarian, Muriel Green, 1973

BELOW: Aerial view of the 'Wrap', c.1973

1950/1 Denis Richards appointed Principal.

1958/9 HRH Queen Mother opens new building on 29 October.

1962/3 The new Refectory murals by Edward Bawden are opened.

1963/4 College begins to plan its extension project in King Edward Walk.

1964/5 College celebrates 75th anniversary of its foundation and formalises appeal for its building project.

1965/6 Barry Till succeeds Richards as Principal.
The Inner London Education Authority (ILEA) replaces the London County Council (LCC) as funding body, though fees remain mostly unchanged.

1967/8 Upper floors of the visual arts building, in the converted King's Arms pub on the corner of King Edward Walk, in operation.

1968/9 Jennie Lee, Minister for the Arts, opens the Gallery in February.

1969/70 Baroness Seear succeeds Lady Walton as Chair.
The College launches a new appeal for what was to become the 'Wrap' extension.

1973/4 The 'Wrap', designed by John Winter, opened by HM Queen Elizabeth II in Dec 1973.

1975/6 Sculpture Studio opens at Pelham Hall in Lambeth Walk.

1980/1 Morley no longer considered a 'literary institute', following restructure of ILEA adult education provision. Morley expands as a result, operating over six branches, in addition to Westminster Bridge Road, to undertake 'more general adult education' in the locality in such subjects as home studies and physical education.

1981/2 Fresh Start courses aimed at getting people into employment and Second Chance courses 'for those whose past experiences … have made them chary and lacking in confidence' become a major feature of the College's programme; a new Basic Education department provides courses in literacy, numeracy and English as a second language.

1982/3 Ground floor of the Nancy Seear Building in King Edward Walk is brought into use; remainder of building remains uncompleted while fund-raising continues.

1984/5 Beginnings of threats to the continuation of the ILEA prompts a 'Safeguard Adult Education' campaign: 'Let not Emma Cons' Inspiration die'.

1986/7 Susan Fey succeeds Till as Principal.

1988/9 Morley's future is 'safeguarded' in a Government House of Lords statement, but funding (now directly from the Department for Education and Science) is significantly reduced. The College is now expected to generate more of its own income: the registration fee doubles to £1 – the first rise for 26 years – and unsubsidised courses are introduced from April 1989. Janet Roberts succeeds Fey in January.

1989/90 Centenary year – one of the most difficult the College has faced. The College Council commissions Lord Henderson of Brompton to head a review panel to look at problems facing the College and growing disquiet amongst staff. In December the ILEA freezes its grant due to concerns over College management and its subsequent funding is closely overseen by the London Residuary Body. Nevertheless, a leak of the Henderson report leads to headlines in press on 'Morley's mutineers' and their allegedly left-wing infiltration.

With dissolution of the ILEA, Morley becomes an independent institution from April 1990, governed by a Foundation Governing Body and Board of Trustees.

Roberts leaves and is replaced in spring 1990 by Vice Principal David Normand-Harris as interim Principal.

A CHANGE OF CAREER

ANTHONY GILBERT

As a former Morley student (in Russian, Spanish, and then harmony, counterpoint, music history, orchestration and conducting), and from 1972 as teacher of composition myself, I was asked to write a quiet fanfare for the visit of the Queen to open the College's new extension in 1973. Perhaps it was too quiet, because halfway through, Her Majesty rose and walked out into the area where we were all to gather for a glass of champagne. She did apologise, however, and we had a brief chat about the Sydney Opera House which she had just returned from opening. She showed herself very aware of the internal politics which had forced the sharing of the various halls in the opera house to be renegotiated.

In 1956, when I was studying advanced Russian and Spanish at Morley, as class secretary it was my job to collect the class register from a little office in the building. Noticing that the young lady sitting at the desk had a pile of songs there, I asked whether she was studying music, and she replied 'Well, sort of'. We got chatting, and on telling her about my wish to pursue studies in composition, she told me to contact Anthony Milner, who taught theory and composition. I did, he took me on, and from then on I slowly changed profession, from translator/interpreter to composer. The young lady at the desk was Janet Baker!

At the end of the 1950s, I enrolled in Iain Hamilton's orchestration class. We were all sitting waiting for him when a charismatic young man strolled in. Someone said, 'Come and sit here – Mr Hamilton will be here shortly.' The young man said 'No, I'm afraid I'm taking his place.' A better-informed member of the class exclaimed, 'Oh, so you're Alexander Goehr!' And so he was. As well as his brilliant lessons in orchestration, he also agreed to take me on as a private composition student, declining any fee. The important thing for me was that I learnt, in the 12 or so years I was a part-time student at Morley, far more than I'd have done on a full-time conservatoire-type course at the time. Sandy Goehr's orchestration class began to fill up with people from the music colleges: David Blake (now retired professor at York); Roger Smalley and the late Brian Dennis, both in their time eminent composers and in Roger's case, pianist and conductor; John Tilbury, pianist; eminent Scandinavian composer Gunilla Ormerod (later Loewenstein). Through Sandy Goehr, I became first a copyist for his publisher, Schotts, and later their chief music editor. And of course in that role I got to know Michael Tippett very well, though I hadn't known him when he was on the staff at Morley. In other music classes the standard of teaching was sufficiently high to attract practising members of the profession. For instance, in Lawrence Leonard's conducting class which I attended for two years from 1967, among other students were harmonica player Larry Adler; composer Francis Chagrin; the chief *répétiteur* of Covent Garden; and composer Nicola LeFanu (who was also to become a Morley tutor for a while).

The portrait of Bev Walters by Maggi Hambling in the College's collection

1990/1 Bev Walters appointed Principal in January. Morley's curriculum offer is now much reduced, due to its grant 'no longer covering work which is primarily local in character', and most of the branches consequently discontinued.

1992/3 From April 1993 Morley is funded through the new Further Education Funding Council, which according to the Principal has the 'voracious appetite for numbers, budgets, charts, graphs, floppy discs and strategic plans' which have become a way of life ever since.

1994/5 A full-time Access Studies programme is introduced to replace the more dispersed Fresh Start courses.

1996/7 'Morley College at Waterloo – Learning for Life' adopted as a logo.

2003/4 Philip Meaden succeeds Walters as Principal.

2007/8 Ela Piotrowska appointed Principal from April.

2008–14 'Morley Renaissance' programme of renewal and refurbishment.

2014/15 Morley celebrates its 125th anniversary.

Morley's stall in Lower Marsh Market, Waterloo, 2014

In the early 1990s, Morley faced the challenge of reinventing itself as a significant provider of adult education in London, following the disappearance of the ILEA. When the College brochure came out in the summer, there were doubts about how well news of the Morley offer was circulating to libraries and other institutions promoting courses in lifelong learning. There was not the money to pay others to do it on the College's behalf.

So on a very hot day in July, I went to a white van hire company near The Oval and took responsibility for a delivery van which was loaded with hundreds of Morley prospectuses. There then followed what were the worst two days of my life. From that time I was never rude about white van drivers. Imagine driving around London with a map spread out on the front seat trying to locate the delivery points that were marked. It showed where a library was located. However the vagaries of local government meant that the library now sat in the midst of a pedestrianised area. Yes, I was informed, there was an alternative way of approaching the

GETTING THE WORD OUT

MURRAY ROWLANDS

library for delivery purposes, but that involved a complex path of navigating each borough's one-way system, then trying to attract the attention of those inside to open the door. After all this, in a few sniffy libraries there was a discussion about whether the Morley prospectus would be accepted at all. Late one afternoon hot, bothered and lost, I was driving the wrong way up a one-way street and came face to face with a police car!

In order to survive, Morley had to promote itself in Lambeth and Southwark throughout the year; we would go across to Waterloo Station and promote Morley there. Morley also sought to cement its identification with Lambeth through active participation in the Lambeth Country Show, which not only involved producing leaflets about the College

to interest the hundreds attending the event, but also having a stand for the two days of the fair. Here Glen During, the office manager of Morley, did sterling work in liaising with Lambeth Council about our site on a vast campus of stalls at Brockwell Park. During the show, Morley offered a range of activities including arts and crafts, dance and physical education.

We also stood at the entrance of Brixton Station and it was nice to greet potential students, who pounced on our prospectus because they had thought the College had closed. We were less successful at the Elephant and Castle. On one occasion, I had to return to the College to pick up a display for the stand we had been granted and left the prospectuses in an alcove. Imagine my reaction when on my return I discovered all the boxes of prospectuses had disappeared! There then followed a desperate search among the rubbish skips for the missing boxes. After all this, I wish I could claim that our stall in The Elephant elicited great interest among the shoppers ...

Denis Richards

DENIS RICHARDS was born in 1910 and raised in London. He graduated with a double first in History from Trinity Hall, Cambridge in 1931. From 1931 to 1939 he taught history and English at Manchester Grammar School, and then at Bradfield College near Reading until 1941, when he joined the Royal Air Force (RAF). Recalled from active service, he headed up a team of historians to prepare the official history of the RAF, which appeared in three volumes in 1953–4.

After the war, he was appointed as principal in the Air Ministry, but he found Civil Service life dull, so he applied for the post of Principal at Morley in 1950; his appointment was greeted with some hostility in feminist circles, since most principals previously had been women. Undaunted, he set to the unenviable task of rebuilding Morley. In his first article in the *Morley Magazine*, he recalled a conversation with a journalist in which he said, 'I shall make a nuisance of myself in all the appropriate quarters until we get our new building.' His trials with the LCC have been well documented in his history of the College, *Offspring of the Vic*, and later in his memoirs.

One of his innovations was to set up the Friends of Morley in 1952, to 'help make the College a still more useful, vigorous and beautiful place than it already is', by providing items not covered by the usual funding. One of

The portrait of Denis Richards by Ruskin Spear in the College's collection

the Friends' gifts – a bar – would not have been approved by Emma Cons!

Denis Richards was already a published author when he joined Morley, with several popular school history books to his name. He wrote in the mornings and worked at Morley from 3pm till 10pm. His desk, together with that of the entire College administration, was in the Library until 1958. He commented that at Morley, 'news travelled faster than in a Welsh village'.

Richards encouraged other organisations to make use of the empty building in the daytime. These included the Bagot Stack College, which was the training section of the League of Health and Beauty, the National Opera School, the Sigurd Leeder School of Modern Dance and the Central Tutorial School for Young Musicians, now better known as the Purcell School.

By 1963 Morley was expanding at such a rate that the new building was not big enough, and Richards put together funding to buy some property in King Edward Walk. This comprised a derelict pub, some prefabs on a bomb site, a garden and four terraced houses. This additional property portfolio helped Morley to expand in future years.

Denis Richards left Morley in 1965 to have more time for his writing, and became a Longman Fellow in History at Sussex University. He was awarded an OBE in 1990. His two volumes of memoirs: *Just to Recall the Flavour* and *It Might Have Been Worse: Recollections: 1941–1996*, were published in 1999. He died in 2004.

ELAINE ANDREWS

Denis Richards at the summer fete at the College's sportsground in Eltham, 1950s

LEFT: The Yorkshire Society School building after Morley's acquisition, c.1924; and the Gymnasium, 1927

TOP: Maufe's sketch of the new 1937 wing; and ABOVE: the extension from the courtyard

BELOW: Broadbent's sketch of the new building

Morley's Architecture

IN 1923 MORLEY COLLEGE moved into a building on its present site, occupied from 1812 to 1917 by the Yorkshire Society's School. The architects Lanchester, Lucas & Lodge, successors to the partnership that designed Westminster Central Hall, were responsible for adding a wing to the rear, opened in 1927, containing a large Concert Hall with a Refreshment Room and Gymnasium below. It was a plain, Georgian-inspired building, in the manner of the time. The direct hit by a bomb in October 1940 destroyed both parts of these buildings. However, the wing added in 1937 to the west by Sir Edward Maufe, architect of Guildford Cathedral, containing the Library above and the Holst Room below, survived, and provided the only accommodation for the College after the war, until the completion of the replacement to the original building in 1958.

The long wait was caused by the need to obtain planning permission and a building licence, and to satisfy the demands of the War Damage Commission, which required as far as possible a like-for-like replacement. The architect appointed was Charles Cowles Voysey, son of the more famous Arts and Crafts house designer C. F. A. Voysey. When he retired in 1954, the practice became Brandon-Jones, Ashton & Broadbent, and it was J. D. Broadbent who became chiefly responsible for the project, including coping with a late-stage budget cut of one-eighth. The partners were doubtful about the practicality of some aspects of the lightweight Modernist style

of the 1950s, and so the yellow London stock brick of Maufe's wing was adopted, with a projecting cap on the parapet to protect it from rain. The slight bow at the entrance adds a reminiscence of Regency gracefulness.

In 1972, John Winter, who had extensive experience of study and practice in America, was chosen to design a steel-framed extension to connect the existing buildings at the rear, known as the 'Wrap'. It was his first major

1889-1956

MORLEY COLLEGE.

commission, and a complete contrast to the earlier buildings, designed according to the Modernist principle that the exterior should express the construction materials and methods. The Morley building was an adventure to beat the clock over a summer vacation and use up a sum of money that had suddenly become available, but was in danger of being clawed back if unspent. Winter added a further building in King Edward Walk in 1982 (usually known as the 'yellow building' from its brightly coloured trim.) Having used it for his own house in Highgate in 1967, Winter chose Corten, a type of steel that develops its own rusty patina out of doors, and was originally developed for railway goods trucks to avoid the need for painting. In 2012, in an article berating the post-modern style of the 1980s, the *Evening Standard*'s architecture critic celebrated Morley's 'yellow building' as one of the 'hits' of the decade.

ALAN POWERS

The 'Wrap' under construction, c.1972

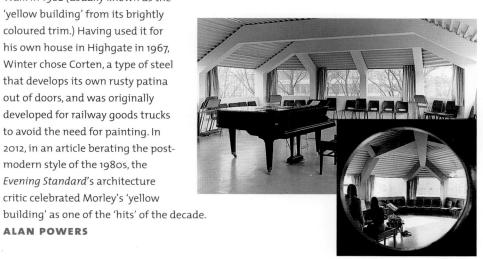

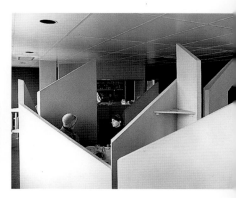

Views of the interior spaces of the 'Wrap', 1973, including the music room (left) and the former College bar (above)

BELOW: The 1983 Nancy Seear Building

Morley's Library

THE LIBRARY WAS FIRST mentioned in the Royal Victoria Hall's Annual Report of 1890/1: 'The library is very little used because [it is] only open one or at most two evenings a week and that not very regularly. If six librarians could be found to take one evening a week each, and would send a substitute when prevented from coming themselves, the students would know that the books were available.' The Library was described in 1894 as 'a beautiful room which runs the whole width of our premises from Waterloo Road to Webber Street, and is lighted by a lantern roof'. The Library was also used for social occasions, such as the Debating Society, and for free lectures; the mock trial involving Mr Perks ('Skrep') in 1901, reported in the *Morley College Magazine*, delighted a large audience. Most of the books, and some of the furniture, was donated by well-wishers and friends of the College in the early days, including generous gifts from Caroline Martineau and Lady Ottoline Morrell. Librarians came and went rapidly in the early days, and one notable appointment might have been Miss V. Stephen (Virginia Woolf), who wrote to her friend Violet Dickinson in 1905, 'I am going to be Librarian at Morley. Miss Sheep[shanks] says that she thinks my gift is rather influence than direct intellectual teaching.'

In 1924 Morley moved to the present site in Westminster Bridge Road and inherited the library from the Yorkshire Society's School. From the beginning, students had to pay an annual subscription to borrow books, and there is a note in the Library reports for 1932/3 that the unemployed did not have to pay, a concession which continued throughout the 1930s.

The extension, opened by Queen Mary in 1937, offered a bespoke library for the first time, with oak shelving,

I was Morley's Librarian during 1980–95. From time to time a firm of solicitors would contact us: someone had left their books to Morley College Library. The deceased person had usually been a student at Morley – often many decades ago – and had appreciated the service. Whilst we received many excellent and valuable donations, more often than not the books turned out to be in poor condition, old and outdated, and we were disappointed. This took us to all kinds of places, little cottages in the Home Counties or attics in London.

Once we were called to a house in Greenwich to collect books left to us in the lady's will. The solicitor warned me not to wear my best clothes! It was a large house, but much neglected from the outside. Inside we entered another world. Two sisters had been born here and lived here all their lives. There was no electricity, but the rooms were lit by gas lamps on the walls. The original wallpaper was interesting, but in shreds. Downstairs the

MORE BOOKS?

ANNE BRACHT

kitchen had not been touched since the last war, when the sisters decided to move upstairs. Old tins lined the shelves, a grate full of ancient ashes, and on a string across the corners hung the remains of old dishcloths. Upstairs in a wardrobe, the splendid uniform of a beadle of Lewisham – could that have belonged to the ladies' father? The books downstairs were as expected. The librarian of the City Lit was already at work, as she had also been left the books, and between us we decided the damp and mouldy heap was not worth moving. We signed our piece of paper declining the acceptance of the gift and left, stepping back into the 20th century.

Another time we were contacted by the police regarding some stolen books. We had noticed some systematic stealing which included the entire set of a valuable reference work. There had been reports in the press that a book thief had been prosecuted who had stolen thousands of books from all over the country. We were invited to go to Norfolk and retrieve them. It was the summer holidays, and the Head of Art and I set off north. After an enjoyable pub lunch, we eventually found the huge barn where the books were housed, guarded by the police. A place the size of an aircraft hangar, stuffed full of books in no particular order, neither ownership nor subject. How could one man have stolen and stored all those books? We had an impossible task. I found a lot of highly desirable books, but was not allowed to take any that didn't belong to us. We found none of our own books and left disappointed. I sometimes wonder what happened to all those stolen books.

solid tables and chairs from Heals, some still in use today. The room had innovative uplighters set in the bookcases, and individual reading lights on each table. Over the years more bookcases were added to cope with the expansion of stock. The Library became the hub of the College after the rest of the building was destroyed in 1940. The Principal and his assistant were still working there until the new buildings were completed in 1958.

John Winter's 'Wrap' extension of 1973 gave much-needed space for the ever-expanding library stock. This room, furnished with easy chairs and a coffee table for comfortable browsing and also study carrels, became known as the 'Art and Music Library'. As the stock continued to expand, the easy chairs gave way to a central bookcase, purchased by the Friends of Morley.

The lower library in 1973

The lower library
today

Over the years the Library has had to respond to the changes in audio-visual items, and the excitement on receiving huge donations of gramophone records had dimmed by the end of the 20th century with the advent of compact discs.

Computer use for students was slow to develop, and it was only at the end of the 1990s that another room was added to the Library, named after a former student, Ursula Hyde, who had left a considerable bequest. This enabled the College to set up a proper suite, which could be used as a classroom and for drop-in access. The College's first Virtual Learning Environment was called Digitalbrain, now superseded by Moodle, which allows students to download resources, catch up on missed classes, communicate via forums, and become part of an online community. Tutors can set online tests, receive assignments from students and respond. Now users can access e-books, e-resources and the Library catalogue at any time of the day.

This is a long way from 1890 when only one book could be borrowed at a time!

ELAINE ANDREWS

Barry Till

BARRY PLAYED AN IMPORTANT role in transforming
Morley College and establishing it as a centre of
excellence for the creative arts and adult education. He
believed that people from all backgrounds should have
access to the best teachers and facilities, and was
committed to community and social inclusion. His work
raised the profile of adult learning, often described as a
Cinderella service.

Barry arrived at Morley in 1965. Educated in Cambridge,
he served in the Coldstream Guards in the Italian
Campaign and after the war he was ordained and held a
number of roles in the Church. After four years as dean of

A MORLEY MARRIAGE

ANTONIA TILL

You could say that Morley *was* the first half of
our married life. Barry Till became Principal of
Morley in 1965. I had been singing in the
Chamber Choir from 1962, and a friend said I
should meet 'the new Principal' – and we
married in 1966. So Morley became the focus
and framework of the whole family for
21 years.

Barry had decided to open the College all
day with a crèche and playgroup for mothers
starting or resuming education, so I became a
helper at the new playgroup. Soon afterwards a
literature tutor dropped out suddenly so, as I
had teaching experience, I was asked to tutor a
poetry class. And I went on singing, both in the
Chamber Choir (in which my sister-in-law now
sings) and Hilde Beal's 'Enjoy Your Voice'. And I
cooked and cooked and cooked! There were the
Christmas puddings and mince pies for the
Christmas Fair, quiches and cakes for Open Day,
and ambitious dinner parties for people Barry
hoped would contribute when he was fund-
raising for the new building, and for
distinguished guest speakers. We recall with
special delight entertaining Judi Dench and her
enchanting husband, the late Michael Williams.

By this time we had two daughters and,
once, I asked if they could come down to meet
Ernst Gombrich, the eminent art historian, and
his wife. Barry said they were too distinguished

to be bothered with young children, but as
soon as they arrived the Gombrichs asked to
see the girls in their bunk beds. I glowed. The
girls were quickly embraced by Morley, coming
on Saturdays to sing with Guy Woolfenden
(they can still sing one of his songs all these
years later) or to participate in various
activities. They were dressed in their best when
the Queen came to open the new building
and, as they grew up, attended more and more
Morley occasions and came to know many of
the staff. Nick, Barry's older son, lectured at
Morley too. Many of the tutors were and

Antonia Till in conversation with Peyton Skipwith,
co-curator of the exhibition 'Edward Bawden,
Storyteller', 2014

remain dear friends. Nancy Seear, Chair of
the Council, would join us for Christmas
and lent us her sweetly ramshackle house
in France for summer holidays. Morley and
the people who worked there became the
background, the context, of our family.

Long after he had left, Barry kept his love
for and interest in the College, seeing his
time there as his greatest professional
achievement. It remained a powerful and
heartening memory even as he grew more
frail and forgetful. So it was fitting and
consoling that it was at Morley his life was
celebrated in November 2013. There was
wonderful music of course: the Chamber
Choir sang two of the spirituals from
Michael Tippett's *A Child of Our Time* (which
I had sung with both John Gardner and
Michael Graubart), Martino Tirimo
generously and magnificently gave us two
great piano pieces, and the London
Sinfonietta performed Schubert and
Harrison Birtwistle with grace and
intensity. It was a glorious occasion to
which we were welcomed by Ela with a
warm tribute and with speakers from other
phases of Barry's career. Any melancholy
was dispelled by the characteristically witty
tribute of the last speaker, the
incomparable Maggi Hambling.

the Cathedral in Hong Kong, he returned to England in 1964. Appointed Principal at Morley in 1965, he began a journey which was to become his passion and life's work.

At the time Morley was one of the smaller ILEA Adult Education Institutes, with some 150 classes. In his second year, Barry appointed Raymond Rivers as Vice Principal and together they started work which established Morley as a considerable force in adult education. Barry admired the College's strong heritage, particularly in music, and wanted every other department to be equally distinguished and professional. He started with the visual arts.

In 1965 art courses were only run as evening classes and there was limited space to develop a curriculum. Barry earmarked the King's Arms pub, a bombed-out shell opposite the College, which had been purchased by the previous principal, for development as the new visual arts centre. He made sure that a gallery was included in the plans, believing that visual arts students needed the equivalent of the performance spaces enjoyed by the

The Queen with Barry Till, 1973

College's musicians. Supported by the chair of Governors, Baroness Seear, Barry embarked on years of fund-raising. With excellent art facilities for painting and printing finally established, he added sculpture to the curriculum by buying a former mission hall which became the College's bespoke sculpture studio.

Barry's vision for Morley as a centre for a broad programme of adult education to meet the needs of an increasingly diverse London population continued to grow and, in 1969, he launched an appeal for a new

Bridget Riley's mural in the foyer

extension. He chose John Winter, a young up-and-coming architect for the project – in preference to another up-and-coming figure, Norman Foster. The new extension was opened by the Queen in December 1973, and doubled the College's capacity, providing disabled access and classrooms designed to encourage informal methods of teaching, unequalled at the time.

His support for young artists characterised his approach to developing the College. Bridget Riley was commissioned to produce a work for the new extension and during his principalship, Morley extended its reputation for employing foremost musicians to professionals in other fields, including artists such as Maggi Hambling, writers, historians and philosophers, as well as adult educators who were to develop new programmes addressing the needs of disadvantaged communities. He also pioneered inclusive education for all. Influenced by Gavron's *The Captive Wife*, in the late 1960s he set up childcare provision to enable women to attend courses at Morley. Further influenced by the Russell Report in 1973, Barry inspired a new range of courses designed to reach out into the local community and provide first steps back into learning for some of the most disadvantaged communities in Lambeth and Southwark.

But these developments needed yet more space and so again, Barry launched an appeal to fund a new community building on the College estate where prefabs providing accommodation for the College's childcare provision had stood, and commissioned John Winter again to design a user-friendly building. The Nancy Seear Building was 'a sort of a bridge with the local community', providing an important element of his vision, reflecting Morley's original mission of the 1880s, but also bringing Morley to the forefront of new developments such as training preschool playgroup leaders, courses for the unemployed and community education. During this period, Morley also became a centre of excellence for Fresh Start, providing access to higher education for adults.

Barry was conscious that he didn't conform to the image of some of the educators emerging in the late 1970s. He once said that some of the new students attracted by the development of community education, literacy and numeracy programmes at the College might find him 'rather grand and upper-class'. But he was a radical, believing that learning was immensely liberating and should be available to people from all backgrounds,

and that Morley was about 'people finding and fulfilling themselves and their lives, and learning, in their own way, how better to live them'.

Over the 21 years that Barry was Principal, the College grew from about 3,300 students to 12,000, making it the largest adult education centre in London at the time. He was an inspiring leader as well as my mentor and friend. Barry was charming, eloquent, occasionally irritable, with a great turn in Latin phrases and a penchant for chips. He often ruled with his heart for which he was respected, and remained forever an adult educator and learner.

After retiring from Morley in 1986, he assumed the directorship of the Baring Foundation, steering the charitable arm of the merchant bank towards a number of key social welfare projects. He served as a trustee or board member of a wide range of institutions, including the Victoria and Albert Museum (V&A), Fitzwilliam Museum, Mary Ward Foundation and, most significantly, as chair of the London Sinfonietta. He also returned to his scholarly activity in ecclesiastical history, and in 2008 was awarded the rare honour of a 'Lambeth Degree' DD (Doctor of Divinity) by the Archbishop of Canterbury.
ELA PIOTROWSKA

Morley in Waterloo Today

OVER THE LAST 30 YEARS, the social and cultural diversity of the College has significantly broadened, reflecting the changes in our local population. Essential Skills, Access to Higher Education courses and a range of other qualifications have been introduced to respond to the needs of London's communities and now play an important part in the College's community engagement work. These programmes reflect the College's roots in education for

Art Club at the Waterloo Action Centre

The opening of Morley's stall in Lower Marsh market, 2013. L to r: Carole Powell (Enterprise Co-ordinator), Ela Piotrowska (Principal), Helen Santer (Chief Executive of Waterloo BID) and John Stephens (Chair of Morley's Governing Body)

the working classes and its mission to build confidence and self-esteem in its students, support social and educational mobility, and offer qualifications and opportunities to progress to further learning or employment.

Amongst these is a recently developed range of courses in enterprise and business to support the interests of students who are thinking about running a business or perhaps becoming self-employed. Just as 125 years ago, Morley's impact on its local area and on people's lives was a response to the social, political and economic drivers of the times, so too is its impact in the second decade of the 21st century. Here, Helen Santer reflects on how some of this work has made a difference to the Waterloo of today.

* * *

WATERLOO IS A singular place. It is an area that is changing massively and rapidly. An area with an established local community and a lot of new faces. An area with a mixture of extreme wealth and significant deprivation, where multinational businesses rub shoulders with launderettes and corner shops.

And yet it excites surprisingly similar reactions from all who experience it, with the most common of those being the extraordinary sense of community that seems to exude from the place. Yet how, in the context of this diversity, can this community be defined? And for a college such as Morley, how can it make itself relevant to all the people who live and work in this area, or are simply passing through?

Over the seven years I have worked in Waterloo, I have witnessed a sea change in how Morley has reached out to the local community and engaged with new groups that historically may not have realised the relevance and proximity of the College to them.

Businesses are the lifeblood of local communities, providing employment and amenity to all who live and work in the area. The College has become more businesslike in its dealings both with residents and the large community of people who work in the area. Never in a way that sacrifices its principles or the sheer delight of learning for learning's sake, but with an increased awareness of the importance of developing skills that can help make not just this community but other areas continue to thrive.

Waterloo Quarter, the Business Improvement District for the area, recently had the pleasure of working with Morley College on the Portas Pilot programme – an initiative, funded by the government and mayor, to test innovative solutions to address the national decline in high streets, which focused on Waterloo's prime retail streets of Lower Marsh and The Cut.

This programme was the clearest demonstration of Morley's determination to reach out to the broader community, proudly and publicly to put the College's work in the public domain, and to support local people in developing skills and practical experience required to start a business. Through the development of an 'Introduction to Market Trading' course, Morley worked with Waterloo Quarter to develop an initiative that brought a total of 35 students out onto Lower Marsh market to sell products that they had made in a college environment.

The enthusiasm of the staff and students was a pleasure to witness. From the College's perspective, being 'out there' in the community seems to have become a passion – the experience proved so popular that we even investigated the possibility of creating a permanent 'Morley Shop' in Waterloo.

Morley in Waterloo today feels utterly relevant. I can think of no greater compliment to give the College than that – it is an organisation that knows its community and their needs and is determined to continue to evolve to meet them.

HELEN SANTER

Morley's Place in Adult Education

IN HAROLD NICHOLSON'S FOREWORD to Denis Richards's marvellous 1958 history of Morley College, *Offspring of the Vic,* he identified six themes which he saw as distinctive, and they make a good starting point for recognising the distinctive place that Morley plays nationally in adult education.

The first characteristic he noted was Morley's 'organic vitality', its ability to rise phoenix-like from the ashes, and to adapt to changing circumstances. He was writing just as new buildings were being completed to replace those destroyed by bombing in the Second World War. That initiative, like its successor in 1973 when the extension was added, was the result of Morley's extraordinary ability to create effective alliances between grass-roots community organisations and the great and good of the day to further its interests. (It was, incidentally, the first publicly funded new building for adult education in Britain after the war.)

Nowhere was that ability better illustrated than in the run-up to the 1988 Education Reform Bill, which abolished Morley's principal funder, the ILEA, and jeopardised the future of adult education in the capital. Nancy Seear in the House of Lords, backed by Sue Fey, then Principal of the College, put together a coalition of support, arguing that London's four literary institutes (the City Lit, Mary Ward and the Working Men's College, in addition to Morley) should have their status and distinctive character protected in legislation, and funded nationally. The success of the coalition was remarkable, protecting the blend of programming that combined cultural studies and practice of the highest order with access to education for people failed by the school system and returning to learning for the first time since school.

The phoenix-like qualities of Morley can be seen in its periodic reassertion of the community engagement that had fired its creators. Just as its first lectures, classes and performances were offered to ameliorate the bleakness of lives lived in poverty in the North Lambeth of the 1890s, so in a different way were the daytime classes for the unemployed mounted during the recession of the 1930s. And when the ILEA offered the four London literary institutes the opportunity to take responsibility for the broader community education in its area in 1980, Morley was alone among the four in taking up the challenge, and

Harold
Nicholson

voluntary body, aided but not owned by the local authority. Not only does it inform the provision of space for learners' voices in the governance of the institution (which impressed me in the short time I was a governor of Morley), but also, critically, the negotiation of the curriculum between tutor and students in individual classes.

This commitment can be linked to Nicholson's fourth theme, which was the College's emphasis on 'social intercourse, and on providing entertainment, congenial companionship, clubs, and opportunities for outside activities'. What Nicholson recognised is that there is far more to the College than the sum of its individual classes, inspiring though they are. Adult education centres as communities focused on learning had their heyday from the 1920s to the 1990s, supported by the work of the Educational Centres Association. But the changes to public legislation, linking funding solely to courses provided and students enrolled on approved courses, led to the closure of many centres. Morley, however, demonstrates just what richness is to be had from the life around the class: from the interaction in the canteen and the performances offered to students and the wider public, to the art on the walls and the sheer celebration of curiosity. It certainly inspired our work at Brighton's Friends Centre, a smaller version of the same kind of centre, when I worked there in the 1970s.

Harold Nicholson's third theme is Morley's early groundbreaking commitment 'to proclaim and inculcate absolute equality, not merely between the several social grades, but between the sexes'. The language about 'social grades' may seem dated now and reinforce distinctions it was designed to overcome, but the commitment of the College was genuine. The scale of the challenge on gender equality can be seen from the arrangements for pay for LCC-funded adult education principals in 1946. As a result of LCC policy, Morley's Principal, Eva Hubback, was on a scale that started £200 lower than her colleague at the City Lit, her annual increments were smaller, and the top of her scale lower than her colleague across the Thames. Like other women principals, she was paid a lower salary solely on account of her gender; a man in post would have been paid a higher sum. Despite this institutional discrimination characteristic of its day, Morley has enjoyed throughout its history the leadership of brilliant women, from Emma Cons at its inception, through Eva Hubback from the 1930s to the 1950s, to Ela

its resultant championing of Access to Higher Education programmes, English as a second language, and adult literacy programmes created routes to further learning that offered breadth, richness and challenge.

The second of Nicholson's themes was the democratic principle that guided the work of the College as a

Bertrand
Russell

Piotrowska today. There have, too, been inspiring men –
none more so than my own mentor and friend, Barry Till.

Each of these themes has had an important role in
Morley's development, but it is Nicholson's fifth and sixth
themes that mark out Morley's absolute distinction as a
centre of adult learning. His fifth was the close link
between Morley and the arts. The institution grew out of
the Old Vic, so there was always a relationship between
learning and performance. But the extraordinary
standards of its teaching in music and art are unparalleled
in adult education anywhere in Britain or abroad. Its
traditions of excellence have been established and
sustained by Nicholson's sixth theme – the quality of its
teachers. Morley has benefited from a stellar roster
including Gustav and Imogen Holst, Michael Tippett,
Ralph Vaughan Williams, Virginia Woolf, Bertrand Russell,
and more recently Maggi Hambling and Margaret
Drabble. But it has also secured the commitment of
dedicated adult education professionals to the mainte-
nance and enrichment of those traditions, and to opening
them to as wide a community of learners as possible.

All in all then, Morley College is a precious institution
with much to celebrate. However, the College has a heavy
responsibility to face in the years ahead. At a time when
education in school and after is ever more narrowly
focused on utilitarian outcomes, there is an urgent need
to reassert the values of learning that enrich lives and
stretch the soul, and for that kind of learning to be
available to all. And who is better placed than Morley to
make the case for that revaluation?

ALAN TUCKETT

ABOVE: A beginner's piano class in the keyboard
studio; and BELOW: an exhibition of students'
photography

C&G Photography | Level one, two and three | 09.00

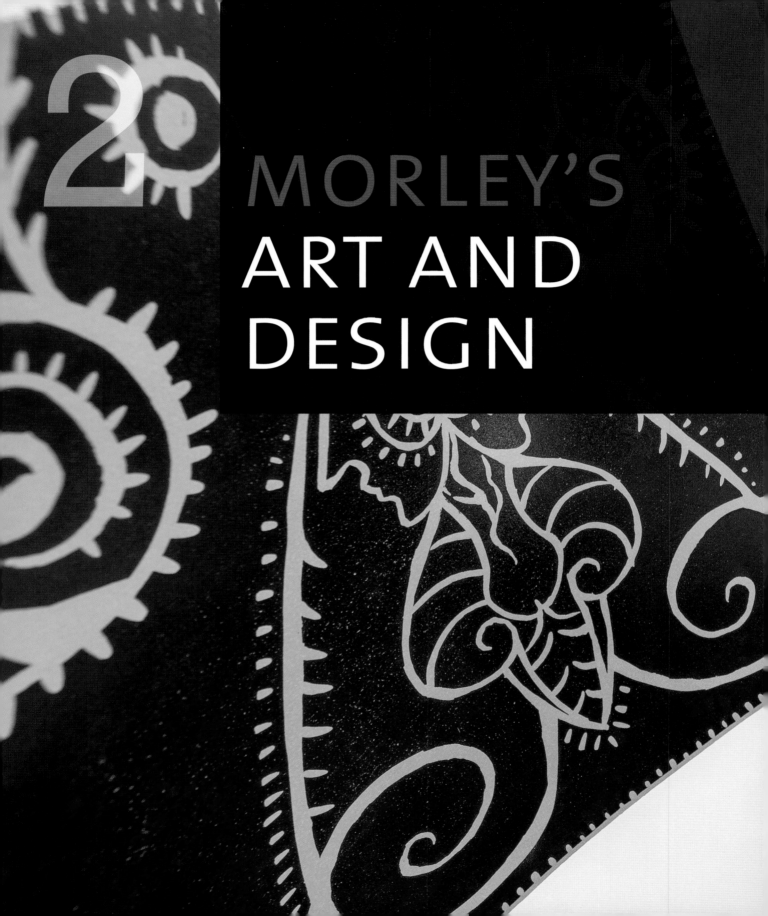

MORLEY'S
ART AND
DESIGN

> " People of all ages from all walks of life are offered a chance to discover the selves they never knew they had: that is Morley's huge and enduring gift to everyone " MAGGI HAMBLING

A Rich Mix

TODAY THE ART AND DESIGN department is the largest in the College. It is a rich mix of the visual, applied and digital arts, secure in its success and its dual role of being at once the depository of some old and precious skills and traditions, and at the same time alive and responsive to the contemporary scene. The department changes annually, growing and adding new ideas for courses, and continues to attract talented practitioners who, along with students, contribute fresh insight and edge. And of course there is the Gallery, a unique and precious resource within the Community Learning sector.

Throughout its history, Morley College was well known for music. It was reported in the 1927 Board of Education inspection that music was on a scale 'quite unique in the whole field of adult education in England', while the work in English language and literature was superior to any with a couple of possible exceptions. Classes in the visual arts were few, but the College's links in the visual arts establishment were deep. William Rothenstein was commissioned to oversee some of the decorations of the College: Edward Bawden and Eric Ravilious worked on the Refreshment Room and Cyril Mahoney on the Concert Hall. Denis Richards was later to write that the response to these murals brought more publicity to Morley than anything since the musical activities of Gustav Holst and were heralded as a renaissance in British mural painting. Actual art classes however remained few throughout the 1930s (there were a total of just 134 students studying the visual arts in 1938). In the 1937/8 academic year, there were only four classes: painting and drawing, crafts, and two classes taught by a Miss Clarice Moffat entitled 'What is Art For?' and 'Everyday Art', both illustrated by lantern and epidiascope. In 1938/9 the programme was virtually the same. The following year was the outbreak of war. Nevertheless, Miss Moffatt continued with 'Your House and Mine', just as houses came toppling down.

After the bombing, in the 1940/1 academic year, only two art classes were offered, one taught by painter Graham Sutherland, who became an official war artist in the War Artists Scheme (1941–4). With typical sangfroid, the only reference to war in the syllabus for that year was the mention of an official air-raid shelter on the premises.

The post-war period brought a renewal of interest in adult education, particularly in the visual arts. Morley's Art department grew during the late 1940s, and student numbers stood at nearly 300 by the end of the decade (a simultaneous decline in languages and social studies enrolments occurred). At this time, David Bomberg was in post at Borough Polytechnic just down the road, forming the Borough Road Artists Group and, later, some of Bomberg's students had links with Morley: Dorothy Mead taught here and Dennis Creffield exhibited at the Gallery in 1974. In 1950, however, there were still only five art classes on offer; by the end of the decade there were nine. Photography was introduced in 1957 with two leading technologists at Kodak, but it was part of the Science section.

Throughout the 1950s expansion was on the cards. After years of fund-raising under Denis Richards, the main building was opened in 1958 for which, again, murals were commissioned, from Edward Bawden, John Piper and Martin Froy for the Refectory, the Common Room and the Emma Cons Hall. However, before 1960 the Art department was tiny, entrenched and a little conventional and stale. It did have some wonderful tutors and good ideas that attempted to respond to the times; but any change year on year was minor.

In the early 1960s, the College also acquired the King's Arms public house in King Edward Walk, originally intended for the Music department, but when Barry Till became Principal in 1965, it was redesignated for Art as a response to the closure of places for part-time evening

students at art schools. Up to this time there had been only evening classes at Morley, but Barry Till opened the College during the day, starting in September 1967. From the beginning of the 1960s, particularly from 1966, there was a large expansion in the art on offer. Photography was merged with art courses. There were some noteworthy new tutors on the books: Peter de Francia, painting professor at the Royal College of Art, who had been teaching at Morley since the early 1950s, was joined by Mario Dubsky, Gerald Marks and Dorothy Mead who taught painting; Jeremy Leach, pottery; and Adrian Bartlett, printmaking.

Lawrence Toynbee arrived in 1968 and became the first part-time Director of Art with a brief to develop a gallery in the new Arts Centre. He appointed Birgit Skiöld, the Swedish artist who had set up the Charlotte Street print studio, to assist them. She promised to get some of her 'chums' to attend classes: David Hockney and Allen Jones showed up. Printmaking, painting and sculpture were all in the new converted Arts Centre which was opened in 1969.

In the mid-1960s, despite a slight snobbishness around 'craft' at the College, there was a real engagement with the applied arts. Jewellery's reputation was built by Barbara Christie and Nuala Jamison over many years. Bookbinding was established with its own studio, along with glass engraving. Pottery, which had been under Hermann Nonnenmacher since the early 1950s, was taken over by Jill Crowley, appointed by Barry Till after he saw her Royal College of Art (RCA) show in the early 1970s. A proper studio followed with a new kiln funded by the

recently formed Friends of Morley. Textiles, which harked back to Miss Moffatt, was rejuvenated under the quilter Jenny Hollingdale in the top studio of the new Community Education Building in King Edward Walk. Like the other applied arts this went on to flourish under Alex Meyer and latterly Marian Lynch.

Maggi Hambling and Jane Joseph arrived in 1969. Jane Joseph subbed for Anthony Fry's Thursday daytime painting class. She recalls that many of the art students were essentially 'posh': so keen was Barry Till to build the Art department that he invited many of his friends to enrol. In time both women took over the 'Advanced Painting' class, coveted because it paid a higher rate, with many a rueful joke about the 'advanced' referring to the age of the participants and the medley of sounds emanating from both music classes and whistling hearing aids. In all her time at Morley (until 2012), Jane Joseph felt she had great freedom as a tutor; no one ever told her what to do, except in the 1990s, when the staff were drilled in how to behave if an inspector showed up. The most important bit of protocol was to give them a chair to sit on, she said. Good outcome guaranteed!

From the 1970s, there was a pub named The Tower opposite the main entrance where everyone decamped after work. Lawrence Toynbee was always there so it was an essential place for departmental business. It was knocked down in 1988. Perdoni's café on the Kennington Road was another favourite port of call from the earliest years and continues to this day, despite a change in name.

BELOW: Lawrence Toynbee taking an Art class

BELOW RIGHT: A feature on the Art department in the *Illustrated London News*, 1969

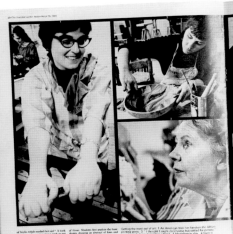

In 1962, the year in which I arrived at Morley, there were no daytime courses at all. And there were no departments either, in the way we have them now. There were two evening classes in painting, taught by Gerald Marks and Mario Dubsky. There was some pottery, and one class each of woodcarving and wood engraving.

There was no change to this pattern until 1965, when Barry Till replaced Denis Richards as Principal. With Barry's arrival the visual arts were about to enjoy a great expansion. He invited the painter Lawrence Toynbee to become a part-time Director of Art. Lawrence lived in Yorkshire and was to travel down to arrive at midday on Monday; he taught on Monday afternoon and evening, and all day Tuesday. He invited other artists whom he admired to teach on other days, notably Anthony Fry and Colin Hayes. Colin was to work at Morley for many years, but Anthony had difficulty in remembering to turn up; he

ART DEPARTMENT

ADRIAN BARTLETT

solved this problem by getting a couple of his former students to stand in for him – Jane Joseph and Maggi Hambling. They took it in turns, week by week, to take his class. I believe this was a confusing experience for some of the students.

An important part of the new Arts Centre was to be a gallery and planning this took a lot of Lawrence's attention. However, the teaching studios were ready for occupation sooner, and more courses were created. Mark Wickham took another painting class, and there was sculpture in the basement, tutored by Glen Hellman and Mark Harvey; bookbinding initially shared the printmaking studio on the second floor. There were some new courses

started in the main College building too: Gunilla Treen was employed to teach jewellery, the pottery was expanded, and there was a new course in glass engraving.

Jennie Lee, Minister for the Arts, officially opened the Arts Centre in February 1969, when the Gallery was ready to be unveiled. Student numbers increased rapidly and there was a growing interest generally in the value of adult education. Lawrence, having got the Centre off to a great start, began to find travelling between London and Yorkshire something of a strain and retired in 1972. His place as Director was taken by Cyril Reason.

Cyril retired in 1980, and I took his place. The role was still very much a part-time one, in terms of remuneration, but with growing numbers of courses, it was increasingly demanding. A general reorganisation of adult education in London as a whole resulted in the creation of full-time heads of departments. I did not apply for this, but continued to run the Printmaking and the Gallery. John Flemons was appointed as Head of Art.

Morley was thriving, but for various reasons Barry Till tendered his resignation in 1986. This was a cause of great sadness to many. He had put so much love and energy into Morley over a period of 21 years. His loyal interest and support continued until his death in 2013.

Having handed over the running of the Gallery some years earlier, I retired from the Printmaking section in 1999.

I started trying to teach drawing and painting as a substitute for a substitute on Monday afternoons late in 1969. As there was no model I placed, rather nervously, three large Suffolk onions on the table in the centre of the studio with students at their easels in a circle around this rustic still life.

It was all new to me – eye-opening and surprising. But I began to enjoy it. In due course I was officially appointed by Barry Till to the ranks of his 'bloody artists', as he always referred to us. Thanks to him the King's Arms was purchased and transformed into Morley's Arts Centre. At the invitation of Lawrence Toynbee (then Head of Painting) I had my first London exhibition in 1973 at the Gallery: portraits from memory of solitary drinkers in South London pubs and landscape drawings made in Suffolk.

Without Morley, I would not have met the distinguished printmaker and teacher Frank Connelly. He introduced me to the medium of monotype, reinvigorated my long-lost love of etching and, since our first encounter in 1988, I have refused to make prints with any other practitioner. He is a master.

The aim of my teaching is to encourage students to realise their own personal vision by the discipline of training the eye, the hand

45 YEARS AT MORLEY

MAGGI HAMBLING

and the heart to act as one. Commitment to hard work is de rigueur, as are cross-dressing and performance at our Christmas parties. My classes are run along the lines of *Dad's Army* in which I play Captain Mainwaring aided and abetted, over the years, by a succession of Sergeant Wilsons.

I still teach in the same studio in the ex-pub on Thursdays, which are for some reason almost inevitably dark just as the flaps of Morley envelopes inevitably never stick. Morley remains marvellously idiosyncratic despite the annoying efforts of the bureaucrats. The Suffolk onions have been replaced by a rich variety of naked humanity.

People of all ages from all walks of life are offered a chance to discover the selves they never knew they had: that is Morley's huge and enduring gift to everyone.

Wendy Taylor and her sculpture *Opus*, 1982–3, outside the Nancy Seear Building

The department continued to grow and flourish through the 1970s and 1980s. In the late 1970s, Sculpture was moved to its own specialist studio in a disused mission hall on Lambeth Walk, where Alan Thornhill ran courses. In the early 1980s the architect John Winter, who had designed the 'Wrap' extension in 1972, was commissioned to design the Nancy Seear Building in King Edward Walk. The aim of this building was to increase the College's appeal to local people. On the top floor, a wide range of art and textiles classes took place, including soft sculpture, taught nowhere else in London and introduced by Victoria Bartlett and Marta Rogoyska. Jean Mumford came in the 1980s to build the Fashion section. Barry Singleton developed the art history on offer. For each new addition to the College, external sculptures were commissioned, from Glenn Hellman (tutor) for the Arts Centre and from Wendy Taylor for the Nancy Seear Building.

How is the department different today? It is unrecognisably larger, more complex and with a great range of subjects on offer. The curriculum is very responsive to change and new courses are offered every year to thousands of students. Each Head of Art brought their own particular contribution; in 1972 Cyril Reason took over from Lawrence Toynbee; Adrian Bartlett, then John Flemons followed. Patrick Goff became Head in 1990, followed by Janet Browne. She was considered warm, responsive 'and came to be loved', not least because she said yes to everything! Under her leadership, the department expanded and diversified. She was followed by Kathy MacLauchlan, under whose watch the department gained a grade 1 in the Ofsted inspection of 2011. The department enjoyed generous funding for many years, but like everywhere else, funding loss over time meant tuition fee rises. Jane Joseph commented that in those days there was a greater cross-section of people in the student body.

The first Art Foundation course started in the mid-1990s under Patrick Goff. It was a one-year programme and a more integrated and complex educational tool for students than had hitherto been attempted in art at Morley. Course tutor Joanna Hyslop led a team teaching painting, drawing, sculpture, printmaking, ceramics, textiles and art history. The students went on to London art schools with a solid foundation that aspired to merge ideas, materials and techniques and how they interrelated. As a result, they could survive the tough environs of art school, could 'posit questions and find answers for themselves without relying on tutors' (itself a telling commentary on the state of teaching in art schools). As she put it, 'We taught students how to generate ideas as a tool, as part of one's practice, alongside the practical, making side. It is all about looking and being confident about it.' The course has re-emerged after a gap, still aspiring to the same high standards. In a sense it is a condensing of all that is great about teaching and learning for students of art and design at Morley.

Tens of thousands of students have attended art classes at Morley over the years. For some it has heralded major change; unemployed students became textiles artists, taking commissions; bankers became jewellers; and clerical workers became painters. For others the change was simply making work for personal pleasure.

CASS BREEN

OPENING DOORS

SUZAN SWALE

I have taught at Morley College for 35 years. Morley is a place where people still open doors for you. Literally, when you are laden with books in the corridor, and also metaphorically, opening doors in your mind, discovering new skills and gaining self-confidence.

Because of Morley, I have learned as much from my students as they have learned from me. All the students that I have taught in life drawing and painting and in art history possess a unique experience and knowledge in their own fields and backgrounds.

I first taught at Morley in 1979, deputising for Evelyn Ballentine. Soon afterwards I took over John Epstein's class, which had a female student as a caretaker. This was D.H., who was the class secretary. The class had been without a tutor for quite some time, and I had to work really hard to convince D.H. and the class that I was a fit replacement for teaching life drawing and painting, despite the fact that I had taught full-time BA and MA Fine Art courses since leaving the Royal College of Art.

Over the years, I have experienced further education classes where you could enrol for £1, when the Greater London Council (GLC) were in charge. I have taught while heavily pregnant and my baby was born on the day after teaching at Morley. My son was in the Morley crèche while I taught all day on Wednesdays.

I have had a police detective working on a case for which I was a witness join my class, I have had my life drawing class provoke a debate that ended up in the national press, and I have taught with a chemo-pump around my waist, when I was ill with cancer, during which time Morley was fantastic. I have laughed and cried at Morley and I have made a large number of friends there. Many of the students are now practising artists and they continue to support the College. Morley is like a second home. I have had students who have said that they will continue to attend classes as long as they can manage to get there. That says everything.

Morley's Murals

THERE MUST BE MANY people for whom Morley College means murals, and in particular the ones painted between 1928 and 1930 by Edward Bawden, Eric Ravilious and Cyril (alias Charles) Mahoney. For those who know something of these paintings, sadly destroyed by a bomb in 1940, the story of the later murals in the College buildings, mostly still in place, may contain surprises.

The three walls of the basement Refreshment Room in the old building were painted by Ravilious and Bawden with scenes from Elizabethan and Jacobean dramas. Small, rather doll-like figures enacted their roles, giving a comic edge even to the tragedies, while in the zone above their flimsy pavilions, deities and allegories floated in the sky. The sophisticated mockery was even more apparent in Ravilious's depiction of an open-fronted doll's house with figures in each room, apparently derived from activities across the road from the Kensington lodgings he shared with Bawden. This was a survivor from the first proposal for depicting 'London Life', rather than illustrating the drama theme. The section was photographed in colour at the time, giving a sense of the pastel colours to dispel the gloom of the basement on a winter's evening.

These paintings were the gift of the art dealer Sir Joseph Duveen, who had previously sponsored Rex Whistler's work in the Tate Gallery Restaurant. The Morley

ABOVE: 'Life in a boarding house', a detail of the mural by Eric Ravilious, reproduced in *The Graphic*, 1930

LEFT: *Faust, Pomona, Arraignment of Paris* by Eric Ravilious, 1930

BELOW: Ravilious and Bawden working on the murals. From the *Evening Standard*, 3 February 1930

commission was arranged through Charles Aitken, the director of the Tate. Eva Hubback at Morley was keen, having seen how the dreary basement at Millbank had been transformed, and the artists were selected on the recommendation of William Rothenstein, the principal of the Royal College of Art.

While Ravilious and Bawden lifted the spirits with the frivolity of the Bright Young Things, Mahoney, described to Duveen by Aitken as 'a clever student who works more like Poussin', struck a more sober note. In the recess over the stage of the Concert Hall, his mural showed a ring of folk dancers to reflect one of the main uses of the Hall, and modern dress personifications of arts and letters were seated below. This was the sort of highly structured, modernized Renaissance classicism that students in the 1920s were encouraged to follow, and if in photographs it seems a little stiff and solemn today, at the time the

contemporary clothes and hairstyles must have made a strong connection with everyday life. The colour accents were blue and red.

The paintings were a huge public relations success for the College, not only from the art critics, but from the opening ceremony performed by the leader of the Opposition Stanley Baldwin, which was reported around the world. In it he thanked God for a place such as Morley that 'opens a window in one's soul completely remote and alien from one's daily work'.

In 1938, John Anthony Greene, a pupil of Bawden, added murals to the vestibule between the original building and the recent extension by Edward Maufe. The design had much in common with the Refreshment Room, with spindly structures like Victorian seaside piers carrying costumed figures against a large blank background. These too were lost in the Blitz.

LEFT: Cyril Mahoney's folk dancers, and ABOVE, his Melpomene from *Pleasures of Life*

RIGHT: One of John Anthony Greene's murals

The Canterbury Tales, 1958–61, Edward Bawden's murals in the refectory.
LEFT: 'The Tale of Sir Topaz', 'The Clerk's Tale' and 'The Pardoner's Tale'. CENTRE: 'The Wife of Bath's Tale' and 'The Nun's Priest's Tale'. RIGHT: 'The Squire's Tale', 'The Knight's Tale', 'The Prioress's Tale' and 'The Manciple's Tale'

Eva Hubback's belief in the value of murals remained firm and she engaged the artist Angela Latham, in 1948, to teach a weekly class on design and technique. The students, mostly drawn from other art schools, were offered walls to paint in the upper 'B' corridor of the 1938 building; a 22ft × 7ft painting by Fred Millett (who went on to a notable career as a muralist and architectural artist) and Brian Probyn was executed, showing 'working-class life and dwellings', more decorative than social realist in style. The surface was coated in 'Presafix', a new varnish. It is possible that the work lies beneath coats of paint and could be recovered.

As the new building took shape, the War Damages money from the lost 1930 murals was used to commission replacements, even though the official estimate of £3,900, based on tripling the original Duveen donation, hardly represented the value of what had been lost. Edward Bawden agreed to come back and decorate the new Refectory, replacing the Refreshment Room on the first floor. He chose subjects from Chaucer's *Canterbury Tales*, giving him scope for comedy and the grotesque that he enjoyed, in a flattened perspective reflecting some of the style of his work with Ravilious. One of his students, Justin Todd, painted one of the panels in a compatible style.

ABOVE: The 'lost' mural was painted by Fred Millett and Brian Probyn in the short-lived class on mural painting in 1948–9

RIGHT: Justin Todd at the opening of 'Edward Bawden: Storyteller' in September 2014.
FAR RIGHT: His mural illustrating 'The Reeve's Tale', 'The Merchant's Tale' and 'The Miller's Tale'

Bridget Riley, *The Morley College Mural*, 1973

John Piper, *Abstract: Nailsworth Mill, Gloucestershire*, 1958

John Piper had connections with Morley from before the war, and although he had become one of Britain's most famous artists, he agreed to paint a long canvas of a semi-abstract landscape that was installed on the wall facing the entrance in the Common Room/foyer. In the new Emma Cons Hall, Martin Froy, a former Slade School student, then in his early 30s, continued the abstract evocation of outdoors in the form of watery shapes and colours in his two long friezes, completed in 1959, achieving the difficult task of decorating without distracting an audience from a performance, for which Mahoney had been commended.

Bridget Riley's Morley mural, 1973, was funded by the Edwin Austin Abbey Fund at the Royal Academy, and was chosen by Barry Till to be positioned in and reflect the style of the new John Winter building, bringing a completely Modernist item to the collection. Like the Piper, it is a moveable canvas, and having first been placed by the courtyard entrance, it has currently found its home where Piper's mural originally hung.

The most recent addition to the Morley murals was a collaborative work organised by Patrick Goff for Adult Learners' Week, executed in 24 hours as part of a 'Paint-in' in 1994 – the idea behind it is thus more representative of Morley's participatory ethos than any of its august predecessors. It adds interest to the apse-like space created by Edward Maufe beyond the staircase at the end of the Library wing. After the extreme of abstraction represented by Bridget Riley, this exhibits a Postmodernist return to figuration, although there is still a controlling geometrical grid in the background to give structure to the gigantic and richly coloured blooms.

ALAN POWERS

Morley's Art Collection and the Artists' International Association

Morley's history as a 'College for Working Men and Women' attracted those who believed there was a social function for art. It is, therefore, hardly surprising that the works of art that Morley has accumulated over the years largely reject the notion of the autonomous art object and, instead, actively engage with human activities. This is not to say that their art is traditional, but rather to be classed as 'figurative modernism': art that approaches the surface of the painting and the medium of paint in ways that assert modernism, but that retain an interest in the figurative, a concentration on the human condition.

Many of the artists viewed on the College's walls were involved with the Artists' International Association (AIA), an organisation that grew out of the anti-fascist movements of the 1930s. The Depression of the 1930s and the rise of fascism gave the arguments around the function of art a greater urgency, and the AIA encouraged debate and involvement. Robert Medley, represented in the Morley collection by *Bus Stop – Fulham Road* (c.1960), says in his *Memoir* that as an artist 'it was impossible to ignore the tragic consequences of the slump'. He describes group readings of *Das Kapital* with Misha Black and Clifford Rowe, founders of the AIA, in the early 1930s, and chairing meetings 'that preceded the founding' of the AIA. Julian Trevelyan, whose *High Tide on the Thames* (1954) is held by Morley, was involved in the Mass Observation movement in the 1930s, making collages of Bolton (known as 'Worktown' in the Mass Observation surveys because it epitomised the working towns of the north of England heavily hit by the Depression). He was horrified by the conditions he observed and remained active in AIA political debates, defending the revolutionary nature of surrealism in the 1938 AIA debate on socialist art. Gerald Marks, who taught painting and drawing at Morley from 1955 to 1965, was for many years a member of the Central Committee of the AIA and chairman in 1950. His *Man and Machine* (1958) in the Morley collection is a work that in its choice of subject matter, a factory, shows this desire to engage with ordinary life and elevate it to the importance formally accorded only to grand places or beautiful vistas.

Morley artists were also the beneficiaries of the AIA Artists' Refugee Committee, established in 1938 to help

Julian Trevelyan, *High Tide (The Thames)*, 1954

ABOVE: Gerald Marks, *Man and Machine*, 1958

LEFT: Robert Medley, *Bus Stop – Fulham Road*, early 1960s

European artists escape, firstly, Czechoslovakia, and then as war began, other parts of Europe threatened by fascism. Oskar Kokoschka, who was commissioned to paint Morley's director of Music, Sir Michael Tippett (1963), escaped Czechoslovakia with their aid.

The AIA organised exhibitions throughout the 1930s in aid of Republican Spain and then post-war in aid of Peace and Reconstruction. Ruskin Spear, whose *Portrait of Denis Richards, Principal of Morley*, 1963 (see page 27), is held by the College, and Peter de Francia, whose *Chinese Acrobats* (1956) is part of the collection, were both involved in exhibitions run by the AIA. De Francia had arrived in England in 1939, ahead of the invasion of Brussels where he had been studying. Post-war he studied in Italy with the communist painter Renato Guttuso before returning to England, where he continued a commitment to politically engaged art. He taught part-time at Morley College in the 1960s.

Lawrence Toynbee, who taught at Morley from 1965 to 1972, is represented by a large painting, *The Rugby Tackle* (1965), a perfect example of the artist reconnecting with a wider public that artists in the 1930s sought. Dorothy Mead, who taught at Morley in 1963–5 and 1973–5, is represented by *The Pianist 1* (see page 132), a work that evokes the intensity of the pianist and the listening experience. The neo-humanism of the Morley collection shows even in the landscapes. Kathleen Allen's *The Rebuilding of Morley College* (1957) uses a fleshy pink, as though humanising the building process, tying together the human loss of the war with its reconstruction. Jane Joseph, who taught at Morley for over 40 years, places her *Thames from Kew, October, Tide Rising* (2008) firmly in a

tradition that recognises the real world as the place where art belongs. The very specificity of the title places the human there, even if the figure is absent from the painting. Maggi Hambling's paintings *Barry Till* , 1986 (see page 33) and *Bev Walters*, 2003 (see page 26), both portraits of former Principals of Morley, are more than portraits: they fizz with energy and a sense of the individual, there, in front of the viewer.

Oskar Kokoschka, *Portrait of Sir Michael Tippett, Director of Music 1940–51*, 1963

Peter de Francia, *Chinese Acrobats*, 1956

LEFT: Kathleen Allen, *The Rebuilding of Morley College*, 1957

RIGHT: Jane Joseph, *The Thames from Kew, October, Tide Rising*, 2008

Lawrence Toynbee, *The Rugby Tackle*, 1965

The Morley collection represents the concern with ordinary humanity that emerged in the 1930s; a neo-humanism in art that rejected the purity of abstraction for the chaos of life. This did not mean a Soviet-type realism, but a reintroduction of meaning, content and social, if not always political, engagement on the part of the artist.
JENNY VUGLAR

LEFT: The Queen Mother with pottery tutors Hermann Nonnenmacher and his wife

Ceramics

THE FIRST RECORD OF CERAMICS ('Pottery and Modelling') taught at Morley College is in 1948 with Hermann and Erna Nonnenmacher. Hermann had studied sculpture at the Royal Academy in Dresden, Germany, and emigrated to England in 1938. He taught pottery without using the wheel.

The Ceramics section has a link to the influential Studio Pottery movement created by Bernard Leach with his grandson, Jeremy Leach, teaching at the College from 1963 to 1969. Jeremy studied at the Central School of Arts, as did Colin Saunders, who taught in 1967–70. Alan Thornhill, sculptor, studied at Camberwell and Farnham Schools of Art and taught in the section between 1975 and 1979.

Jill Crowley, the first MA Ceramics graduate to be employed, started in 1970 whilst still studying at the Royal College of Art. Jill was head of the section for over 30 years and is still teaching. She set up Morley's first family pottery course in 1980, where children and adults learn specific projects together, developed and taught for many years by Annette Welch and now by Caroline Tattersall.

During this period, Jill visited Paul Soldner in America. He was a student of Peter Voulkos, one of America's most influential ceramic artists, and together they created the 'California School' of ceramic arts by combining Western materials and technology with Japanese techniques (raku) and aesthetics. On her return, Jill set up the first raku course at Morley. Raku teachers at Morley have included David Roberts, Christine Constant and Annette Welch, who

is still keeping the flame alight. Jill can also be credited for training over 15 technicians, giving them invaluable experience of running a studio, mixing glazes, and packing and firing kilns. Our current technician is Alex Huber.

Other notable potters who have taught ceramics are Naine Woodrow (1981–4) who set up North Street Potters, an ongoing successful workshop in South London; Linda Gunn-Russell (1977–81); Angus Suttie, a significant maker and tutor from 1982 until his untimely death in 1991; and Sophie MacCarthy (1993–9). Many, such as Takeshi Yasuda and Kate Malone, have come to demonstrate and teach on short courses or give lectures.

Morley has had a close relationship with London Potters, a voluntary organisation formed in 1986, associated strongly with Emmanuel Cooper, a sadly missed figure in the world of ceramics. It is the only London-based society offering membership to both professional and non-professional makers, and provides a forum for the exchange of ideas and experiences for those interested in the subject. It has an annual exhibition in the Morley Gallery and the College hosted their lecture series on Friday evenings for many years. A packed Holst Room assembled to hear Emmanuel Cooper discuss the work of Bernard Leach.

My first teaching job at Morley was in 1988, working with Jill Crowley, Annette Welch and Angus Suttie, who were exhibiting both nationally and internationally with figurative and object-based sculptural ceramics. My functional and sculptural approach with the wheel offered something new to the section.

I feel privileged to be head of this thriving Ceramics section, where we have a newly refurbished modern studio, and the materials and equipment to explore a wide range of contemporary ceramic approaches. As an outward-facing section, we work increasingly in partnership across the College and cultivate a diverse range of external relationships, including an ongoing series of masterclasses developed with the national Craft Potters Association. We have also run educational programmes with the prominent London-based Kids Company and have a recent collaboration with Tate Modern and the local Dragon Café.

We introduce our students to other professional makers to broaden their outlook and understanding of what clay is and what can be done with it. Our current students range from 20- to 80-year-olds. Interestingly, we have had a number of undergraduates attending who are seeking to complement their chosen degrees in graphics, fashion, illustration and fine art. Many students set up their own workshops alongside classes at Morley and sell their work at craft fairs and retail outlets. In class they explore techniques, take creative risks, and experiment with a wide range of clays, glaze textures and surfaces. It is wonderful to see the level of confidence and achievement that develops in students as a result of learning new ceramic skills.

DUNCAN HOOSON

through the dynamics of the student body and with the help of the College, they slowly started to build a workshop that could run regular jewellery courses.

Principal Barry Till saw the potential for developing jewellery courses. He applied for funding from the Goldsmiths' Centre and the jewellery studio was soon equipped with jeweller's benches and torches. Barbara Christie took on the role of section head for Jewellery, and the workshop and courses developed into a well-established and reputable section offering morning, afternoon and evening courses for different levels. In 2009, Barbara Christie decided to move on from Morley and develop her flourishing career, and Helen Smith took over the role of section head for Jewellery.

At that point the studio was on the ground floor and was surrounded by music classes and general teaching rooms where exams took place. The sound of hammering and forging metal would be timed to follow the rhythm of salsa or classical music. There were several occasions when frustrated music tutors would march into the studio and ask us to stop making so much noise.

In 2010, with the Morley Renaissance in full swing, the jewellery studio was able to move to its present location, which proved a great success. The new jewellery studio is spacious and well equipped with hardwood jeweller's benches, a fully extracted hearth system, an enamelling room and all the latest technology. Since then the section has continued to expand. The courses have doubled in volume and now run regular masterclasses and weekend courses with leading jewellers in their field.

As with all sections in Morley, the students have been an inspiration. The loyalty and passion they show for their subject has carried the jewellery section to new heights. Showing their work regularly through Morley's excellent Gallery has spread their reputation far and wide.

HELEN SMITH

Jewellery

OVER THE YEARS, the Jewellery section at Morley College has undergone several transformations. In the early 1970s, Gunilla Treen and Catherine Mannheim took the first tentative steps to developing what would become a thriving section. They were soon joined by Barbara Christie and Nuala Jamison, all influential jewellers at the start of their careers. As well as the jewellery courses, Joan MacKarell was running an enamelling course.

When the College first started offering jewellery courses, the studio was very basic. The students remember sitting on nursery chairs and working at low tables. They would bring in a G clamp and a piece of plywood to use as a bench peg, and shared tools and equipment. They organised sales and collections, and

RIGHT: Ring by Frances Ling and 'Wind in the Willows' piece by Victoria O'Connell

Life modelling
class, 1950s

Sculpture

THE PELHAM MISSION HALL (the Henry Moore Sculpture
Studio) is off-site from the main College and is a local
landmark as one of the last remaining Victorian buildings
on Lambeth Walk.

Patricia Leigh
sculpting 'The Wave',
which won a prize in
the competition
'Inspired by the V&A'

Pelham Mission Hall was built in 1910, with the
Archbishop of Canterbury at the time, the Most Reverend
Randall Thomas Davidson, laying a date stone on 18 July
1910. The Hall was initially used by St Mary's church (now
home to the Garden Museum), and was famed for its
open-air pulpit from which preachers would address the
shoppers visiting the Lambeth Walk market stalls. It still
blows hot air today with the ceramic sculpture kiln
extraction unit exiting from the pulpit. The crypt below
the church, accessed by a trapdoor in the floor, is used to
store materials for our triennial bronze-casting courses.

Morley College acquired the lease of the building for
£6,000 in 1978, following a fund-raising drive by Principal
Barry Till. Donations were received from the Gulbenkian
Foundation, the Baring Foundation and the Sainsbury's
Foundation. Sculptor Henry Moore donated a small
sculpture which was sold at auction and helped to raise
£2,000; in return, the College named the new sculpture
studio after him. The freehold of the building was
eventually bought by the College in 2006.

Gavin Cordeiro joined the Morley sculpture courses
soon after their inception in 1979, wanting to learn woodcarving and techniques for making his own guitars. He
recounts that the Art department held their end-of-term
dance parties in the Hall in the early 1980s. Gavin still
attends the Tuesday afternoon 'Exploring Sculpture' class,
working in wood being a great asset to the class sharing
his skills.

The sculpture studio went through a major refurbishment in 2011, and now provides one of the best

further-education sculpture facilities. There is an extensive range of courses including metalwork, clay life modelling, stone- and woodcarving, and bronze casting, thanks to the expertise of the diverse practising exhibiting sculptors teaching and giving technical advice. There is also a good tradition of progression in the Sculpture section, where several of our valued technicians and tutors first started as students.

Giles Corby, a valued technician and tutor, helped to develop the expert metal sculpture facilities, following on from Derek Howarth and initial courses by Sheila Vollmer (present Programme Manager for Sculpture), all of whom were past technicians to sculptor Sir Antony Caro.

The talents of the Morley sculpture students are reflected by several of our learners being exhibited in the annual national adult learners' competition 'Inspired by the V&A'. This year student Patricia Leigh won the sculpture prize.

The excellent facilities and ambient space at Morley's sculpture studio are often praised by our students. Today, the Hall sees approximately 250 students of all ages, backgrounds, experiences and approaches, pass through its doors each week, undertaking sculpture courses in its unique Victorian surroundings, producing sculptural work in a variety of materials, techniques and craftsmanship, reflecting the talent and creativity of Morley's adult learners.

SHEILA VOLLMER

Wood-carving class
past and present

SCULPTURE FILM

DAVID-PAUL PERTAUB

Although I've been interested in photography for some time, I only began making films at an evening course ('Filmmaking for Beginners') at Morley College in the autumn of 2013. I can thoroughly recommend it – not only was it great fun for all involved, but it was extremely well organised and comprehensive.

Following up on my new skills and interests, in the winter of 2013 I enrolled on a Masters module in Documentary Filmmaking at University College London (UCL), in the Department of Anthropology, with Academy Award-winning producer Vikram Jayanti as

tutor. The brief for the final piece of coursework was to plan, produce, film and edit a 10–15-minute documentary film on a topic of personal interest.

I live right round the corner from Pelham Hall, Morley's sculpture studio, and I've always been intrigued by what goes on there,

so this was a perfect excuse to find out more. I was really lucky: as a student of the film classes, Morley College's Sculpture section welcomed me into the Hall for filming with open arms!

I didn't only aim my camera, I tried my hand at clay modelling in the life class and bashed away with a mallet in the stone-carving class. Anthropology does involve fieldwork after all! The result was the film 'Modelling at Morley', a profile of a life-modelling class and a professional life model at Pelham Hall, which was very well received by my tutors at UCL.

Printmaking

I ARRIVED AT MORLEY COLLEGE in 1962 to take over the wood-engraving evening class. At that time there were only evening classes. None of my students were making, or hoping to make, wood engravings; lino cutting was the preferred medium. There was a very good Albion type press which is still going strong today.

When Barry Till became Principal, he declared that he wanted to build up the Art department to equal the already illustrious Music department. He appointed a former fellow Coldstream Guard, painter Lawrence Toynbee, to execute his plans. Fortunately for me, Lawrence felt that a good Printmaking section was essential. Barry's conversion of the abandoned pub on the other side of King Edward Walk as his new Arts Centre was an exciting time.

Neither Lawrence nor I had sufficient experience of setting up a print room which would cover etching and lithography, as well as the relief printing we were already doing. He invited the Swedish artist Birgit Skiöld to discuss the project. Birgit and I got on well immediately. She was very interested in the idea and we all settled down to detailed design and equipment. She was full of ideas; I had the minivan.

It was decided that there would be a gallery on the ground floor, sculpture in the basement, a painting studio on the first floor, printmaking on the second and a small lecture room at the top. Birgit and I were a bit dismayed to learn that we would have to share our space with the bookbinding class — an unfortunate combination of messy and clean crafts. However, very sadly for the book-binders, their tutor died not long later and their class was ultimately housed elsewhere.

The new Arts Centre was officially opened in early 1969 by the Minister for the Arts, Jennie Lee. There was considerable media interest. A young Stephen Frears came to film a programme about it for the BBC and, as a result, we learnt the nature of our neighbours in the tall building on the other side of Westminster Bridge Road: MI6! One of their security guards on an upper floor had seen the glint of the BBC's camera lens in the print room and a posse rushed over to see if we were spying on them.

Birgit agreed to do a little teaching on Tuesday mornings, which she continued to do on and off until she died in 1982. I did the rest of the teaching as we gradually accumulated new students. David Hockney looked in to give us moral support and offered to join our classes if we needed an extra name on the register. After a few years we had expanded at a gratifying rate and employed more tutors — Susan Jameson, Terry Shave, Dorothea Wight, Frank Connelly and Marc Balakjian.

Fees were very much lower at that time. Our expansion was rapid, running courses every day except Sunday and most evenings. We also invited well-known artists to visit and talk to our students, such as Anthony Gross, Michael Rothenstein and Julian Trevelyan. Akira Kurosaki came over from Japan to teach a course on Japanese woodcut. We had long waiting lists and most sessions were overcrowded which prompted concerns about health and safety. In the one studio we had acid baths, perpetually giving off fumes, and an aquatint box exuding resin dust, quite apart from other chemicals and solvents. The head of the Art department by this time was Patrick Goff, who was very supportive of the Print section and solved our problems by letting us move into the rooms on the top floor.

Boy and Fish
by Chris
Salmon

I stopped teaching in 1999 and my place was taken by Frank Connelly until 2013. It continues to thrive under Michelle Avison, who had originally come to us as a postgraduate student from the Slade, had done some teaching and then took over from Frank.

ADRIAN BARTLETT

Textiles

TEXTILES, A RELATIVE NEWCOMER in the Art department at Morley, began with Victoria Bartlett's classes in soft sculpture in 1975. Cyril Reason, then head of Art and commuting up from Brighton, appointed Victoria, a notable artist in her own right. Classes were first housed in the basement of what is now the Arts Centre, with the Lambeth relief sewer gurgling beneath the floor. Victoria's students worked in sync with the cloth sculpture of Pop artists such as Jann Haworth, one of the first to 'cast in cloth' in the 1960s and at a time when feminism was a visible influence in the public sphere. Cloth, stitch and stuffing as media referenced a female language, playfully poking fun at a male-dominated art world. Making use of recycled materials, the classes were cheap to run and produced elegant, subversive and witty work.

The Morley Soft Sculpture Group made its mark locally, winning first prize for their 'soft' fence for the new Lambeth Walk development, and were interviewed for the BBC TV Arena arts programme. Later they exhibited in the National Theatre foyer.

Victoria also introduced papermaking. Her classes were filled with non-working women during the day, making use of the College crèche, and in the evening with ILEA teachers topping up their skills, as did London's art school students, particularly those studying costume and theatre design.

Keen to expand and promote a fine-art slant to Textiles, Barry Till was the driving force in establishing 'Classical Tapestry Weaving' with Marta Rogoyska as tutor. Her legacy survives today with tapestry at Morley as a unique class for adult learners in London and currently enjoying a renewed popularity under William Jefferies.

In 1983, when the 'yellow building' (later named the Nancy Seear Building) was completed on King Edward Walk as a centre for community education, Jenny Hollingdale was appointed by Barry to occupy the top floor. With dedicated studio space and an inclusive agenda, Textiles expanded to offer patchwork and quilting, embroidery, crochet, dressmaking, basketry and hat-making. Fridays offered a drop-in Arts and Crafts Workshop for £1. In the mid-1980s, machine knitting was introduced under Alex Mayer, who was to become head of Textiles from 1999 to 2012.

Experimental Textiles', combining a wide range of dry and wet techniques, and giving students an exciting introduction to the breadth and scope of the section.

Such diversity and industry took its toll on the studio. In 2013, a timely refurbishment was undertaken and today students work with visual imagination in a congenial atmosphere of artistic freedom, producing work of value, ingenuity and quality. Regular exhibitions and collaborations affirm the flow of creative currents and multiple approaches that coexist in a studio full of life, energy and colour.

MARIAN LYNCH

Jenny firmly established high standards in patchwork and quilting at the College, with students winning City & Guild national medals. In 1990, when the plight of babies and young children in Romanian orphanages hit the news, the Textiles section responded through a community quilt project. A hundred and forty cot quilts were designed and constructed from donated cloth by 70 participants, ranging in age from 11 to 82, supervised by tutors in their free time.

The section expanded further when the studio space was divided by a partition of cupboards, enabling two classes to run simultaneously. Janet Browne, head of Art with a textiles background herself, supported Alex Mayer in developing new courses giving students the opportunity to participate in wet and messy processes, including dyeing, felt and print. Together, over tea in the Refectory, they wrote the Textile Foundation course. Janet introduced Debby Brown, who established 'Creative and

By the time a City & Guilds patchwork and quilting course drew me to Morley College in 2007, both my parents were dead. The course was just what I was looking for; a place to test myself within an established structure. Successful completion of that course led me to take the Morley Textile Foundation course that in turn encouraged me, aged 52, to apply to university. I graduated with First Class Honours in 2013. Thank you, Morley.

Morley College had another resonance in my family: I had always known that this was the place that my parents had met. He from London, a student at the Brixton School of

THE PLACE MY PARENTS MET

KATE VICIC

Building who had taken advantage of a scheme to educate young men who had completed their National Service (three years in post-war Palestine, in his case). She, granddaughter of a Durham miner, for whom education was the route out of a colliery village. She had made the journey south to teacher-training college, where she could escape her fate of miner's wife. He lived in Brixton with his widowed mother; she in 'digs' with medical students from St Thomas's Hospital. She loved to dance; he to socialise. Both met at a student 'hop' at Morley College. The rest is history.

Fashion

Dressmaking classes were introduced in 1892, just three years following the establishment of Morley College. They were popular enough by July that year to hold a Women's Holiday Prize Needlework Competition. Prizes were offered for plain sewing ('for the best nightgown, hand work only'), knitting ('for the best pair of socks or stockings, adult size') and darning ('for the best darn – the hole to be worn, not cut, and not less than a penny in size').

The following year, an April entry in the *Morley College Magazine* states that there was 'a very wide difference of opinion . . . as to the best method of teaching . . . dress-making'. Many students thought 'the scientific system' had all the advantages, whilst others praised 'the good old-fashioned method', so much so that Miss Frost, the tutor, undertook to give 'two distinct classes' the following term, which would give 'the members of each . . . the opportunity to prove . . . how superior is the *method* they have adopted'.

Sewing machines could have been provided from the beginning, but in 1907, when the College became home to one of the County Council's trade schools for girls, machining would have been a priority. Certainly by 1917,

courses list 'machining skills' in the first term.

Dressmaking classes were not offered from 1927 until 1981, when the College took over various smaller adult education centres in an ILEA reorganisation; in 1981, the course guide lists five

ABOVE: Tutu by Alice Angus

BELOW: Shirts by Aneeta Patel

tutors teaching dressmaking, crafts, design and 'Dressmaking for Asian Ladies'. Classes took place in a variety of venues for the next eight years, including the Charlotte Sharman School, West Square, a short walk from the College.

The Charlotte Sharman School was where I took up my appointment as fashion lecturer in 1989. The equipment was shockingly outdated. I had a maximum of 18 students and struggled to teach my seven courses a week using one iron, with one wooden ironing board and eight old sewing machines sporting brass plaques claiming 'Property of the LCC', which had been abolished in 1965!

Although three other tutors were listed in the guide as teaching in other centres, I never met them at all. At the end of that year, when the ILEA was abolished, I became the only tutor teaching these skills and 'Making Clothes' was moved to Room E14 in the Nancy Seear Building, where we have been ever since.

I would like to say that the clothes-making section really took off then, but despite improved equipment and the introduction of other subjects over the years, such as tailoring and hat-making taught by professionals, what is now known as the Fashion section has only been able to prosper since the 'Morley Renaissance' began to take shape from 2008. Studios became available at weekends and we were able to run a course for every day the College was open, increasing the number from 45 to 92 courses in 2010–11. This reflected an interest in fashion which hadn't been met till then. With an extra studio added in 2011, more equipment and a complete renovation, we now offer nearly 200 courses.

It is true that some of our more esoteric offerings such as 'Dress Your Pets' and 'Making Women's Clothes for Men' may not have been successful, but many other entirely new and niche courses are. Costume-making, dancewear, accessories, corsetry and lingerie, tailoring, vintage fashion, design and styling are some of the areas now firmly part of what we do, building on the wide range of garment construction and pattern-cutting courses that form the foundation of our work.

While we no longer run competitions for darning holes in socks, we have moved with the times and set the agenda for professional skills taught by experts in the subject. It's a simple but winning formula and long may it continue.

JEAN MUMFORD

Dress by Patsy Burrows

Digital Design, Film and Photography

DIGITAL DESIGN IS ONE OF THE youngest sections in Morley College. It was initially formed out of two sections, Computer Studies and Computing for Art and Design, both small areas when first established around the year 2000, but which rapidly grew. In 2003, the section officially became Computer and Digital Design, and soon there was a whole range of classes in computer software and new media technology.

Early courses offered opportunities to study desktop publishing, digital graphic design, image editing and web design, alongside more traditional computer classes such as word-processing, spreadsheets and using the Internet. Yet, while basic computing courses were popular for a short time, within a few years there was less demand for them. Consequently, the section started to build the programme of art and design courses in creative computing that it now offers. Firmly established within

the Art and Design department, there was further expansion in 2010 as Digital Design joined up with Film and Photography.

The first course, in what later would be called media production, was the television class, launched in 1973, where students could learn about aspects of studio production and camerawork. The class took place in the College's brand new purpose-built TV studio and control room. Video and media production classes continued throughout the 1970s and into the 1980s, and photography joined the programme during this time. Early photography classes included processing and printing film in the new darkroom facilities in the Nancy Seear Building, and then later accredited City & Guilds courses in photography.

By the early 1990s, the old TV studio facility had become rather neglected. Video courses were taught for a while outside the College at the Pimlico Arts and Media Centre, but by 1999, media production had moved back again to Morley. The old studio underwent some refurbishment, and became the temporary home for film and video.

The next big transformation was going digital: old analogue editing equipment was replaced by computers with video-editing software, and Super VHS camcorders gave way to the higher definition mini-DV format. In photography, the switch was to digital SLRs; the use of software for digital image manipulation also became more popular. Also, during this period, Film and Photography transferred from Humanities to Visual Arts.

Morley has always been keen to embrace new technological advances and provide facilities for students to pursue their studies in a professional environment. In the 1970s, there was the innovative teaching space of the TV studio, while more recently the learning experience has been enhanced by the welcome

My story from Congo to Britain is a very long story, full of loads of emotions and things that were really difficult. I was an artist before I came to England: I had the opportunity in my country to do a BA in Fine Art. I started to work as an independent artist. I was always passionate about helping children, and things that were happening at the time in my county with children living on the streets were just horrible. This affected me, and I began to make art about these children. I wanted to support children who live on the streets, to raise awareness about child abuse, to promote education and protection for children everywhere in the world. So, I started that back home in the Congo, and it was going very well, until it got to a certain point when people started to notice and unfortunately some of them were not happy with the work that I was doing. That's the reality, and I couldn't carry on anymore, because I was being threatened all of the time. I also didn't want to put my family in danger. So the only way to survive was just to leave: it became too dangerous for me to stay, so I decided to go and find a new home.

I came to Britain. I started studying at Morley. I was doing many things: ceramics, photography and English level 1. Then someone at Morley told me about the Art Foundation course. It sounded really good to me. They told me I had to apply for an interview, and I was a bit afraid because of my English, which is very limited: I thought they may not give me a place. But it was fine, I did get a place and I was really happy because that changed a lot of things. Not just about my work, but about my life as well, and so I can never forget that. It was really a good thing for me.

Doing the Art Foundation, I've had the opportunity to learn things that I didn't know

MY STORY

CEDOUX KADIMA TSHIZANGA

or that I hadn't tried before. As an artist, I understand that there are no limits in everything we do: there are so many possibilities. Artists can explore ideas and share a message, or communicate with people. This year I had an exhibition in the Saatchi Gallery, which was about my experience as a refugee from the Congo. It was a very successful exhibition, because

after that I had loads of good and positive feedback from people.

My dream is one day to go back to the Congo and carry on working with children, so I again have the opportunity to teach them how to draw, how to paint: that was my happiness, something that makes me *me*, who I am today. It was a really incredible experience to work with children, to hear their stories, and just to spend time with them. Also, it is important for me to tell their stories in my art: that's why I decided to carry on now.

I will continue with my art. Art is my life. I always say that art is my magic key, so I can never stop it: I will always carry on with art.

addition of the digital design studio, with its state-of-the-art iMac computers, and up-to-the-minute software.

Digital Design, Film and Photography now offers an amazing range of courses, including stop motion and 3D animation, sound design, blogging and social media, HTML5 (latest Hypertext Markup Language for web applications) and CSS3 (most recent version of Cascading Style Sheets for formatting of layout of web pages), alongside more traditional classes in portraiture, fashion and travel photography, and filmmaking. In the year that Morley celebrates its 125th anniversary, the section is launching an exciting new programme of Digital Media Foundation courses to help students build skills for the future.
FAY HOOLAHAN

Morley's Gallery

MORLEY COLLEGE DID NOT always have a gallery space and there is little evidence of artwork on display other than the magnificent murals by Ravilious, Bawden and Mahoney, and the very occasional exhibition, such as the one that helped start the career of Julian Trevelyan. It was not until 1969 that the College could enjoy a dedicated exhibition space in the old pub, the King's Arms, opened by the Minister of Arts, Jennie Lee. It is testament to the optimism and enthusiasm of the era and the particular energy of Principal Barry Till that we have this amazing resource 45 years on.

The Gallery was thoughtfully designed and has served the College very well with little need for updating. One notable improvement was made fairly early on; at the end of the 1960s it was à la mode to have hessian walls, and the Gallery followed the fashion for this rustic sacking. I am not sure how long it was before some wise person took the plunge and painted the whole space white, perhaps prompted by the then arts editor of *Time Out*, Sarah Kent, who allegedly refused to visit the Gallery with hessian walls! The designer had thought of everything: large picture windows, making us the best possible attraction on Westminster Bridge Road; storage space hidden in the walls; moveable screens, a generous number of power points, a beautiful red eucalyptus floor, and strip and spot lighting. Little has changed over the years with one exception: the addition of state-of-the-art LED lighting, part-funded by the Friends of Morley, who have always been so generous and supportive to the Gallery.

When the Gallery opened it was a smaller world and one that relied on being well connected. The Gallery's first director was celebrated artist Lawrence Toynbee, best known for his sporting canvases, his links to the art world and the Leicester Galleries, not to mention his aristocratic connections with the Earls of Carlisle and Castle Howard. He came well equipped to steer this modest but beautifully formed space into a well-respected and unique arts venue. Those heady early days saw the most extraordinary programme of shows, including, in 1970, pictures

Advanced Painting
End of Year
Exhibition 2011

THE KING'S ARMS

MARGARET FOLLETT

We lived in the pub from early 1933, when I was just over two years old. Those years were so interesting; Morley College was already built as far as I remember. I have a photo of myself on the flat roof of the pub (I used to play there) with part of the College in the background.

There's quite a lot I remember; as an only child, I had a great deal of freedom and could go wherever I pleased on my own. Consequently I saw much of the poverty in the back streets and listened to customers talking whenever I went into the bars. It was a lively pub, not least because of the characters of my parents.

The College received a direct hit in 1940 and, amazingly, the pub survived. My parents

were living there at the time and were given shelter by friends in Reigate after that night. Fortunately, a few weeks earlier, I had been sent with the Notre Dame Convent to Northampton, so was not at home.

My father was taken to hospital (the wardens insisted, although he was not badly injured) and on returning a few hours later, found that the bars and wine cellar had all been looted and the beers and spirits gone. Apparently there were empty bottles all around the pub. He managed to retrieve some of the furniture from the first floor and it was put in store until we returned to London the following summer to take over another pub in North London.

Maggi Hambling's exhibition 'Father', and the International Small Print Biennale.

Building on the success of our Rootstein Hopkins Drawing Competition, open to all in adult education in London, the Gallery held the first 'Inspired by . . .' exhibition in partnership with the V&A in May–June 2014. Students from over 40 adult education institutions throughout the UK submitted work for this competition, inspired by collections in the museum. The exhibition, which was selected by curators of the V&A, showed 112 artworks. Using new technology, the Gallery created an online catalogue which was available on iPads throughout the space. This seminal exhibition can be seen as a precursor to the celebration of Morley College's 125 years with a programme of exhibitions to demonstrate its forward-thinking and innovatory profile.

The Gallery has survived through thick and thin, and without the support of Morley students and staff in the early 2000s, when the College seriously considered selling the Arts Centre where the Gallery is housed, it may well have disappeared. However fortune cast her glance our way and with the appointment of Ela Piotrowska as Principal in 2008, a new chapter of Morley began. She saw the importance of a dedicated exhibition space which would support the development of students through offering valuable exhibition experience, as well as enhancing the profile of the College, and with an engaging programme would contribute to the unique qualities of the College.

In earlier days, it was remarked that the Gallery was south of the river, which was deemed deeply unfashionable and too far to travel. However with the opening of Tate Modern and the development of the South Bank, it can be argued that it is now eminently more fashionable to be on the south side of the Thames!

JANE HARTWELL

Rootstein Hopkins Drawing Exhibition 2011

from Castle Howard, and works from the personal collection of Sir Herbert Read; in 1971, an exhibition of works by Mark Gertler, and 'The Art of War' showing works by Lewis, Nash, Nevinson and Roberts, curated by Peyton Skipwith; in 1972, an exhibition of works by Eric Ravilious and Camille Pissarro: drawings from the Ashmolean Museum, Oxford; in 1979, paintings and drawings by John Minton; this impressive list goes on and on.

I came to the Gallery in 1992 and have seen 22 years of exhibitions, on average 12 a year in this space. Adrian Bartlett, who was then head of Printmaking but had been director of the space some years earlier, was one of the most supportive mentors one could wish for. He taught me a lot about the art of hanging an exhibition for which I am very grateful. Highlights over the years have been many. The annual student exhibitions are a real testament to the creativity of people who come to Morley and their tutors; the standard of student work is astonishing. There have been too many exhibitions to mention them all, but 1999–2001 was particularly memorable for me with 'A Cabinet of Curiosities from the collections of Peter Blake' in 1999, curated by Andrew Lambirth; 'March into Holloway' showing work from the inmates of Holloway prison, opened by Cherie Blair in March 2000, and the sound art exhibition 'Strange Attraction'; in 2001,

3
MORLEY'S MUSIC

> **The spirit of combining work of the highest standard in all kinds of music with openness to people at all levels of musical experience** MICHAEL GRAUBART

A Commitment to Community

RECENTLY I HAVE contributed a chapter to a book which examines Britten's commitment to the community around Aldeburgh, Suffolk, where he lived and worked. Britten said, in his famous 1964 acceptance speech for the Aspen Award, that he was less interested in writing music for posterity than he was in being of use in the community in the here and now. This statement prompted me to look at other modern British composers and to ask if this commitment to community was a particularly British phenomenon. Morley College appears repeatedly in the story. While working on the

LEFT: One of Morley's choral groups rehearsing Tippett's *A Child of Our Time*

BELOW: Peter Racine Fricker, Director of Music 1952–64, rehearsing a section of the orchestra in the Holst room, 1950s

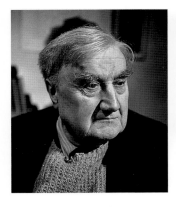

ABOVE: Gustav Holst

LEFT: Ralph Vaughan Williams

book, I spent many hours in Morley Library, sifting through press articles and old programmes, and it was brought home to me forcefully what a central role this institution has played at many important moments in British, and indeed world, musical history for well over a century.

My explorations started at the beginning of the 20th century, when Vaughan Williams and Gustav Holst, two close friends from student days at the Royal College of Music, were determined to invent a new kind of English modern music. At that time, German scholar Oskar Schmitz looked back on the barren landscape of British 18th- and 19th-century music, and came up with the stinging quip 'Das Land ohne Musik' – 'the land without music'. But, just as he penned his famous barb, a renaissance in British music was taking place. Elgar was the first composer for two centuries to have international standing, but he was regarded by the younger Vaughan Williams and Holst to be too influenced by the sound of Brahms and Wagner. In search of an authentic English music, the two friends went out to villages and used the newly invented recording cylinder to capture the music of agricultural workers, partly to preserve these traditions and partly to provide material with which they could build a uniquely English modernity in music. They also revived the music of a more distant past, that of Purcell, Tallis, Wilbye and Weekes, encouraging its performance and using it as source material for their own compositions.

Gustav Holst had a strong sense of the role of a composer as a musical leader in the community. Composer Judith Weir has written: 'Holst was an important professional composer who nevertheless worked a full-time schedule devoted to women's and workers' education. A good deal of his music was written for these people to perform.' Holst had strong socialist beliefs and, without Vaughan Williams's private means, he also had a need to earn a living. Early in his career, he led the Hammersmith Socialist Choir and, in 1907, became Director of Music at Morley College. Morley was, in the words of Holst's daughter Imogen, 'his musical home', and he was to remain in this position until 1924.

All were welcome to the Morley ensembles, choirs and classes. 'There was no weeding out at Morley,' writes Imogen. 'People who could hardly hold their violins were surrounded by more competent players. Among the singers, there were several whose voices would not have passed an audition in a more orthodox choir.' He taught his enthusiastic amateurs harmony, counterpoint and original composition. His teaching philosophy was forward-thinking, and he scorned the prevalent 'music appreciation' approach: 'If there isn't time for theory and practice, let us have practice only.' The performance programme was full of new discoveries from early English music, including Purcell's *The Fairy Queen*. There were no existing performing materials for *The Fairy*

Queen, so even this was achieved as a community exercise. In the *Morley College Magazine* (November 1910), Holst makes the following appeal: 'Any extra help in copying the parts of Purcell's "Fairy Queen" would be welcome.' By way of encouragement, Holst draws attention to the fact that history is being made: 'No performance of this masterpiece will have taken place for three hundred and fifteen years!'

Holst's other major educational commitment was as director of music at the newly founded St Paul's Girls' School. During the First World War, Holst brought his Morley and St Paul's students together in the Whitsun Festivals centred around Thaxted church in Essex, where he had his home. Vaughan Williams supported his friend by writing challenging music. He wrote his Mass in G Minor for Thaxted and dedicated it to Holst and his Whitsuntide Singers. 'How on earth Morleyites are ever going to learn the Mass I don't know,' wrote Holst to Vaughan Williams. 'It is quite beyond us, but still further beyond us is the idea that we are not going to do it.' Vaughan Williams wrote to Holst, 'We don't take music as part of our everyday life half enough – I often wish we could all migrate to some small town where there could really be a musical community – London is impossible from that point of view.' But the politics became too much for some of the St Paul's Girls' parents and the Festival moved from Thaxted back to London and eventually ceased.

THE DEL MARS AND MORLEY

ANTONIA DEL MAR

The Del Mars and Morley College go back a long way. My uncle, Norman Del Mar, conducted the Morley College Symphony Orchestra (aka the Hoffnung Symphony Orchestra) in all their Hoffnung concerts, starting in 1956. Four years later he conducted the London Symphony Orchestra and Morley College Choir at the Royal Festival Hall. When I was older, Norman fetched me each Tuesday, and drove me to Morley Symphony Orchestra which he was conducting each week whilst Lawrence Leonard had a sabbatical. We played amazingly huge works (Richard Strauss springs to mind, naturally) followed by chicken-on-a-spit on Waterloo Bridge, before I was returned home, little thinking that one

day I would myself be teaching at Morley. Thirty-three years later and I am still teaching there. During some of that time my cellist mother Pauline (not to be confused with Norman's wife Pauline, who played viola and floor polisher for a Hoffnung concert) played in Morley Chamber Orchestra, but her earlier memories are of accompanying Roy Budden, when he played the Marcello Oboe Concerto in

a concert in the Holst Room. The circle seemed complete when the Morley Symphony Orchestra was chosen by Norman's elder son, Jonathan Del Mar, to give the first informal performance of his acclaimed new Bärenreiter edition of Beethoven's Ninth Symphony, with all three generations represented for the evening: me playing viola, and my mother and my daughter Morwenna sharing a desk in the cello section. The conductor on this occasion was Mark Fitz-Gerald. On 29 September 2014, which was the 125th anniversary of the opening of Morley College, I was at the celebration tea party and concert, and it felt extremely special. I treasure all that Morley has given me over the years.

It was in 1957 that Lawrence Leonard formed the Morley Symphony Orchestra; by this date Michael Tippett's South London Orchestra had long been eclipsed by the Morley Choir and it was time for Morley's orchestral legacy to be reinvented. Lawrence was just the man to do it – a charismatic character who could cajole and scare his student players to far exceed their normal abilities. My first experience of this band was in 1958 as a visiting E-flat clarinet player performing in Ravel's *Daphnis and Chloe* Suite No. 2. Previously, this piece would have been considered off the radar for a non-professional orchestra but, with Jimmy Galway on flute and Tony Camden on oboe, it garnered rave reviews in *The Times* the following morning.

In the 1950s and 1960s, the Morley Orchestra was fulfilling a function not available in London's music colleges; it gave students and keen amateurs a chance to explore a vast orchestral repertoire. This tradition continues. Today's orchestra is the Morley Chamber Orchestra which, in 1967, was formed by Gordon Kember to complement the activities of the 'big' orchestra. I remember telling Gordon that I'd find a few players for his first rehearsal and he could then take it from there. He did, to produce a notable first concert at the Camden Festival in 1968. This included a first performance of John Taverner's *Grandma's Footsteps* and a 'scintillating performance' (to quote *The Times*) of Milhaud's *La Création du monde*.

MEMORIES OF MORLEY ORCHESTRAS

TERRY TRICKETT

On Lawrence's departure for Canada, Guy Woolfenden produced magic with the main Morley Orchestra. A performance of Tippett's Symphony No. 3 was a high point in which, as ever, a sense of tension and excitement permeated the Emma Cons Hall. In those days, an audience loyal to both Morley and Tippett came to re-experience the creativity of Morley's continuing musical tradition.

This is a series of personal reminiscences in which all the conductors I've mentioned were personal friends, as was Malcolm Binney; he held sway with the Chamber Orchestra in the 1970s until, eventually, Lawrence returned and became even more closely involved with the fortunes of Morley's music-making. His influence was paramount for nearly half a century. How fitting it was that his wife Rose, whom he met at Morley, arranged a grand send-off for him at Southwark Cathedral, in which the Chamber Orchestra, conducted by Gerry Cornelius, stunned a packed house almost into silence.

The tradition of creating a powerful connection between the highest level of music-making and ordinary people continued to thrive at Morley College under subsequent Directors of Music. Michael Tippett had much in common with his near contemporary, Benjamin Britten. They both trod the delicate path of being a gay public figure at a time when this was illegal, both espoused left-wing and pacifist beliefs, and both believed in the idea that music can be of use in people's lives. Tippett came to maturity in the years of the Great Depression and, to earn a living, he found work which was in keeping with his growing interest in socialist politics and desire to make a difference. He conducted the South London Orchestra for unemployed musicians, mostly comprising players from cinema orchestras made redundant by the rise of the talkies. He also went to Yorkshire to mount a community production of John Gay's *The Beggar's Opera* with miners whose colliery had been closed. Seeing the poverty and undernourished children, Tippett questioned everything: 'Had I the right to turn away from such reality, to shut myself up to write abstract music?'

Tippett tackled this question by becoming involved with music education for working people at Morley College: in 1940, just after the Morley building had been devastated by a German bomb, he became Director of Music. Tippett continued Holst's tradition of excavating old music, as well as putting his own music to service. In 1944, at the height of the war, the Morley Choir joined

ABOVE: Walter Bergmann

ABOVE RIGHT: Alfred Deller

BELOW: The Morley Wind Ensemble performing at the College summer garden party in the 1950s

forces with the London Region Civil Defence Choir and the London Philharmonic Orchestra to perform the premiere of Tippett's oratorio *A Child of Our Time*. The work, with its dark but ultimately optimistic theme, clearly touched many people in those times, and it had repeated performances in the wake of its premiere.

Tippett defied the prevailing nationalist mood and brought in musicians from continental Europe escaping the rise of Nazism, including three Austrian string players who later formed the basis of the Amadeus Quartet, and another Austrian, Walter Bergmann, an early pioneer in the revival of the recorder. Alfred Deller, also part of the early music revival, gave a vivid account of the importance of Tippett's musical community at the height of wartime:

Those who were fortunate enough to be members of the Morley College choir and orchestra in those days will agree that to have made the 'black-out' journey, often punctuated by sirens and bombs, and then to enter the Holst Room at Morley to a hubbub of voices with Michael in the centre shaking with laughter, was an assurance that all was right with the world – the true world of the spirit.

In 1943, Tippett was called up but made a stand as conscientious objector, and not even influential representations attesting the importance of his work at Morley College could prevent him from being sentenced to three months in Wormwood Scrubs. Vaughan Williams spoke in his defence at his trial and wrote to *The Times*: 'As regards [Tippett's] teachings at Morley College, it is distinctly work of national importance to create a musical atmosphere at the College and elsewhere. We know music is forming a great part in national life now: more since the war than ever before, and everyone able to help on with that work is doing work of national importance.' From Wormwood Scrubs, Tippett wrote, 'There is a baby prisoners' orchestra here whom I conduct and try to improve ... it's a sort of light café orchestra, and with instruments all of a different pitch – in fact – throw-outs ... On Sunday we are to play in chapel, in the middle of a recital by Peter Pears and Benjamin Britten.' The performance by Britten and Pears in Wormwood Scrubs, for which the prisoner Tippett turned pages, is a touching episode in British musical history.

Tippett left Morley in 1951, but Morley College remained crucial to the story of British composers and the community into the 1960s and 1970s, when Cornelius

ABOVE: John Gardner taught at Morley for 25 years and was Director of Music 1965–9

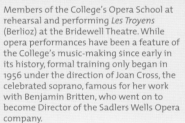

Members of the College's Opera School at rehearsal and performing *Les Troyens* (Berlioz) at the Bridewell Theatre. While opera performances have been a feature of the College's music-making since early in its history, formal training only began in 1956 under the direction of Joan Cross, the celebrated soprano, famous for her work with Benjamin Britten, who went on to become Director of the Sadlers Wells Opera company.

Cardew was teaching an experimental music class. Out of this emerged the Scratch Orchestra, formed in 1969. It had an open membership with no auditions and performed experimental music. But Cardew's increasingly hard-left political focus eventually caused the group to fragment, and it ceased to perform in 1974. Composer James MacMillan, while out of sympathy with Cardew's politics, sees him as an important figure in the line of British composers with a commitment to music in society.

As a younger man, I was very interested in the way that Cardew thought to engage the community in music-making, even if this was politically motivated. In that sense you could say that he has had a big impact on the development of musical education and outreach work undertaken by many ensembles and organisations in the decades since his death. I am specifically referring to those projects which aim to take music into communities which, traditionally, don't have much contact with the world of 'art' music – schools and prisons, for example.

In more recent years, I have been lucky enough to observe the story of Morley College and how it remains at the centre of new and important ideas in music. One recent development under the current Director of Music Andrea Brown is modest in scale, but has the capacity to have a seismic impact on the world of music. The creation of a course for young women conductors was an imaginative response to the chronic lack of women from the podium in our concert halls. It was particularly sparked by the media storm surrounding Marin Alsop's appearance in 2013 as the first ever woman to conduct the first night of the BBC Proms. The course is aimed at teenage girls, and hopes to build confidence and skills at an early stage in their development; course leaders include conductors Alice Farnham and Sian Edwards. Watching a film of the course was a moving experience for me, realising what a unique sight it is, even in the 21st century, to see not one but several women conducting. As ever, Morley is at the forefront of big, new and important ideas in music, and the rest of the world just needs to catch up.

GILLIAN MOORE

Morley's Choirs

THE CHOIRS AT MORLEY COLLEGE have always played a central role in the Music department and the College ethos. The first choral society at Morley started in 1906, conducted by Director of Music H. J. B. Dart, but it was the following year when the group and the department started to flourish under Gustav Holst. Imogen Holst writes:

> The college in those days was next door to the Old Vic . . . the music classes held in a gloomy, ill-ventilated room, and often the members would arrive thoroughly tired out after a hard day's work. But he managed to make them happy, and after that it was comparatively easy to make them sing Bach. Of all the ways of making music this was perhaps the way that he enjoyed the most. As for the students, they revelled in it, and one of them was heard to describe Morley as 'a sort of heaven we go to on Mondays and Wednesdays'. The enthusiasm of the students was tremendous. Sometimes they would turn up at the college with influenza and a high temperature rather than miss a single rehearsal.

It was Holst's commitment to 'amateur music-making' – that music should be open to all – which resonated with the College's own vision. 'Morleyites were eager to seize every opportunity for informal singing', inviting Edmund Fellowes to the College to sing madrigals, serenading Vaughan Williams on his 50th birthday, and joining other singers for performances at the Whitsun Festivals.

The choirs continued to flourish in the 1930s under Arnold Foster, performing works including Dvořák's *Stabat Mater*, Vaughan Williams's *Benedicite* and *Fantasia on Carols*, and other works by Warlock and Holst. In 1940 Michael Tippett became Director of Music when Foster was evacuated.

Charles Stuart of the *Musical Times* remarked: 'Tippett has the personality which takes the fancy of musical amateurs and enables them to achieve the impossible as a matter of routine. At first he worked on a shoe-string. On the first Sunday but one after the bombing, not more than ten singers showed up. They sang madrigals and knew in their hearts that all would be well.'

At the behest of the Arts Council, an ambitious series of concerts was programmed for the Festival of Britain and the opening of the Royal Festival Hall in 1951. The indefatigable Morleyites performed Monteverdi's *Vespers of 1610*, Tallis's *Spem in Alium*, two works of Stravinsky and Tippett's *A Child of Our Time* within a fortnight during the inaugural season, going on to perform, with

ABOVE: The Chamber Choir, 1950s

BELOW: Programmes for *The Fairy Queen*, 1911, and a choral concert in 1943

'LET THERE BE LIGHT . . .'

MICHAEL GRAUBART

On one occasion, while I conducted the Morley College Choir, we were going to perform Handel's *Samson* in Southwark Cathedral with the Chamber Orchestra, and decided to do a public run-through with piano in the Emma Cons Hall a few days earlier. It was late spring or early summer and the performance was scheduled to start at 6pm or 6.30pm, so I failed to think about timing and we started by daylight. As the music progressed, I suddenly realized that the light was fading and the

singers, too, were beginning to hold their copies obliquely to catch what daylight there was. I got seriously worried (and, no doubt, so did the singers).

We got to 'Let there be light – and light was over all', and dead on cue the house lights came on. We all nearly collapsed, but managed to carry on. After the end of the run-through, I rushed around the building to find the part-time assistant caretaker, who was on duty that evening, and said, 'Thank you so much for turning on the lights. But you have no idea of the coincidence . . .!' He drew himself up tall and said, somewhat indignantly, 'Coincidence? I *know* the oratorio!'

That's Morley!

Goldsmith's Choral Union, 'one of the first performances in this country' of Carl Orff's *Carmina Burana* ten days later. All were relatively unknown works. Geoffrey Otton writes in the *Morley Magazine*: 'My wife and I joined the Morley College Choir in 1950 . . . Under the direction of Michael Tippett, it had for some years been establishing a high reputation as an adventurous organisation concentrating on "works outside the normal repertoire which are of cultural, educational or historical interest".'

The choirs continued to be a tour de force in the department in the 1960s. The College Choir was conducted by the then Director of Music, Peter Racine Fricker, the Madrigal Choir by John Gardner, the Chamber Choir by Denys Darlow and the Opera Group by Miss Joan Cross. Dame Janet Baker, too, worked in the administration department to help fund her studies.

Denys Darlow conducts the Chamber Choir, 1960s

REMINISCENCES

HAZEL ELAM

My links with Morley College go back to the 1940s. Not my own personal memory but that of a dear family friend, Rosina Binder. She came over from Linz in Austria in the early war years. Whether she learnt English at Morley I do not know, but she was an enthusiastic Morley student from the late 1940s until the early 1960s. She attended a variety of classes, including tailoring, and proudly wore the clothes she made. In later years, her favourite class was in comparative religion. As a single woman with no family here, she valued the social life of Morley, its clubs and the parties she attended.

My own first acquaintance with Morley College was in 1965. Newly arrived in London, I had just begun work with the ILEA in County Hall. Back then there was a huge enthusiasm for adult education and many of my young contemporaries eagerly perused *Floodlight* to decide what classes to attend. The class I especially recall was Morley Singers. I felt too timid to audition for the prestigious Morley Choir, but felt happy to apply for the Morley Singers, which required no audition. The initial interview with John Carewe, the conductor and our tutor, was delightfully informal. But he brought together a happy group and we sang

a variety of ancient and modern pieces. Later his place was taken by Michael Graubart and again we explored a variety of religious and secular music, performing at Christmas in the lobby. I still retain a copy of an original work by Alexander Goehr that we sang then.

I appreciated the involvement that Morley offered to students. I was class secretary for a time with the Singers; back then class secretaries had more to do with the register than they do now. I can remember organising class end-of-term meals in an Italian restaurant at the Elephant and Castle.

In the late 1960s and early 1970s, I had a different view of Morley as I worked in the Further and Higher Education division of the ILEA. The ILEA exerted considerable control over what went on in colleges: all prospectuses were submitted to them for approval and printing, and no new subject could be introduced without the consent of the Education Committee. I remember, for instance, preparing the report on Hatha Yoga

(Iyengar method) so that this could be taught in adult institutes.

I especially enjoyed my direct contacts with Morley and remember the annual meetings to discuss the budget for the coming year. Principal Barry Till defended the needs of staff and students ably and persuasively. Though it was a time of greater benevolence and understanding of the needs of adults, there were always budget restrictions.

When I retired in 2000, I saw in the Morley prospectus a class in 'Enjoy Your Voice' which sounded inviting. I was drawn in from the start by the amazing warm-up session of the tutor, Rita Godfrey. That helped in overcoming the terror of getting up on the stage in the Holst Room and exposing my voice to the judgement of others. Now, I still love Rita's musicality and deep humanity and continue to learn in the original Singers' studio. I have also enjoyed the erudition, gentle humour and guidance of Lydia Glynoer's French classes. At all times I have appreciated the contribution to learning made by the excellent Morley Library with its helpful staff. Though I have attended other establishments, it is the unique ambience of Morley College and the friendships I have made there that I especially value.

MORLEY COLLEGE, MY MOTHER'S SECOND HOME

ANNE-MARIE NEWLAND

My mother, Joan Christina Khachik, lived at Morley College – I think! She joined so many classes that she always said that after she retired, she didn't know how she had time to work.

Joan Khachik was born in Leicester in 1928 to an Aberdonian father and English mother. They came from different classes and in those days that was unusual.

Joan had a happy childhood with memories of music in the house and self-education as a pillar of man's own endeavour. She married an Iraqi in 1953 in Lebanon and moved to Iraq within weeks. Both she and my father, Abdul, were human rights activists and their life was soon shattered by my father's arrest in 1960. Our mother and us, her three children, escaped to England, leaving our father behind to a fate we could only imagine. It was in 1979 that they both moved to London after his release, thanks to Amnesty International. Soon after Joan discovered the 'University of an Older and Wiser Age', as she called it: Morley College!

Mum did everything in that College that her meagre allowance allowed. She joined the Iyengar Yoga class, the 'Can't Sing' Choir and the Country Dancing Club. The 'Can't Sing' Choir became her passion. She travelled to concerts, was on TV, did outdoor performances and, after being told all her life she could not sing, she sang with a newly found voice that made her very happy. After her death I found a tape of her singing both with the Choir and on her own; my favourite was 'Over the Rainbow'. Bless her!

As the Right Honourable Mayor of Southwark (1997/8), she also danced and sang at any tea dance going, usually with a rendition of

Joyce Grenfell's 'Dancing Cheek to Cheek'! People used to say, 'Your mum likes a tipple!' And I would reply, 'My mother doesn't drink! She doesn't need to!' The soul of any party, any group and anything going when it came to Morley College, she loved that place deeply.

My mum was diagnosed with gall bladder cancer on 8 July 2009. We brought her to Leicester so I could care for her. She did not know then that she would not return to Morley for the new term, or ever see her home again. She still focused on the Country Dancing Club's Christmas party and really believed she could still be there. Before she died, she cried so hard for Morley College, my heart broke for her.

This is how Joan lived her life, with a deep belief that every moment should be both joyous and full of a personal endeavour to pursue knowledge, friendship, the arts, and challenges until the last heartbeat! I want to thank you personally for the richness of life you gave my mother right up to the end. I know you miss her as much as we do.

However, the ambitions of Morley tutors sometimes were at odds with the College and its funds. Michael Graubart writes that one tutor

had begun to feel that there were members of the Morley College Choir that were no longer up to scratch and had re-auditioned all the members of the choir, asking those who had failed to come up to his standard to leave the choir. There were quite a few of these, and they went to the Principal [Barry Till] or to the [then] Director of Music [John Gardner], in indignation and demanded that another choir be founded that would allow them to continue singing choral music at Morley. This new choir was established and called the Morley Singers, and I became the conductor.

Another Director of Music, Robert Hanson, wrote about a Morley College Choir tutor whom he 'strongly

Combined Morley choirs rehearse Purcell's *The Fairy Queen* at the Southbank Centre, 2011

The College Gospel Choir in 2010

advised ... that a programme entirely in Danish and comprising mainly contemporary music was proving too esoteric for the choir in its present state, and that he should announce immediately a programme for next term which would be much more attractive'.

Charles Stuart further wrote that 'an ambitious series of Royal Festival Hall concerts in 1952 ended in financial disaster', not helped by the 'extremely large fee for the young Elizabeth Schwartzkopf' to perform alongside the students, and that as a result 'the music department reverted to its original role: to foster educational, recreational and social activities with the emphasis on process rather than end-products'.

Today we strive to uphold Holst's initial vision for the department, and our choral offer continues to be wide and diverse, including the brilliantly named 'Can't Sing' Choir, Jazz Choir, Gospel Choir, Choral Society, College Choir, Chamber Choir, and lunchtime choirs including the Meridian Choir. Our tutors are all professional musicians who have a commitment to community singing and music-making, and include Alexander Chaplin, who conducts the East London and Harlow Chorus; Cerys Hogg, who conducts the Lambeth-based choir The Kenningtones; Michalis Angelakis, who works with the Royal Opera House's Community Choir in Thurrock; David Dellaire, who conducts the Tulse Hill Estate Singing Group; Andrew Tait, who conducts the Peckham-based community choir Koruso!, and David Revels, who works with the excellent Morley Choral Society.

Most recently, our project 'A Choir of Our Time', which won an award from the National Institute of Adult Continuing Education (NIACE), hit the headlines when some 400 singers, including Morley staff and students, eight community choirs in Lambeth and Southwark, the BBC Singers and London Philharmonic Orchestra performed Tippett's *A Child of Our Time* at the Royal Festival Hall, in June 2013. The project enabled community singers, through the spirituals in the work, to perform in an international venue with an orchestra, some for the first time.

Antonia Till writes of the Tippett spirituals that 'they were extra poignant for me, because I had sung them with John Gardner who became a great friend – and genial participant in the after-rehearsal pub'. *Plus ça change ...*

ANDREA BROWN

A Harmonica at the Feast: Holst and Thaxted

HOLST'S HUGELY DIVERSE musical output was shaped by his eclectic range of interests, which encompassed folk song, 16th-century polyphony, mysticism and the English landscape. His appointment as Morley's Director of Music in 1907, on the recommendation of his great friend Vaughan Williams, gave the College's music a new focus and energy, but also provided Holst with a platform to pursue another of his fascinations: the music of England's past, particularly that of the then neglected 17th-century composer Henry Purcell.

Already by 1909, Holst had built up an orchestra and choir proficient enough to perform extracts from Purcell's *King Arthur*, which had been 'rarely heard – never in London within living memory'. In 1911, the College staged the first full performance since the late 17th century of Purcell's score of *The Fairy Queen*, which had disappeared soon after his death and been rediscovered less than a decade before. Morley's students not only performed the work, but under Holst's supervision 'a little army of volunteer copyists' had fashioned the parts from the transcription of the manuscript. The performance, 'one of the most interesting events in the London musical season in the year of the Coronation', according to the *Morley Magazine*, attracted critical acclaim and national attention, and formed the bedrock of Morley's distinguished musical heritage. Scenes from *The Fairy Queen* were often performed in College concerts over the next few years and in the 1914/15 season the College produced *Dido and Aeneas*, Purcell's celebrated, but then little-known, opera.

Yet there was a further, less acknowledged, preoccupation that Holst's time at Morley was to highlight: his

LEFT: Holst at the Thaxted Festival in 1916. Jack and Sylvia Putterill and Dulcie Nutting are amongst the musicians

RIGHT: The College's portrait of Holst by William Rothenstein

Choral parts meticulously copied by hand by Morley's students for Holst's revival of *The Fairy Queen*, 1911

commitment to the early 20th century's emerging socialist movement with which Morley, founded for 'the advanced study by men and women belonging to the working classes', was hardly unconnected. In 1914 Holst made his home in the Essex village of Thaxted, where the vicar was the outspoken socialist Conrad Noel. Noel embedded dance and music in the life of the church as a way of reaching out to ordinary people, brightening up the church with banners and flags, controversially establishing a *mixed* choir, encouraging the congregation (where he had abolished segregation between gentry and working classes) to sing by placing the choir amongst them, and inaugurating a 'Midsummer Festival of Faith' – a week of special services, music and dancing culminating in a colourful 'People's Processional' through the village.

Holst met his wife, Isobel Harrison, at the Hammersmith Socialist Club and, before Morley, had taught at the Passmore Edwards Settlement (the antecedent of Morley's fellow Adult Education Institute, the Mary Ward Centre). He found he had much in common with this 'socialist with an unrivalled sense o humour' and soon involved himself in Thaxted life by helping to train the choir and playing the organ.

Noel was a cousin of the left-leaning politician Charles Roden Buxton, Morley's third, if somewhat part-time, Principal of 1905–10, so it was unsurprising that Holst should bring Morley singers along to bolster Thaxted's choir for Christmas 1915. The following summer, Thaxted's Festival featured 15 Morleyites together with 10 Thaxted singers (most of whom were factory workers) and 10 musicians from St Paul's Girls School, where Holst was also musical director. The music included Bach's Missa Brevis and cantata 'Sleepers Wake!'; choral works by Palestrina, Lassus and Victoria; and string orchestra pieces by Bach and Purcell.

But while this 'official' programme was performed within a series of church services, the Morleyites used every spare moment to make music informally. Driven indoors by the rain at the Holsts' tea party, they 'resorted to Elizabethan love songs, rounds, and part-songs accompanied by violins, penny whistles, piano and even a mouth organ', and to more folk songs and morris dancing at the Noels' party the following day. For Holst himself it was 'a feast – an orgy. Four whole days of perpetual singing and playing, either properly arranged in church or impromptu in various houses, or still more impromptu in ploughed fields during thunderstorms or in the trains. It has been a revelation to me ... We weren't merely excited – we were ... rather more alive than usual.'

Around 30 singers and 21 instrumentalists took part in 1917. Byrd and Victoria were now joined by Holst's own music, his *Three Festival Choruses* of which the last, celebrating Thaxted's church bells, proved especially popular and was repeated the following year. Holst's eight-part round proved especially memorable, placing its eight groups of musicians around the

church, the socialist connotations of this egalitarian musical form being not unnoticed. Morley students added their own banner to the Processional that year, quoting Bach: 'The aim of music is the glory of God and pleasant recreation.' The latter as much as the former characterised Morley's contribution, as Holst recounted: 'We kept it up at Thaxted about 14 hours a day . . . it was heaven . . . as a girl in Thaxted said to me: "The great point of all this is that there is no reason why it should ever stop." '

'Long live Thaxted and its vicar!' concluded the *Morley College Magazine*'s account of the event. However, Holst's Festival involvement was to last just one further year. More Victoria and Byrd comprised 1918's formal proceedings, and Holst introduced his *Tomorrow Shall Be My Dancing Day*, dedicated to Noel. More ambitious works by Morley students found their way into the festivities, as did a performance of the parody 'Opera as She is Wrote', which had been performed at the College in March. The *Morley College Magazine* sombrely reminds us of the context in which such jollities were taking place: 'At a time like the present let us cling to our music . . . for it is to be cherished as an ever-present witness for sweetness

and sanity in a world deliberately giving itself over to madness and passion – the abiding voice . . . raised in eternal protest against the Realism which has turned Europe into a slaughterhouse.'

It was perhaps this slaughterhouse that prompted Conrad Noel to preach what one Morley participant called a 'dotty sermon about communism'. Having already upset the Church authorities by hanging a red banner outside his church in support of the Russian Revolution, his festival address that year attacked its participants as 'camp followers', more committed to Bach's 'pleasant recreation' than the cause of Christian socialism. This was more than the gentrified parents of the St Paul's Girls could tolerate and the school ordered Holst not to return to the Festival.

Holst continued his association with Noel (who was amongst the invited few to hear the first, private performance of *The Planets*) and to organise Whitsun festivals involving Morleyites in London, then Canterbury and finally Chichester. However, 1918 was not the last time Morley was to appear at the Festival. In 1964, the conductor Graham Treacher, an established presence at Morley, resurrected the Thaxted Festival with Holst's

MUSIC MEMORIES

GRAHAM TREACHER

As a young conductor some 50 years ago, I found Morley College an exciting place in which to explore music, to teach, to meet people from all walks of life, including students from the Academies in search 'of something different'. The Orchestra, the Morley College Choir, the Opera Group were all thriving, and we could often rely on professional soloists to join us for rehearsals and concerts.

Highlights in my memory are visits to Thaxted in Essex with Imogen Holst to revive the Morley Midsummer Festivals, and Dulcie Nutting from Morley singing Vaughan Williams's songs (which he composed for her) beneath the candelabra late at night.

Another memorable occasion was a children's concert of music by Bartók and Stravinsky in Emma Cons Hall, with the English Chamber Orchestra and children playing piano pieces and singing. And I remember Oda Slobodskaya, the doyen soprano for whom

Stravinsky wrote his opera *Mavra*, sweeping on to the stage, declaring, 'I've never sung so early in all my life!'

The choir took part in an International Choral Festival in Cork, performing a new

commission by Elizabeth Maconchy. After the performance, a group of us ended up late that night in a local fish-and-chip bar, singing for our supper part of Byrd's Five-Part Mass, an event that somehow reached the local press the following day!

Graham Treacher and Peter Racine Fricker auditioning Delia Woolridge, accompanied by Gerald Smith, for the Holst choir

Composer and politically engaged musician Elizabeth Maconchy is an inspiration to many and, as I found out through my involvement with WRPM (Women's Revolutions Per Minute) Music by Women in the 1980s, she was also a woman of great strength, curing herself of TB. I, like others, paused to reflect on her life during her 100th anniversary in 2007. At that time, I was an Access to Music student at Morley College, returning to a college where I had taught philosophy in the 1970s to pursue my passion for music. I was intrigued, but not surprised, to discover that Maconchy had been involved with Morley and began to uncover the story.

It started with a chance comment midway through the course from the composer Nicola Lefanu (Maconchy's daughter and a composer in her own right) who told me that that her mother had written several pieces for Morley, for both choir and orchestra. The choral piece was *Nocturnal,* commissioned from Maconchy by the Cork International Music Festival in 1965. I decided to research *Nocturnal* for my seminar presentation in the 'Form and Analysis' part of the Access course with Bob Hanson, and tracked down the original, beautifully crafted ink manuscript given to the College and lodged in the Lambeth Archives.

ELIZABETH MACONCHY (1907–1994)

HILARY FRIEND

I also visited the Maconchy Archive at St Hilda's College, Oxford, where I had been a reluctant student in the mid-1960s.

Nocturnal had its first performance in Cork in 1965 with Graham Treacher leading the Morley Choir. A richly textured piece in three sections, it skilfully brings three poems

together to powerful and evocative effect. The dedication to the Morley Choir is clearly visible in the manuscript, but not in the published score. The organisers in Cork said this was because the way in which acknowledgements were made were not systematised at that time. It would be good to see the dedication in new copies! I heard from Treacher about working with Maconchy at the Thaxted Festival where the Morley Orchestra performed Maconchy's piece for wind and brass in 1966.

In 2007 while I was researching *Nocturnal*, Virginia Firnberg, one of my tutors, was working with Lontano music publishing company on the recordings for the anniversary year of Maconchy's vocal and instrumental works. Virginia made sure *Nocturnal* was included and the CD with the BBC Singers came out in 2007, the first modern recording. *Nocturnal* was performed in Dublin later that year and also broadcast.

This was a highlight of my music studies and I have a continuing interest in music by women composers and in securing the integration of their work into musical life and education. The WRPM collection is now in the Special Collections of Goldsmiths Library, London University, and readily accessible to all.

composer-conductor daughter, Imogen. The challenging programme demonstrates how far Morley had built on the musical foundations laid by Holst, and in addition to Imogen and Treacher, boasted some notable performers: the choir of St Paul's Girls School conducted by composer and Morley tutor John Gardner (soon to become the College's Director of Music); Morley's then Director of Music, the composer Peter Racine Fricker; the singer John Shirley-Quirk, on the cusp of international fame; and as organist, a young student who was to become the renowned conductor Sir Andrew Davis.

The co-operation of the incumbent, 'red' Jack Putterill, was required, of course, and hardly likely to be withheld: Putterill had been one of the Morleyites at the 1916 Festival, and became Conrad Noel's son-in-law, curate and then successor as rector. Noel's principles and enthusiasms, if not his dotty sermons, were maintained in every

respect: 'The price of the tickets will need careful consideration – keeping as low as possible'; 'I think it would be good if we could link the fanfare with processions ... we could have a lovely dance through the town'.

The Festival in 1964 included Holst's *Four Songs for voice and violin,* sung by Dulcie Nutting and accompanied by Putterill's daughter, Sylvia. Holst had written the work after hearing one of his Morley students, Christine Ratcliffe, at the 1916 festival playing the violin softly to herself while improvising a vocalise. Three of the songs had been premiered at the 1917 Festival, sung by Dulcie with Christine playing the violin part. A member of the Morley Orchestra since 1914, Dulcie Nutting was to return to the College as a teacher, having worked as a copyist, including for Holst. Nutting was largely responsible for encouraging choirs of first-time singers and she continued to take her scratch groups to Thaxted, even

after Morley's role in the Festival dwindled once Treacher had moved on in 1966.

The *Morley Magazine* of 1976 celebrated not just 60 years of the Festival, but also the birthday of 'a great lady [Dulcie Nutting] who has done so much for song since she first came to the College when it was situated at the Old Vic' and who, at 80, had organised that year's visit. The egalitarian legacy of Holst and Nutting live on in the College's 'Can't Sing' Choir, its classes for adults with disabilities, its fostering of community music, in making accessible to all its immense range of performances and its continuing conviction that music can make us all feel 'rather more alive than usual'.

NICK RAMPLEY

Tippett at Morley

SIR MICHAEL TIPPETT, ONE of the greatest composers of the 20th century, was Director of Music at Morley from 1940 to 1951 – years through which he led both himself and the College to national reputation and success against a backdrop of personal and political turmoil. He arrived relatively unknown as a composer, with few professional performances to his name; he left with an established reputation. Before becoming Director of Music, Tippett was the conductor of the South London Orchestra for unemployed musicians based at the College and which premiered one of his (now) most famous works, Concerto for Double String Orchestra, in 1940. (Myra Hess was the soloist for their performance of Beethoven's Fourth Piano Concerto.) His full-time appointment came after the declaration of war.

Tippett ends his first opera, *The Midsummer Marriage*, with a quotation from Yeats's poem 'Lapis Lazuli': 'All things fall and are built again | And those that build them again are gay.' Tippett certainly had to rebuild musical life at Morley once war broke out, and did so gaily, despite suffering personal troubles. He was emerging from a period of intense psycho-analysis following the break-up of

Sir Michael Tippett in 1994 with the College's portrait of him by Oskar Kokoschka

Programme for concert by South London Orchestra with Myra Hess, 1939

his first major love-affair; his father died shortly after being caught in an air raid; his closest friend, Francesca Allinson, committed suicide in 1945. In 1943 he was imprisoned in Wormwood Scrubs for failing to comply with the terms of his conscientious objectorship. His irrevocable pacifism would not allow him to give up what he believed his true wartime role to be, namely, musical life at Morley – but such life faced almost insurmountable difficulty. On 15 October 1940, the main building of Morley College had been almost completely destroyed by a bomb, and there was little to no rehearsal space. Buildings, and ensembles which would use them, had to be rebuilt from scratch. The South London Orchestra was never revived. Tippett's first choir rehearsal was made up of only 10 singers – but numbers tripled within a year.

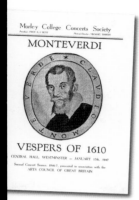

ABOVE: Programme for the Morley College Concerts Society production of Monteverdi's *Vespers*, 1947

RIGHT: The dedication page of the score for Tippett's *Two Madrigals*

Mátyás Seiber

Tippett's conducting style was, by all accounts, including his own, eccentric, but he had an innate ability to work carefully with choirs and orchestras, of all ages and skills, in order to produce performances of hugely challenging repertoire. He taught no classes at Morley, his responsibilities being to conduct ensembles and to programme concerts (although he once played percussion for a Bach concerto). Tippett established a series of concerts open to the public, which soon secured the College's reputation as a place of serious music-making; William Walton became honorary chairman of an official 'Concerts Society' which received some funding from the Arts Council. Performances were of immense scope and ambition, including premieres by major contemporary composers, and the joyous resuscitation of long-neglected works. Tippett conducted the Choir; conductor Walter Goehr eventually took over the Orchestra. The situation in Europe at the time meant that, for the concerts, Morley was able to employ distinguished Jewish refugee composers who had emigrated to England, including Goehr (who had been a pupil of Schoenberg), and Mátyás Seiber whom Tippett employed to teach composition.

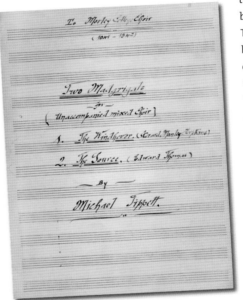

Vaughan Williams didn't take kindly to this foreign influence, but Tippett, aided by the College's Principal, Eva Hubback, was able to stand firm. Hubback seems to have been something of a mother figure to Tippett; his correspondence details therapeutic night-time conversations with her about the vexed issues of his life.

The concerts (mostly held in the Holst Room at Morley, but occasionally at larger London venues such as Wigmore Hall) regularly featured early English composers alongside the music of Bach, Monteverdi, Buxtehude, Pergolesi, Vivaldi, and Handel. Many of these scores Tippett had literally picked out of the rubble to which Morley had been razed. The Choir, under Tippett, is widely regarded as having played a major part in a complete restoration of Purcell's reputation. Tippett also 'discovered' the counter-tenor Alfred Deller, then a lay clerk at Canterbury, who performed and briefly taught at the College, and has been credited with rejuvenating the counter-tenor voice into mainstream repertoire. (It was Tippett who reintroduced the word 'counter-tenor' – as opposed to 'male alto' – to musical vocabulary.) Works now regularly performed, such as Handel's *Messiah,* or Tallis's 40-part motet, *Spem in Alium*, were then much less frequently performed and only in excerpts. Tippett's complete performances at Morley drew great notice. The Tallis motet (which had taken two years to learn – Tippett was nothing if not persistent) was recorded and released on record (still available, in crackly splendour, on disc).

It was the combination of such rediscoveries with performances, even premieres, of more obscure contemporary music that put Morley on the map: concerts were broadcast on the BBC, and the College was establishing itself as a place where unknown and challenging music could be heard in London. Composers such as Hindemith, Kodály, Bartók, Busoni, Schoenberg and Stravinsky (Morley gave the UK premieres of

Dumbarton Oaks and Babel) were featured with reasonable regularity.

Speaking on Desert Island Discs many years later, Tippett told Roy Plomley (who must have been startled to be addressed by his castaway as 'love' throughout): '[Morley] got this reputation that was a great deal larger than its buildings'. A performance of the Monteverdi Vespers of 1610 (the first in Britain) was, he recalled, a 'world-beater'. Other notable figures flocked to Morley at Tippett's invitation, including Benjamin Britten and his partner, Peter Pears. Not so much Tippett was played as might be supposed, although his First Symphony cropped up, as did two madrigals (The Source and The Windhover), which he dedicated to the College. His compositions from this period are indebted to rhythms and formations in the 'early' music of, say, Purcell and Gibbons. It was at a performance of Gibbons's verse anthem My Beloved Spake that Tippett first met Britten and Pears. A confused German cellist in the orchestra supposedly asked afterwards, 'What exactly is a "spake"?'

It was the Choir of Morley College under Walter Goehr (with Peter Pears as the tenor soloist) which premiered Tippett's A Child of Our Time, at London's Adelphi Theatre, on 19 March 1944. The work, according to his own programme note, 'springs from an impassioned protest against the conditions that make persecution possible'. It is a tripartite oratorio documenting the dark state of man and his place in the world, and the fate of the 'child of our time': the boy (never mentioned by name) Herschel Grynszpan, whose assassination of a Nazi official provided, in 1938, the catalyst for Kristallnacht, in which the Nazis destroyed thousands of Jewish homes and businesses. The piece is punctuated by arrangements of five Negro spirituals taking the place of the communal Lutheran chorales in the Bach Passions. Tippett loyally claimed that the Morley Orchestra would be skilled enough for the premiere, but eventually they had to cede to the London Philharmonic Orchestra. The Morley Choir, aided by the London Regional Civil Defence Choir, did perform. The alto soloist, Margaret

A CHILD OF OUR TIME
An Oratorio by
MICHAEL TIPPETT

The first performance of this work will be given at the ROYAL ADELPHI THEATRE, on Sunday, March 19th, at 2.30, by JOAN CROSS, MARGARET McARTHUR, PETER PEARS, NORMAN WALKER, LONDON REGION CIVIL DEFENCE & MORLEY COLLEGE CHOIRS, and the LONDON PHILHARMONIC ORCHESTRA conducted by WALTER GOEHR. (It will be preceded by the Maurische Trauermusik (K477) and the Symphony in G minor (K183) of MOZART).

AN ACCOUNT OF THE ORATORIO IS GIVEN OVERLEAF

Tickets may be obtained from the Box Office (Temple Bar 7611)
(1d.

Handbill for the premiere of A Child of Our Time at the Adelphi Theatre, 1944

SPEM IN ALIUM AT THE ROUNDHOUSE

SANDRA CLAPHAM

In the spring term of 2012, the members of the Morley College Chamber Choir were given copies of Thomas Tallis's great motet, Spem in Alium, written for eight choirs, each containing at least five singers – soprano, alto, tenor, baritone and bass – and therefore requiring at least 40 voices. In the inclusive spirit of Morley College, this was to be a project combining singers from all the College choirs and we were to be led by the BBC Singers and conducted by Andrea Brown, Morley's Director of Music, in a performance at the Roundhouse, Camden Town.

It was a massive undertaking as we all needed to rehearse our parts in our separate choirs before attending an all-day workshop in Emma Cons Hall, led by Ed Price and the BBC Singers on 17 February. That day, after warming up, we were arranged in a large horseshoe shape and it was thrilling to hear all 40 parts coming together – starting with a solo voice in

Choir 1, quickly joined by another and then the rest of the voices in Choirs 1 and 2, and then voices travelling around the horseshoe, gradually incorporating all the choirs until, at bar 40, all 40 voice parts came together. In order to fill the cavernous Roundhouse with sound, we were to have 80 singers – two to each part. We had listened to the first ever recording of the piece, conducted by Michael Tippett, which had actually been recorded at Morley College in 1948, and also performed in the new Royal Festival Hall, as one of his farewell concerts to Morley, so we had strong tradition to uphold.

Two more full choir rehearsals later, we arrived at the Roundhouse at 9.15am on Sunday, 4 March to take part in the 'Voices Now' Festival, a countdown event to the London 2012 Festival, the finale to the Cultural Olympiad. Sara Mohr-Pietsch, the BBC Radio 3 presenter, announced to the packed audience that almost 2,000 singers were to perform there over the course of the day, and that probably 600 of them were present for the start of the morning's session of choral singing. We were privileged to be chosen as the choir to open the Festival and it was an amazing experience. The 10 minutes that it took us to sing Spem in Alium, to a rapt audience of many school choirs, was over too soon and I think we'd all have liked to sing it again. The BBC were relaying the singing of other choirs at 5pm so unfortunately our contribution was not broadcast but, true to the ethos of Morley, it was the taking part in the Festival that mattered.

MacArthur, also came from Morley. The oratorio has since become the most-performed of all Tippett's works, the unique and moving power of its universal cry for peace recognized throughout the world. In 1945, Maurice Edelman wrote in the *Picture Post*,

What is there in *A Child of Our Time* which receives such an instant and vibrating answer in the feelings of the ordinary man and woman? Perhaps it is that Tippett's oratorio with its pain, its ecstasy and its theme – 'The simple hearted shall exult in the end' – speaks the inexpressible thoughts of us all, children of our time, brothers and sisters in the modern agony.

It was *A Child of Our Time*, and the success of his tenure at Morley, that led to Tippett's wider success, and, eventually, to his resignation in order to compose full time. He lessened his commitments from 1949, particularly after the death of Eva Hubback, and resigned fully in 1951, going on to become one of the country's leading composers, with almost another half-century of music in him. It was hardly surprising that when looking to celebrate Tippett's 60th birthday in 1965, the Institute of Contemporary Arts turned to Morley and the Emma Cons Hall to stage a concert in which Benjamin Britten and Peter Pears were among the performers.

He returned to Morley once more, on 21 May 1994, as 'Sir Michael Tippett, OM', to celebrate the College's acquisition of his portrait by Oskar Kokoschka. In an interview during the afternoon, he gleefully recalled conducting a concert during the war and hearing a whisper between two GIs which reveals the breadth not only of Morley's repertoire under Tippett but of the audience it reached: 'Hey! Monteverdi! Attaboy!'

It is no surprise that, out of his 11 years of war and peace at Morley College, *A Child of Our Time* emerged – a pacifist oratorio with the shadow of war on its lungs. Its composition was much influenced by the music that Tippett had so championed with the Morley Choir. The oratorio harnesses the particular power of community music-making, and community music-listening. Tippett's belief in music's ability to heal, and to bring together, knew no bounds: the unbounded success and influence – still felt today – of his directorship at Morley remains proof of his conviction.

OLIVER SODEN

Michael Graubart, seen here conducting in 1983

The Life and Times of a Music Director

MY INTRODUCTION TO Morley College came long before I had any idea that I might work there. I had been invited to a Morley concert by a friend, and was preparing to enjoy the first piece, a 17th-century six-part *a cappella* work that I did not know. The small vocal group on the stage looked anxious. Suddenly a singer jumped down and rushed up to me. 'The second bass hasn't turned up. Come and sing!' and there I was, sight-singing, suddenly a participant. No bad microcosm of what Morley is about.

In 1966 I became a tutor. Three years later Barry Till, the Principal, called me into his room and said, 'John Gardner is retiring. I have been thinking about whether to appoint a famous composer as the new Director of Music or someone who will do the work, and I have decided on the latter. Are you interested?' I became the new Director of Music, a few years later the first full-time one, and eventually the longest-serving one in Morley's history.

There was less paperwork then and, apart from a rush of course planning and budgeting every spring, my job as head of department was mainly to support classes and tutors (many of them outstanding professional musicians), encourage good ways of learning and deal with very rare problems. So I was able to do a great deal of teaching and conducting myself.

Morley had been the first college in Britain to run an electronic music class. It was taught by Daphne Oram and, in the absence of any equipment at Morley, she invited the students to her own studio at weekends. When she became too busy with her other work, the class came to an end. But in 1971 I was able to buy some VCS3 synthesizers and a few secondhand tape-recorders and revive the class myself.

We started a conducting class, taught by Lawrence Leonard and visiting tutors. It was a paradigm of adult education classes, its members ranging from the head-mistress of a local primary school, who wanted to improve the conducting of the hymns in morning assembly, to the distinguished composer Francis Chagrin and the chief rehearsal pianist of the Royal Ballet. Not to be outdone, I enrolled as a student in it myself.

I once drove the Orchestra for All (which players could join without audition) through Schubert's 'Great' C major Symphony, with all the long repeats. But I also conducted the Musica Viva ensemble, devoted to the most difficult contemporary music. The Morley College Choir, also unauditioned, one of the three I conducted, kept asking me to write a piece for them and I kept saying, 'You'll be sorry if I

Michael Graubart and Nicholas Till prepared an edition of Viktor Ullmann's *The Emperor of Atlantis* for the British premiere at Morley College on 15 May 1981

do!' In the end I did, turning up to rehearsals with successive pages of a very difficult 12-note cantata. Whether they *were* sorry I cannot say, but they performed it marvellously.

The College expanded and returned more and more to its original purposes in those years, and Raymond Rivers, the Vice Principal, had the idea of 'Second Chance' classes for adults who had failed in various subjects at school. My response was the 'Can't Sing' Choir, conducted by Margaret Hopkins, which was so successful that it proliferated into several such groups.

The Music Theatre Group and the Musica Viva, with a few young professional soloists, mounted works that fell outside the remit of the Opera Group (which was primarily concerned with giving intending professional opera singers and proficient amateurs coaching and experience in performing conventional opera, rather than to explore new repertoire and unconventional techniques). The works they performed included the premiere of Nicola LeFanu's *Anti-World,* written for Morley, and the first staged performances in Britain of Viktor Ullmann's *The Emperor of Atlantis,* a profoundly serious satire on Hitler composed and rehearsed, but not performed, in the Terezín concentration camp before

In 1982 I travelled down to Dorset to see a performance of a community play in the town of Sherbourne. The concept of the now ubiquitous community play was still new, having been dreamt up by the Royal Court playwright and literary manager Ann Jellicoe, who pioneered the first such play in Devon in 1978. Jellicoe's method was to invite a professional playwright and production team to work with a specific community to develop a drama about its history or concerns in which the members of the community could also perform. What I saw was a riot of energy and enthusiasm shaped into a coherent and touching dramatic narrative by the distinguished screen and theatre writer Charles Wood, and directed by Ann Jellicoe herself.

I had for several years been working as a director in mainstream opera, including two years at Glyndebourne Opera. I found the social exclusiveness of Glyndebourne increasingly difficult to square with my political convictions, and had started to undertake volunteer work in community arts, in particular at Hoxton Hall in East London. But it was Ann Jellicoe's work that inspired me, for I came to see that opera, in a country like Italy, was a form that had popular roots and allowed the community to express itself through the collective voice of the chorus. Opera, I realised, might potentially be the community art form par excellence. With little experience and no money, I decided to mount a community opera project. Starting with a manifesto that was published in a number of arts periodicals, I built up support for the idea of community opera, and persuaded the Royal Opera that the work should be presented in the big top in Battersea Park, where the Royal Ballet used to perform every summer. At the last moment funding for the 1985 big top season was pulled, and I was left with no sponsor for the project.

I turned to Michael Graubart, Director of Music at Morley, to ask whether Morley might be able to support a more modest version of the project. Michael expressed unreserved enthusiasm for the idea and offered to run the project as a class at Morley, giving us access to facilities. Two other Adult Education Institutes

STREET OPERATIONS: THE FIRST COMMUNITY OPERA PROJECT

NICHOLAS TILL

in South London joined the project on similar terms, enabling us to reach a wider geographical constituency, and we ran a series of workshops to attract possible participants. Maggie Pinhorn of Alternative Arts, who programmed the arts events in Covent Garden Piazza at that time, offered us a coveted Saturday afternoon slot in the Piazza and some funds, and the London Boroughs of Lambeth and Southwark both contributed funds on condition that we also showed the work in suitable locations in Lambeth and Southwark. A production team was got together and we were away.

After six months of preparation, the finished work was presented in Covent Garden Piazza in the summer of 1986. Some 100 performers, including 60 or so children, took part in a piece that told the story of a street stall holder in the market who gave away music from her stall. Her stall was itself a

musical contraption, made for us by the late Hugh Davies, composer and inventor of weird and wonderful musical instruments. A pair of officious men from the Ministry attempted to close down the jollity, but were outwitted by the ingenuity of a child (I forget how!) to general rejoicing.

The project is now recognised as the first large-scale community opera in the UK. Many such projects have followed. Most opera company education departments have since produced community opera projects, including Glyndebourne; Streetwise Opera, which involves homeless people in making operas, is another currently successful offspring of the idea. That first project back in 1984 was flawed in many respects: we had no practical experience of running such a project, and had underestimated the difficulty of creating a sense of community and coherence in a large metropolitan area as opposed to the smaller communities within which Ann Jellicoe worked. But we proved that the idea could work, and that opera is indeed a perfect vehicle for large-scale community engagement and expression.

Scratch Orchestra had grown. Stimulated originally by avant-garde indeterminate music, and allied to Cardew's strong anti-elitist and left-wing political views, the use of graphics and texts instead of music notation and of everyday objects in place of conventional musical instruments enabled people with no musical training to create and perform music. Gradually, Cardew left more and more of the direction of the class to others and its purpose shifted towards rehearsing songs for forthcoming political demonstrations such as IRA marches. At last the Principal and I agreed that the class would have to be closed, but for different reasons. The Principal was concerned about its political activities; I, because it was no longer creating and performing experimental music.

When the ILEA reorganised its many Adult Education Institutes into fewer, larger ones in the 1980s, Morley had the choice of enlarging and taking part or remaining a small, select 'literary institute'. There were many discussions and many meetings; in one of them the Principal, very keen that we should uphold the purposes for which Morley was founded nearly a century earlier but not, perhaps, familiar with everything that that would entail, told us that if we did take over the work of the local Adult Education Institutes, we would be teaching 'Bonzai and other martial arts'!

We did take part in this broadening of our curriculum. Barry Anderson, head of music and dance at the South Bank Institute, joined us as Assistant Director of Music and brought with him his electronic music studio, full of his own equipment, which was thereby able to provide courses applicable to popular music and to recording techniques, as well as to the more esoteric kinds of avant-garde music. We started beginners' jazz classes to complement Gordon Rose's excellent Jazz Orchestra, popular singing classes, and classes in such instruments as the bodhran, the traditional Irish drum.

The College then went through a dark period of internal strife, at the end of which I, in common with all the senior academic staff, left. But I have returned to the fold, and from my vantage point as once more a part-time tutor under the present Director of Music, Andrea Brown, the Music department has regained its old spirit of combining work of the highest standard in all kinds of music with openness to people at all levels of musical experience and none.

MICHAEL GRAUBART

composer and librettist died in the Auschwitz gas chambers. They also premiered Elisabeth Lutyens's last opera, *Isis and Osiris,* a difficult work which inevitably became 'Crisis and Osiris' during rehearsals.

One sad event was the end of Cornelius Cardew's experimental music class, out of which the famous

Cornelius
Cardew

Cardew and the Morley Scratch

IN 2011, THE COLLEGE's *Engine Room* festival marked the 75th anniversary of the birth, and 30th of the death, of one of its more influential former tutors, Cornelius Cardew, considered by many as the founder of British experimental music. Cardew's annotated performing copy of his famous graphic score *Treatise* was exhibited as part of the festival, and on the battered envelope containing these blueprints was a scribbled map, in Cardew's hand, giving directions to Morley. For a time at least, the College was evidently an important focus for this most challenging of artists.

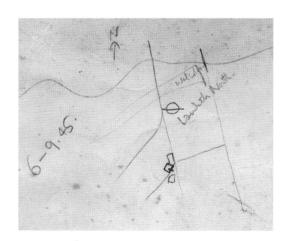

Cardew's map, sketched on the wrapper of his performing score of 'Treatise', showing how to find Morley and emphasising the time his class ran

Morley has enjoyed a symbiotic relationship with many of the distinguished musicians that have passed through the ranks of its teaching staff. They have brought the College high profile and inspired a myriad of students, but even those of the standing of Holst and Tippett have taken something from their time at Morley. That applies no less to Cardew.

When Cardew began his experimental music class in Morley's Holst Room in September 1968, he was the leading light of British avant-garde music: former assistant to Stockhausen, friend and promoter of the American experimentalists centred on John Cage, and a champion of improvisation and new forms of notation. He was able to pursue and promulgate his idiosyncratic ideas at Morley – something far less easy to do at the Royal Academy of Music where he also taught – since it lay outside the mainstream academic establishment and remained true to the pioneering principles of its 19th-century founders. A 'spirit of collaboration and an emphasis on doing something new' is what characterised Cardew's Morley class, according to one of its members.

'Participants in this class will be involved in the performance of indeterminate, improvisatory and electronic music' is how the class was sold. Although it rarely involved electronics, the class explored many and varied ways of stimulating artistic expression, especially through improvisation. Composer Howard Skempton has said, 'Sometimes at a loss, sometimes taking innocent pleasure in our exploration ... we were forced to develop new skills.' Another member vividly recalled: 'You did not have to be frightened; even if you weren't a musician you could do everything. You could make graphic scores, you could scratch chair legs round the floor and make sounds. I did have a banjo which I didn't know how to play, but I was allowed to do what I wanted, like put marbles on it and make noises. So suddenly I could make music!'

The Scratch Orchestra and *The Great Learning*, his huge work in seven 'paragraphs', have proved to be the most enduring and influential aspects of Cardew's legacy. They are inextricably linked and neither would have taken quite the shape they did without Morley. Paragraph 1 of *The Great Learning* pre-dated the Morley class. Rehearsing and developing Paragraph 2 for singers and drummers was the focus of the spring term's experimental music class in 1969, culminating in a performance at the Roundhouse in May. The scale and complexity of Paragraph 2 meant the Morley class needed to be supplemented by others. The idea of a larger, wide-ranging group had been sown and in the summer of 1969, Cardew published the 'Scratch Constitution' in the *Musical Times* and announced the formation of the Scratch Orchestra.

The Scratch owed not only its genesis and nucleus of 'twenty or more stalwarts, most of whom had been members of the Morley College class' to Westminster Bridge Road, but also its core repertoire: the ideas for improvisations and actions from members of the class and from others which Cardew meticulously wrote out as *Nature Study Notes*. As the starting point for the Scratch, *Nature Study Notes*, together with other works devised for the class such as Skempton's *Drum No.1* and Michael Chant's *Pastoral Symphony* (the work which caused Wendy Craig such dismay at a family concert) ensured the Morley class was the primer, and indeed the 'engine room', of the Scratch Orchestra.

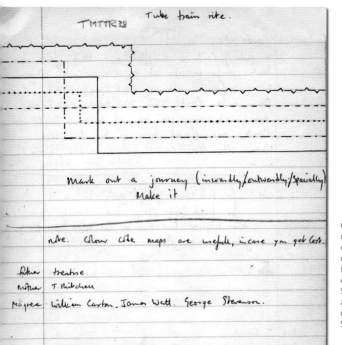

One of the 'rites' developed in Cardew's experimental music class to inspire improvisation, later collected into 'Nature Study Notes' (below) as a resource for the class and for the Scratch Orchestra

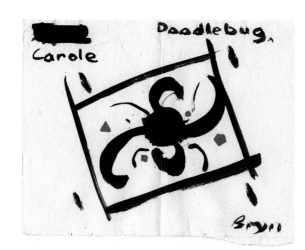

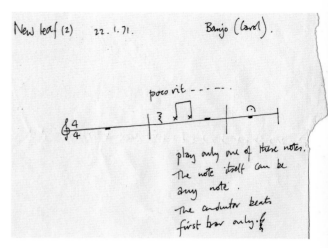

Graphic and experimental scores used in the Morley experimental music class

The Great Learning was to become an important vehicle for the Scratch Orchestra, to whom it was eventually dedicated. But the Orchestra's overlap of membership, ethos and working methods with the Friday experimental music class meant Morley was equally entwined with the Orchestra's emergence, directly involved for instance in the premiere of Paragraph 5, the longest and most complex section, which includes many ideas first trialled in the Holst Room. (And it is perhaps no coincidence that the work's very title should chime with Morley's 'Learning for Life' motto: as Skempton recalls, one of the class members would call the Friday evening sessions a 'learning zone'.) As John Tilbury has observed in his biography of Cardew, '*The Great Learning* was a response to the Scratch Orchestra and the Morley College group … something within reach of everyone but which would curb the woefully anarchic side of the character of both.' By 1972 the identification of the Friday experimental music class with the Scratch Orchestra was such that express mention was made in the College prospectus and it was colloquially known as 'The Morley Scratch'.

The class was cancelled after the 1972/3 session amongst concerns that it had lost its way as it had become acutely politicised. That politicisation had begun in the Scratch and spread to the Morley class with Cardew himself gradually becoming converted to the Maoist cause: 'That political stuff is not for the likes of you and me', one member recalls him saying as she gave him a lift home after a Friday class. But converted he became and in its last year described the class as a 'Music Workshop in the service of the working and oppressed people of England and the whole world', forging 'revolutionary music' in the form of Morley

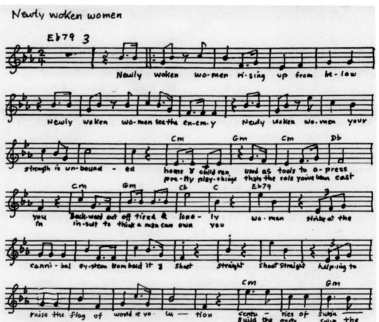

Songbooks of overtly political songs. Diehard class members petitioned against the closure, divining a more politically based objection to its activities than the practical reasons given by the College: enforcement of the 'educational policy of the ruling class'. In his later repudiation of his avant-garde and artistic roots, *Stockhausen Serves Imperialism*, Cardew, now a fully fledged leftist activist, dismissed Morley's aim as merely 'the inculcation of bourgeois values in the working class', somewhat unjustly biting the hand that had helped feed him artistically and materially over the five years of the life of the experimental music class.

NICK RAMPLEY

A page from a Morley Songbook in which class members wrote and collected overtly political songs. The increasingly political nature of the class eventually led to its closure

MUSIC AND POLITICS

THE UNJUST CLOSURE OF OUR EVENING CLASS !

The Music Workshop (originally Experimental Music Workshop) at Morley was set up in 1968. From the start it developed a clear identity, participating on many occasions in the musical life of the college and eventually becoming nationally and internationally known through its offspring the Scratch Orchestra.

Through this activity we gained practical experience of the dilemmas and crises of modern art. At the same time we recognized the growing trend of revolution throughout the world and were greatly inspired by the Cultural Revolution in China. A critical trend emerged and grew strong in the workshop. We realized that all art expresses ideas. These ideas serve either the ruling class, which exploits and oppresses the vast majority of the people, or the people themselves in their struggle to be free from this exploitation and oppression. 'There is no such thing as art that stands above classes.'(Mao Tse-tung) We now see that artists must become politically conscious if they wish to serve the masses of the people.

The workshop has been run consistently on democratic lines and the students have had the initiative and ability to control the development of the class, both as regards form and content. Towards the end of last year the four hour class had become a forum in which current cultural and political issues were freely discussed. Investigation was going forward into: songs from the People's Republic of China; music reflecting the 800 year old struggle of the Irish people for national liberation and other sources. Practical activities such as singing and instrumental accompaniments were developing as well. All these things were done in order to develop a culture which genuinely serves the people.

It was at this positive and progressive stage that Barry Till, the Principal, decided to intervene and close the class. The reasons he gave were as follows: 1) Although attendance was reasonable some of those attending had not paid their fees -- this was immediately rectified. 2) The teachers listed in the brochure were not in fact teaching the class -- this was because our meetings were chaired in rotation by students and 'teachers' alike. 3) the content of the workshop did not correspond to the notice in the brochure -- this was not true.

The real reason for his closing the class is not any of those given, but a desire to suppress the serious discussion of political issues in any connection within the college. In this he is carrying out the educational policy of the ruling class.

Colleges like Morley were designed originally for working class education. Their main function has always been to divert the growing consciousness of the people into safe, bourgeois paths. So we are told that music is music and politics politics, and that the relation between the two should never be examined.

We shall not be deterred by this repressive measure. The members of the music workshop have decided to enroll in other classes in the college and pursue their work within the framework of an Art and Revolution Club. The aims of this club will be to examine in discussion and investigation the relation between art and politics, and to develop a culture of the revolutionary movement in England today using drama, music and painting.

If you are a democratically-minded person and wish either to join this Club or be kept informed of its activities, please leave your name and address or contact us through:

Penny Jordan
21 Prah Road
London N4

01-226 2662

September '73

THE ENGINE ROOM

HOWARD SKEMPTON

For Cornelius Cardew, music was anything but mechanical. He favoured fantasy and informality. If he was delighted by musical 'machines', like those of his friend John White, it was because he viewed them as 'dangerous compositions'. He called his own *Ode Machines* dedicated to White, 'highly imperfect mechanisms'.

Cardew and White performed the latter's *Cello and Tuba Machine* at the inaugural meeting of Cardew's experimental music class at Morley College. This was in 1968, the year of the premieres of Cardew's *Schooltime Compositions* and *The Great Digest* which later became Paragraph 1 of *The Great Learning*, Cardew's monumental achievement of the Morley years. Paragraph 2 was completed in January 1969 and work on this exuberant piece for drummers and singers occupied the class throughout the winter months. A Roundhouse performance in May 1969 prompted the formation of the Scratch Orchestra.

Cardew once likened the Scratch Orchestra to an oracle. The Morley class seemed more disciplined, though the regular free improvisations, like the pipes and radiators of the Holst Room which were sometimes brought into play as percussion instruments, could be guaranteed to generate more heat than light! Morley was the engine room of English Experimental Music, but the engines were human, conjuring from their energies an experimental movement. Alliances and friendships were forged and cemented, and many of these survived the ideologically induced turbulence of the final abortive class of 1972/3. Some of those in the class were musicians: Michael Chant had played the organ in the Cheltenham premiere of *The Great Digest*; Christopher Hobbs and Hugh Shrapnel were students of Cardew at the Royal Academy of Music; Michael Parsons was writing for *The Listener* and the *Musical Times*. Others had attended art school: Tim Mitchell, Carole Finer, Psi Ellison, Judith Euren, David and Diane Jackman. One or two, including the indispensable Bryn Harris, were self-taught. There were friends who dropped in to test the water.

So, Morley was also a hub: one in which dialogue and co-operation held sway. News and views would be exchanged in the refectory during the mid-evening break in proceedings and most of the class would at length gather in the pub opposite for critical reflection, gossip and occasional banter with the locals.

One of its members, David Jackman, remembers the Morley class as 'a learning zone'. A fine balance was maintained between disciplined work on composed pieces and uninhibited improvisation. There was a fertile middle ground of open scores and improvisation rites, both of which called for admirable directness and efficiency. Much of this music remains fresh and characterful. Even its composers delight in rediscovering it and learning from it.

To be at the experimental music class was to be in the right place at the right time. There was nothing comparable, and that it happened at all is a great tribute to Morley College.

Teller by Andrea Byrne in the Sound Art Students at Morley exhibition in the Gallery, 2014

Electronic Music

IT MUST BE THAT THE air is different south of the river – more open to new ideas and to challenging the old. To review tutors in electronic music in Morley College is to see a history of the field in Britain as a whole. A course at Daphne Oram's personal studio in Kent first appeared in the prospectus of 1959 and continued for five years. This must be the first education institutional studio course in Britain by at least six years. In 1968/9 Cornelius Cardew's 'experimental music' class included live electronics as an option. But it was Director of Music Michael Graubart who placed electronic music tuition on a firmer footing in 1971, when he created a coherent and longer-term course structure. While there was still no designated studio, he obtained for the College its first synthesizer (EMS VCS3) and recording equipment. In the subsequent years, Peter Zinovieff, Harrison Birtwistle, Tristram Cary, Lawrence Casserley, Hugh Davies and Lily Greenham all taught classes. This list is interesting in many ways – these are the pioneers, true, but this is also a shortlist for creative diversity, including innovators of new technology, new instruments, improvisation, composition, live electronics, sound poetry and performance. The ideology was inclusive and experimental. Graubart was assisted by Colin Stiff, then later Graham Bradshaw, alongside these more occasional visitors, while Roger Cawkwell led a range of jazz and other improvisation courses, some with live electronics.

In 1981, Morley absorbed a range of smaller institutes on the greater south bank. One was the South Bank Institute itself, which included the West Square Electronic Music Studio which had become very active under its director Barry Anderson from its foundation in 1971 (and its performing ensemble in 1975). Barry became Assistant Music Director at Morley and West Square, the College's more permanent studio (and rehearsal area). In time, space was found in the basement of the art building, closer to Morley's main building, and the studio moved there in 1983/4. Barry believed passionately in public engagement and performed a regular electronic music series around London (with some memorable concerts at St John's Smith Square). In December 1983, the West Square Electronic Music Ensemble toured Britain on the Arts Council's Contemporary Music Network with Dutch bass clarinetist Harry Sparnaay. This increasing profile was sadly cut short by his untimely death in 1987. Two CDs of Anderson's works were recorded posthumously, the ensemble directed by Stephen Montague. Philipp Wachsmann took over as studio director, and, with Ron

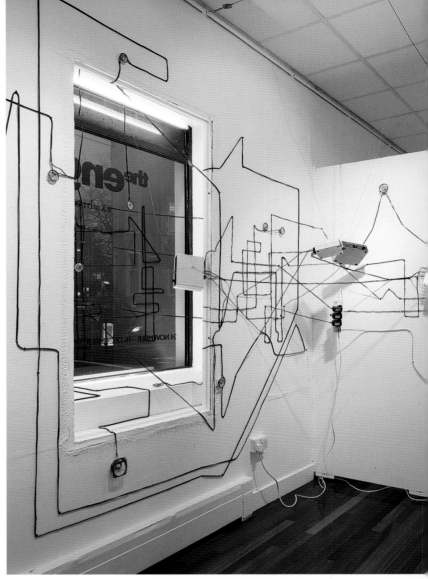

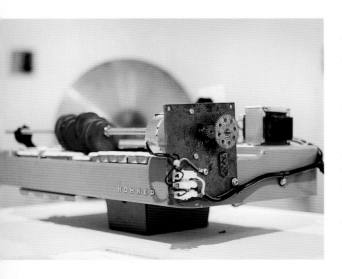

Briefel, who had been a student, then technical assistant in the studio since 1982, Ian Dearden, Javier Alvarez and Julio d'Escriván, took over many of the courses in the inevitable reorganisation.

But the forces of the new digital technology had changed the nature of student needs and teaching approaches by this time. The first generation of analogue studios gave way slowly, but very clearly from the mid-1980s, to small computer-based systems. Atari computers had built-in MIDI ports and the Morley studio installed these soon after their launch in 1985, with Michael Murray teaching a course on MIDI and microcomputers from 1987, and an increasing array of computer music courses in subsequent years. The first hints of the afford-able home studio were emerging and this inevitably

ABOVE: *Dream Sweeper 2.0* by Jenny Pickett and Julien Ottavi in 'The Engine Room' sound art exhibition in the Gallery, 2011

LEFT: *Automated Improvisation for Three Reed Organs and Small Percussion* by Dominick Allen

Barry
Anderson

changed the music and its pedagogy still further. In the 1990s, a new range of tutors versed in these small mobile systems – which rapidly became known as workstations – harnessed new ideas of flexibility, mobility, performance, audio-visuals and composition. But social musical issues have always been a concern at Morley – perhaps the rush to new technology risked boy/toy exclusivity, and Marion Gilbert taught several courses for women in the electronic studio from 1992 to 1996. With Jeremy Arden from 1992 and Holger Zschenderlein from 1996, this generation of Morley tutors are now themselves leading teachers, studio directors and practitioners throughout the UK (and abroad).

The first decade of the new millennium saw steady change and opening out of modular courses across new areas and by 2008 electronic music had been absorbed into a range of music technology provision, many with a creative output. Studio directors have been Stace Constantinou from 2006, Julian Fyson from 2009 and Camilo Salazar, current director from 2011. In 2010 the studios were completely refurbished into the suite of purpose-built facilities we see today – probably the most advanced for an open-access adult education college in the land. The range of creative work from studio classes at this year's SASAM (Sound Art Students at Morley) installation in Morley Gallery was outstanding in quality and range. Daphne Oram's vision of a music controlled by creative graphics had at last come of age in such a wonderful range of sounding art.

SIMON EMMERSON

Jazz and Pop

Pick up Morley's current course guide and you will see a whole section covering jazz, Latin and popular music and a further plethora of courses falling under this broad heading in the Music department's instrumental studies, vocal classes and music technology offerings. Whether it is ensemble playing in such groups as the Afro-Cuban Big Band or the Soul and Funk Band, singing jazz, blues, gospel, soul, pop or rock, world and folk music, or developing skills on keyboards, guitar, bass, saxophone, drums, harmonica – even ukulele: Morley's the place! And while our music technology facilities and expertise support the sort of artistic activity Simon Emmerson writes about on page 95, they are also devoted to training students in the latest software programmes, and teaching skills in sound recording, engineering, design and production, including DJing, urban music, radio production and film scoring.

But it was not always the case. Only with the appearance of the Morley Jazz Orchestra (MJO) in 1964 did the College venture away from the 'classical' mainstream. The MJO was founded by trumpeter Gordon Rose on acquiring the library of William Russo's London Jazz Orchestra, which had featured the very best jazz and session musicians in London, including Gordon himself. This meant the MJO was playing from manuscript works by such jazz luminaries as the trumpeter and composer Kenny Wheeler and continues to do so. Gordon was to carve out for himself a very distinguished career as composer and band leader, accompanying artists such as Josephine Baker and Bing Crosby, conducting no fewer than 12 Royal Command Performances at the London Palladium

and writing the music for six film scores. Throughout, he has continued to lead the MJO which has played a significant role in training many of the UK's top jazz talent. Morley's 125th year is Gordon's 50th as a Morley tutor!

It was nearly another 10 years before the College began to broaden its horizons further with 'A Practical Introduction to Jazz and Rock', followed by a class on Country Music running for just six years during the 1970s and an even shorter-lived Jazz-Rock Ensemble. But despite occasional workshops given by such luminaries as acclaimed folk guitarist John Renbourn, and by Lindsay Cooper composer and performer in the experimental rock group Henry Cow, 'popular' music in any form remained a marginal part of the Morley experience during that decade.

However, jazz – and more particularly big band jazz – was given a boost in 1981 when the Beaufoy Adult Education Centre became part of the College in the ILEA's reorganisation of adult education and with it came the Manor Jazz Orchestra under Bernard Ebbinghouse. Frequently

deputising for Ebbinghouse was Tony Douglas, who became its Musical Director as it became the Morley Big Band, and has taken it from strength to strength, adding two swing bands and a beginners' band to the roster. Tony was awarded a MBE in the 2014 New Year's Honours list for his services to further education, and he and the Band featured in a BBC radio documentary soon afterwards.

Folk guitar classes appeared in 1982 and jazz piano in 1984; jazz and pop grew steadily through the 1980s, at certain points including a Jazz/Funk/Reggae class and a steel band. Twenty years ago the College was providing both the MCO and the Big Band plus lessons in jazz harmony and composing, popular song writing, pop singing, jazz piano, saxophone and folk, electric and bass guitar, while music technology included 'Q:Club Mix' for dance music DJs. Since then the number and variety of Morley's jazz and popular music courses has inexorably increased, not destined to stop in its 125th anniversary year!

NICK RAMPLEY

Supporting Young Talent

MORLEY MAY BE AN adult education institution, but it has not lacked impact on younger generations, not least in the field of musical education. Its long tradition of bringing music to children and families continues to this day. But the College has supported emerging young talent in other ways.

In 1961, the violinist and distinguished teacher Rosemary Rappaport had a vision for a school that would 'provide a good background of general education for boys and girls of all ages who need ample time for musical studies and practice' – Britain's first specialist music school, no less. She enlisted the aid of her friend, a former headmistress, Irene Forster, and the energy and persistence of these two determined women echoed that of Emma Cons and Caroline Martineau in founding Morley College.

Their vision very soon became reality and in January 1962, the Central Tutorial School for Young Musicians (CTSYM) opened its doors, some 18 months before the establishment of the Yehudi Menuhin School; Menuhin himself was one of the founding patrons of the CTSYM. In another echo of Morley's early history, the school operated in accommodation beneath and behind the stage of the Conway Hall in Holborn.

Conway Hall was a less than ideal home for the school and, following his attendance at one of its early concerts, Morley's Principal, Denis Richards, invited the school to

take up space at the College during the day, since the College's own activities were at the time restricted largely to evenings. When CTSYM arrived at Morley in September 1963, it had at its disposal four classrooms, a games room, a music room with two practice rooms, use of an art room and the laboratory, and an office for the school's head, all of which allowed the CTSYM to grow from 12 pupils in

ABOVE LEFT: Members of the Central Tutorial School for Young Musicians at Morley in 1968

ABOVE: Rosemary Rappaport taking a CTSYM chamber group at Morley, its pianist a very young Oliver Knussen

RECOLLECTIONS OF ROBERT HANSON

WILLIAM LEIGH KNIGHT

Bob Hanson was one of the College's longest-serving Directors of Music, 1991–2007. Coming from Dartington College, where he had been a teacher and department head, he made a number of innovations which have been a huge influence on our music-making and study. He revived the Morley Chamber Choir, and ran *Music in Time*, a series of history lectures, which have continued to the present day. They reflected some of his great strengths – the erudition of a scholar combined with a clear and engaging delivery – while his conducting of the Choir demonstrated his love of practical music-making and the sensitivity to bring out the best in people. He also helped reinvigorate electronic music and the development of the recording studio, and increased the courses on offer, especially in areas of non-classical music.

He has always been a great communicator. His way of engaging with students was friendly and sympathetic – two important characteristics needed in a place of adult learning. He did much to forge links by taking performances outside college and also bringing in people from outside, notably in the occasional series of lecture recitals he gave with the Allegri String Quartet. He is also remembered for his exciting compositions for the Chamber Choir. History will doubtless defer judgement, as it always does, but I think in particular his smaller choral compositions (only part of his output) will stand up well, compared with the work of his illustrious predecessors. Despite his academic interest in Serialism and his PhD on Webern, his own pieces, although challenging, are moving and very singable. Members of the original Chamber Choir will always remember his amazing motet for 40 voices, *And There Shall Be No Night There*, written as a companion piece to Tallis's *Spem in Alium*. This is just one of many pieces written especially, or arranged, for the Choir. Other great moments of his music-making with the department included celebrations of Michael Tippett, Director of Music in the 1940s – one concert actually in Tippett's presence – and of Mátyás Seiber, who taught composition here in the 1940s and 1950s.

BELOW: CYM student Coco Cripps taking part in Morley's course for young women conductors

1963 to 30 at the start of the following academic year. The school flourished at Morley and drew increasing attention from the educational and musical worlds. A concert at the College in March 1965 featured an 11-year-old Oliver Knussen, now one of the country's most respected composers, conducting a small choir and ensemble in his own *Three Chinese Lyrics* (billed in the programme as his Op. 47!).

Under Barry Till, the College began to expand its daytime provision, and space for CTSYM was put under pressure. The school acquired Heath House, a former secretarial college in Hampstead, following fund-raising trials and tribulations, to where it moved for the opening of the 1969/70 academic session. Its director of music by that time was the former Morley tutor Graham Treacher. And a further connection 40 years later is that the current writer joined Morley as its Vice Principal, after 10 years as the School's director of finance and administration. Denis Richards had become a governor of the CTSYM while still Morley's Principal and was to serve as its chairman for 11 challenging years during which time it moved to Harrow and changed its name. As the Purcell School, it has become one of the leading musical institutions in the country, boasting an alumni rich in outstanding musical figures, including the most recent (2014) winner of the BBC Young Musician of the Year competition, the pianist Martin James Bartlett.

Morley's support for the musical training of the young did not stop there. In 1970, just as CTSYM was establishing itself in Hampstead, the Centre for Young Musicians (CYM) was being founded as part of the ILEA specialist music provision. CYM moved to Morley in 1993, where its office is based and where every Saturday it fills the College with over 400 talented young musicians. CYM is now a division of the Guildhall School of Music and Drama and is recognised by the Department for Education as one of its national Centres for Advanced Training. It also runs the London Schools Symphony Orchestra and the London Youth Wind Band, both very frequent visitors to Morley's rehearsal spaces. As CYM's director, Stephen Dagg, says, 'We are proud to deliver our service in Morley College, steeped as it is in such a rich musical tradition of its own.' The involvement of CYM students in College initiatives, such as its centenary performance of Purcell's *Fairy Queen* and its course for aspiring young women conductors, would surely have met with the approval of Denis Richards and CTSYM's founders.

NICK RAMPLEY

Family Concerts

THE 1950S AND 1960S saw the rise in popularity of the Robert Mayer Children's Concerts at the Festival Hall and the work of Youth & Music. Robert Mayer himself was a Vice President of the College and, during the 1960s, Morley hosted occasional children's concerts, not least those held under the auspices of the Education Committee of the London Co-operative Society's 'Music for Children' series. These involved the London Co-operative Children's Choir and sometimes 'an orchestra of young people', but were formal concerts exploring 'the World of Stravinsky' or 'the World of Bartók'.

At the start of the 1970s, Raymond Rivers, Morley's Vice Principal, considered and rejected the idea of having similar regular concerts at Morley. He thought Morley's smaller venue, the Emma Cons Hall, would be good for a family audience and Morley had just the right resources – first-class tutors of music and dance, and their talented students. Also, there was nowhere in the country specifically for a family audience.

So, from the 1969/70 academic session, a series of family concerts was instigated that has continued to the present. And what a rich diversity of music and dance has emerged over 40 years! Tiny tots playing violins and cellos, Greek folk dance, Indian Kathak, Chinese ribbon dances, African and Scottish dancers accompanied by live music. Southwark Waits (Morley's Renaissance wind group) accompanied historical dancers, Lucy Skeaping's wondrous medieval dragon caused a bit of a fright, avant-garde electronic works stretched imaginations, singing solo and together, listening to piano (only a three-year-old can get away with throwing a shoe at a concert pianist), wind, brass, jazz and chamber groups, and, of course, the Symphony Orchestras. Two favourite conductors were Guy Woolfenden and Lawrence Leonard, especially when Lawrence brought Paddington Bear to conduct and then invited extremely small people to do likewise!

One notorious early example was given by Cornelius Cardew's Scratch Orchestra. His experimental approach – one 'work' consisted of Cardew himself standing on a chair, removing his jacket and sitting back down again – nonplussed the audience and led to actress Wendy Craig storming out with her offspring in high dudgeon. The year 1974 saw Family Music Making, 'a co-operative effort between parents, children and tutor', added as an

extension of the concert series, which ran for over 20 years under the supervision of the eminent sound and visual artist Max Eastley.

Percussionist James Blades (the sound behind the massive gong for cinema's J. Arthur Rank opening title) proved that giving the most hyperactive child the biggest drum transformed them into a listening child, eager to perform at the right moment. James passed on his beater to Evelyn Glennie, who was starting out on her career and could magically hold a family audience spellbound. We were learning to listen.

Serendipity plays its part in Morley family concerts – sometimes things don't go according to plan but the show goes on. When a group of African musicians were late for their gig, I had to plink a finger piano until they entered the room – fortunately it looked planned! For two or three years English National Opera brought us *Let's Make a Family Opera* directed by the brilliant Peter Kay. There were more older children in the audience in those days. Audiences have changed as society has changed and nowadays we see more families with very young children.

We have welcomed back popular favourites such as Morley's own Un Poco de Flamenco, Lyra Greek dancers from North London, and several London Suzuki groups with their very young performers inspiring audiences of whatever age. We know that to enjoy music and dance together as a family is a happy experience,

creating great memories. As one grateful parent recently wrote:

> I attended the Family concert on Sunday. I want to express my gratitude for such an AMAZING event. The quality and energy of the orchestra and the flamenco performance/workshop was the very best and myself, my 7-year-old son and some friends had a truly wonderful time dancing our hearts out at 12pm! . . . The concert itself was a wonderful gift so please, please make it all happen again!

I bump into people all over the place who either remember their childhood visits or the joy of sharing the concerts with their children. In recent decades, lots of other musical organisations have discovered this too.
SHIRLEY ANDERSON

4

MORLEY'S
MAGIC
CASEMENTS

MORLEY'S FOUNDATION struck at the very heart of the debate at the time about what was the best education for the 'working classes': technical training to improve skills and employment prospects and so contribute to the country's scientific, industrial and economic position; or exposure of the working classes to the liberal arts so that they might cultivate the mind and, in the words of Graham Wallas (later co-founder of the London School of Economics and President of Morley 1928–33), meet 'the need that the working classes should be taught to think'.

That debate has rumbled on in one form or another ever since and as priorities for public funding have changed, institutions such as Morley have had to remain responsive and agile in order to serve both sides of it. But it was clear in its founding aim of 'the study of knowledge

LEFT: Khathak dancing is one of many dance styles offered at Morley today

BELOW: Literature class taken by Monique Rafray, a blind tutor, in the 1950s

and subjects not directly connected with or applied to any handicraft, trade or business' on which side of the debate Morley originally lay. In 1930, the issue was still current. Opening Morley's celebrated murals, Stanley Baldwin thanked God for the fact that places such as Morley and its liberal arts tradition still existed, adding, 'When everyone in this nation ... has had a vocational training it will be time for me to leave it.'

However, while Emma Cons and her circle were at pains to broaden the horizons and ambitions of the working class, the College soon introduced subjects that might 'better the chances of students to earn their daily bread' and promote what we would now term upward social mobility. So even from its earliest days, Morley offered such subjects as shorthand, bookkeeping and machine drawing. And while the introduction of Latin and Greek in the early 1890s was aligned with the College's mission by making accessible 'elitist' subjects to men – and, more particularly, women – of the working classes, these were also subjects needed for entry into professions such as the Civil Service, as noted by social historian Andrea Geddes Poole: 'What Emma Cons determinedly established at the side door of the Old Vic was

both a specific and a virtual space where Lambeth's working men and women could taste the intellectual exercises of the elite, creating new practices of inclusion and participation.'

The 1930s saw a more poetic take on the debate. At a lecture in 1931, Wallas said, 'Here at Morley ... our founders set themselves to create and quicken "wants" among the "wantless" inhabitants of the dreary streets and drearier workshops', while Baldwin's widely reported speech went further: 'Such language and beauty as you are teaching in this college is the language and beauty which opens the magic casements for us, and every life wants its magic casements.' If citizens 'were influenced in their early life by good pictures, good art and good music they would never be taken in by the tawdry, the second-rate and the cheap'.

Morley's 'magic casements' have extended significantly beyond art and music as this chapter demonstrates. At the same time they have had to move with the times as society's 'wants' and ways of attracting the 'wantless' have changed. Kathak dance and flamenco have succeeded 'Movement to Music', dance workout has replaced 'Rhythmical Movement'; we now have Tai chi

Today Tai chi and Latin dance have succeeded other once-popular classes, such as the Margaret Morris dance method

I was very nervous when I took my first class at Morley College in 1969. I had little teaching experience, and had never stood up in front of such a formidable group before. I hoped it didn't show, but it did, because 10 years later one of my most faithful students reminded me of the occasion. 'You did look scared', she said. By then we all knew each other well enough to laugh about it, and I was well into my stride. The class was very good to me. Some of them were old hands, who knew Morley well, and they looked after me. Some, like me, were novices, discovering the College for the first time. They were all ages, from their 20s to their 90s, and from a wide range of educational backgrounds – some retired ex-teachers, some young graduates, some housebound housewives who were grateful for the crèche. We included a nurse, a midwife, an ambassador, a poet, a social worker. We were a mixed group. Some students were Lambeth-based, but some came from far afield. Several American wives, here for a year or two through their husband's postings, found friends. We all looked forward to our time together.

I loved the freedom of being able to create our own curriculum. The Principal, Barry Till (and, not entirely coincidentally, the husband of my good college friend Antonia Clapham), gave us a free rein, and we devised some inspiring reading lists. We studied the 'Woman's Novel', long before it was fashionable to do so, and did a course on 'Literature and the Environment', which included Emerson, Ted Hughes, Mary Webb and Angus Wilson's New Town novel, *Late Call*. We weren't very good at fixing class outings, as most of us for domestic reasons found evenings difficult, but we did memorably attend James Joyce's play *Exiles*, and the film version of my novel *The Millstone*, which

LITERATURE AT MORLEY

MARGARET DRABBLE

appeared under the title of *A Touch of Love*. I know I sometimes set them too much reading; I remember expecting them to read Günter Grass's *The Tin Drum* in a week, which was ridiculous. But they didn't complain.

Students weren't obliged to produce written work, though some of them chose to prepare presentations for class. They received no degrees, no CAT points, no qualifications. They came for the love of the subject, and for the pleasure of sharing their views and learning how to read more carefully. And, being adult, they brought their own experiences into the classroom and applied them, often very usefully, to what they read. One of our older members had taught physics at a distinguished institution and we always appealed to her when our texts led us into scientific terrain. She had also, astonishingly to us, known Joseph Conrad.

I learned Morley's history and imbibed its ethos during my teaching years, and I continue to learn more. I had long known that

Virginia Woolf had taught there, and I knew something of the connections with Emma Cons and the Old Vic, but it was much more recently that I discovered that a Hampstead neighbour of mine (whom I never met, though she was often pointed out to me) had also taught there, and for a while was acting head. Amber Blanco White, born Amber Reeves, was an impressive woman, who became notorious when young as the model for H.G. Wells's New Woman novel, *Ann Veronica*. She also published novels of her own, one of which (*A Lady and Her Husband*, 1914) was very good, and she wrote on banking and psychiatry.

Morley has always had strong teachers – some of them, like Blanco White, impassioned and eccentric – and a tradition of independent thought. During my time there, Barry Till gave us encouragement and freedom to pursue our own agenda. It was a happy place, full of camaraderie and social goodwill. I still meet ex-students, dotted round the globe, and we always greet each other with cries of recognition. I forget some names, but the spirit is unforgettable. In changing circumstances, Morley will surely go on playing its role. It was a very important part of my life and in the life of many of its students.

and Pilates rather than 'Swedish Drill (Women)'. Our language teaching has changed to reflect London's ever-changing demography, offering Arabic, Mandarin, Japanese, Korean, Thai, Vietnamese and a range of Scandanavian languages that would have been

unthinkable not so long ago, just as Esperanto and Gaelic have now gone by the board. What was once just a 'Theatre School' now embraces physical theatre, clowning and even stand-up comedy; photography is no longer a science, but part of our Art and Design portfolio; and the

It's no surprise that my Gran looks as good as she does at 96 – she went to keep-fit classes at Morley in the early 1930s.

This was the pre-war era of economic depression, but the working and lower-middle classes were aspirational and all for self-improvement. So at just 14 years old, fresh out of school and working in her first clerical job at the wool firm Patons and Baldwins, my Gran, Peggy May Clemson, put on her black shorts and white top once a week to join the throng of young women at a keep-fit class at Morley. No Nike footwear back then. Gran remembers doing the class in bare feet to band music played on a wind-up gramophone.

Living round the corner in Gladstone Street, Gran describes a strong sense of community at the time. When I asked her what had made her sign up for the classes, she said that she thought she probably learnt of the class through 'The Youth' at her local church, St Judes. It was an exciting time with the beginnings of real local authority action and responsibility for housing and education, and Gran was all too aware of how fortunate her community was to have Morley at its heart,

KEEPING FIT!

NATASHA BRIANT AND PEGGY ATTEWILL

describing the college as 'a boon to Southwark'. In later years, when she met my grandfather and family, she would attend concerts at Morley. Two of her sister-in-laws were in the choir and Gran said that Morley was a great place to go for those who couldn't afford a concert out at the concert halls of the time.

My own experience as a cello teacher at Morley in 1995/6 shares this same flavour of London community and opportunity. My beginners' cello class was made up of young students (I remember an art student and biochemist researcher), a few professionals including a doctor whom I have stayed in touch with, and two fantastic and memorable ladies from Lewisham. I'm not sure how old Connie and Daisy were but I do remember Connie's tales of being an ambulance driver in the war.

This cello class was not a rarefied classical music experience. I loved the social aspect of meeting and getting to know so many different people through a common interest and love of my favourite instrument. Through Morley's open spirit I also got to meet and perform in a songwriter/cellist duo with one of my closest friends, Craig Snelling, head of Drama at the time and now godfather to my youngest.

Happy Birthday Morley and please stay around to provide something inspiring for *my* granddaughter!

dry- and dusty-sounding 'Basis of Modern Medicine and Surgery' has made way for a range of diploma courses in complementary health.

Morley has seen no shortage of distinguished writers pass through its doors. E. M. Forster and Virginia Woolf (then Virginia Stephen) taught here before the First World War and indeed it has been claimed that Leonard Bast in *Howard's End* and Septimus Smith in *Mrs Dalloway* were even modelled on Morley students. The distinguished poets Kathleen Raine and Charles Tomlinson taught at Morley in the 1930s and 1950s respectively, Margaret Drabble was a tutor at the College for many years during the 1970s, and Angela Carter a not infrequent visiting lecturer in the 1980s. But the emphasis has changed from the study and appreciation of texts to the writing of them, whether writing for children; writing memoirs, short stories or poetry; or screenwriting and writing for radio. The idea of film studies and world cinema must have seemed as absurd in 1914 as 'Elocution and Recitation' does in 2014, though which of 'What is the Soul, and

Choice? What is Free Will and Consciousness?' and 'Why Is Man Aggressive?' belongs to 2014 and which to the 1960s may be less easy to divine.

Space militates against being able to include every magic casement Morley has managed to put before the 'wantless', but those we review below would surely have made Graham Wallas feel less dreary!

NICK RAMPLEY

I was at home with a new baby in 1974 and my friend said, 'We must educate you about Morley.' I had a degree in English so was not sure I needed an education, but my friend and I drove up to the College (could not do that now), deposited the babies in the crèche and had a wonderful two hours thinking about books. One memorable morning when Margaret Drabble was not available, I led the discussion on Conrad's *Heart of Darkness*.

Perhaps that cemented my relationship with Morley. Over the years I have done 'The Hour of Power', an exercise class where we pounded and shadow-boxed to the instructions of a charismatic tutor in tight white shorts; a yoga class with the celebrated teacher Maxine Tobias; and an art history class over three years where Frances Borzello gave me a wonderful introduction to teaching art, both history and aesthetics.

But my children were now at school, their crèche worker who was a poet, Selima Hill, had moved on, and playgroups were no longer part of my life. I wanted to join the Morley team as a tutor and taught 'Preparing to Study with the Open University' (I was an OU tutor in my professional life) and A level English, when I prepared mature students to get places at university, including one to Lucy Cavendish College at Cambridge.

Then I went to classes again as a student at Morley in massage and Alexander Technique and eventually (I expect) I will come to exercise for the elderly and singing for the brain.

The only classes that were never offered at Morley were flower arranging. I did that at Lambeth College and my two years there were quite different (and surprisingly remunerative, though family wedding and funeral flowers can be emotionally rewarding as well). But in the wide and diverse world of adult education, which includes the Open University where I worked for 38 years, Morley is definitely tops and has enhanced my life enormously.

Write Stuff: Creative Writing

MORLEY COLLEGE HAS PLAYED a significant role in providing for those who want to appreciate the art of creative writing and perhaps develop their own skills. This has been partly inspired by the authors to whom budding writers had access through Morley, such as Virginia Woolf, V. S. Pritchett and Margaret Drabble. In the area of non-fiction and social commentary, Maud Pember Reeves worked with Morley in writing her book on poverty in Lambeth. Her daughter, Amber, also made a significant contribution to Morley as a member of staff, teaching philosophy and psychology for 37 years, and became Acting Principal when Eva Hubback died.

When I arrived at Morley, the College's creative writing team was graced by Christopher Reid, one of Britain's top poets. When the demands of Christopher's work at Faber publishers meant he had to resign, he was replaced by two excellent young Irish poets, Matthew Sweeney and Maurice Riordan. My clearest memory was seeing the enraptured faces of the children as they read out poems for young people at one of the children's poetry festivals organised by Morley.

I had known Michael Walker prior to coming to Morley and brought him into the College's creative writing team. Mike was slowly beginning to establish himself as a major radio dramatist on BBC Radio 4. Within a year of taking over our advanced writers' class

Amber Blanco White, cigarette in hand, teaches psychology in the 1950s

ABOVE: Michael Walker

LEFT: Christopher Reid

I started writing when I was in the first primary class in Uganda because we had to learn to write at a very early age. If you did not write as the teachers wanted, they beat your fingers, bottom or even your head. We learnt by writing on sand and slates. You were promoted to writing on slates if you mastered writing on the sand well; then, after the slates, we were given exercise books. Our books had to be neat and clean to avoid being punished for being careless, which could be a beating or sweeping the classrooms after school. Our parents would not be happy when we got home late or if they found out from the teachers that you had been 'dirty', as they called it.

After I studied media at university, my writing got even better. I had to write stories about sports as I was a sports reporter, which I had never done before.

Writing is important to everybody and anybody can become a writer. You just take a pen and a piece of paper and write about what you're thinking or something of interest that has happened. I did not know any of this until I joined Morley College to study drama, headed by Dominic Grant. The tutors not only teach drama, but also give you essays and creative writing projects.

When I was at Morley College there was a competition in collaboration with Penguin to choose a piece of writing for a book about the experience of immigrants. I had joined the Write To Life Group, run by Freedom From Torture (FFT), as I am a victim of torture. I was

IMPORTANCE OF WRITING

JADE AMOLI-JACKSON

a client at the FFT for counselling, physiotherapy and psychiatry, and was referred to the Write to Life Group by my psychotherapist, Mary Raphaely, who helped me with what I was going through for several years. My piece called 'My Painful Journey' was chosen along with 15 other people's and published in *From There to Here*. Though we were not paid for the stories, it gave me confidence to know that I can also take a pen and piece of paper and write something readable.

Writing can be therapeutic because when you are feeling low, you write about what you are thinking and later when you feel better, you can learn from what you have written and sometimes you have a laugh or shed a tear.

At Write to Life we meet every two weeks. We begin with hefty meals followed by writing and reading what we have written on the day, and I go home fed and proud to have written something for the evening and look forward to our next meeting. My mentors from the Write to Life Group are helping me put together all the pieces of writing I have done so that they can be published. It means that however painful your journey, all the mentors, writers at the group, and all the present and former students at Morley can lift up your spirit and make you live again. I know they will all stand by me in my future writing.

and playing a leading role in our summer school, his monumental series on President Johnson and *War and Peace* were being produced on Radio 4. Mike somehow managed to find time to write a book on early women aviators; to come was his series on the Plantagenets, followed by the Stuarts in 2013.

Contacts with the Literary Section of the Arts Council and their funding enabled Morley to offer more courses, expanding into the summer months. Morley was able to run the same kind of courses as are run today by *The Guardian*, for which the newspaper charges hundreds of pounds. Furthermore, Morley did not drop writers after a

week-long lecture and activities programme, but followed some of the most talented with support for months afterwards. At the same time, Morley New Writing began to be published each year, picking up contributions from the College's students. The novelist Wendy Perriam joined the College's writing team and quickly proved to have a wonderful facility to foster and encourage new aspiring writers.

I am looking at the booklet for Write Stuff, a Lambeth-based literary festival in which Morley played a leading role in 2005. The centre spread in purple and blue is devoted to courses offered by the College on

RIGHT: Winifred
Leigh in *The Fool's
Apprentice*, 1982

BELOW: Rupert
Doone (centre)
with Roy Muscott
Walker (left) and
Robert Medley

Saturday 21 and Sunday 22 May; participating writers
included Simon Brett, Moniza Alvi, Melissa Benn and Toby
Litt. As part of the festival, Morley organised a poetry
competition in Southwark and arranged for a prize-giving
ceremony with Baroness Helena Kennedy.

Right from its beginning 125 years ago, Morley has
featured classes devoted to the enchantment and enrichment associated with words in all forms of literature.

MURRAY ROWLANDS

Drama

THE ROOMS USED BY Morley in the early days were
under, above and behind the stage at the Old Vic,
so from the start the students were in the theatre. Later,
Lilian Baylis used the students as 'supers' (extras) during
performances – rewarding them with a cup of coffee
and a piece of cake. Surprisingly, for a college formed
in a theatre, drama was a late addition to the syllabus.
Elocution began in 1890, then in the 1930s more courses
and lectures appeared, including public speaking, history
of drama, and a play reading circle.

The Theatre School began in autumn 1939, with
Rupert Doone as Director, John Piper as Scenic Adviser,
and Michael Tippett as Music Adviser. The course was
designed to cover two years, entrance was by audition
and only a limited number of students were admitted.
The syllabus covered voice and speech training,
movement, stage management and acting of plays.

The College is fortunate to have a very good archive
relating to the Theatre School bequeathed by Miss Winifred
Leigh, who was one of the first students. Her association
with the Theatre School lasted for over 50 years, and her
diary paints a vivid picture of those early days:

> On that first day in the Great Hall of Morley College
> (before it was blitzed), there we were . . . Rupert
> Doone, Francis James, Geoffrey Dunn, Miss Mary
> Skeaping, Miss Gunde von Dechend, about 100
> expectant students and me. The tutors sat in an awe-
> inspiring row, while one by one the students filed up
> on the platform, each reading a few lines of prose or
> verse of their own choosing. Long before it was my
> turn to go up, the session was over, which was as well
> as my knees were trembling at the prospect. This did
> not mean that we were not to be accepted, no one
> was turned away and the outline of the classes was
> explained to us.

The war intervened and classes were moved to
Tavistock Square. The first production was *The
Importance of Being Earnest* at the Tavistock Little Theatre
in 1941. Post-war, the Morley College Actors were given
the opportunity to use the courtyard of the historic

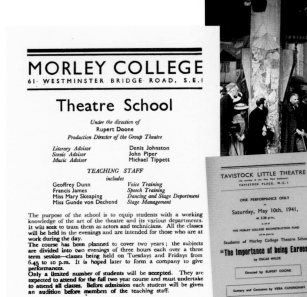

MORLEY COLLEGE
61· WESTMINSTER BRIDGE· ROAD· S.E.1

Theatre School

Under the direction of
Rupert Doone
Production Director of the Group Theatre

Literary Advisor   Denis Johnston
Scenic Advisor   John Piper
Music Advisor   Michael Tippett

TEACHING STAFF
includes

Geoffrey Dunn   *Voice Training*
Francis James   *Speech Training*
Miss Mary Skeaping   *Dancing and Stage Deportment*
Miss Gunde von Dechend   *Stage Management*

The purpose of the school is to equip students with a working knowledge of the art of the theatre and its various departments. it will seek to train them as actors and technicians. All the classes will be held in the evenings and are intended for those who are at work during the day.
The course has been planned to cover two years; the subjects are divided into two evenings of three hours each over a three term session—classes being held on Tuesdays and Fridays from 6.45 to 10 p.m. It is hoped later to form a company to give performances.
Only a limited number of students will be accepted. They are expected to attend for the full two year course and must undertake to attend all classes. Before admission each student will be given an audition before members of the teaching staff.

PATRONS
Sir Adrian Boult   A. P. Herbert, M.P.
C. B. Cochran   Augustus John
Professor Edward Dent   Oliver Messel
Professor Dover Wilson   Ernest Milton
T. S. Eliot   Michael Redgrave
Miss Edith Evans   Miss Gillian Scaife
Anmer Hall   Geoffrey Whitworth
Tyrone Guthrie

Fees : 16/6 per year for the course (including College membership)
See over for syllabus and further information.

TAVISTOCK LITTLE THEATRE
TAVISTOCK PLACE, W.C.1

ONE PERFORMANCE ONLY
on
Saturday, May 10th, 1941,
at 3.30 p.m.
in aid of
THE MORLEY COLLEGE RECONSTRUCTION FUND
Students of Morley College Theatre School
will be given the
"The Importance of being Earnest"
by OSCAR WILDE

Directed by RUPERT DOONE

Scenery and Costumes by VERA CUNINGHAM

ABOVE: A performance by the Theatre School in the courtyard of the George Inn, Southwark; and INSET: students relaxing in the courtyard, 1945

FAR LEFT: Flyers promoting the Theatre School, 1939, and *The Importance of Being Earnest*, 1941

BELOW: Mask for the actor – a drama class

George Inn in Southwark. Six plays were performed, and the impressive costumes were supplied by the Old Vic Wardrobe, maintaining those early links. In *The Winter's Tale*, the scenery was designed and painted by Mary Fedden, and music supplied by the Morley College Telemann Orchestra and Recorder Ensemble, directed by Walter Bergmann. In *Love's Labour's Lost*, two household names made early appearances: Leonard Fenton (best known as Dr Legge in *Eastenders*) in the leading role of Ferdinand, and future newsreader Kenneth Kendall (who was also assistant stage manager).

During the mid-1960s, the British New Wave were shaking up the theatre world at the Royal Court Theatre. One of their number, Keith Johnstone, was developing his groundbreaking improvisational work with learners, including members of his troupe at Morley College, where he taught contemporary theatre. This work led to the publication of the seminal book *Impro: Improvisation and the Theatre*. Throughout the 1960s and 1970s, the department remained a hive of activity and creativity, the courses offered continuing to embrace and reflect the changing times and practices. The 'Groundlings on the Stage' courses were a great innovation in partnership with Shakespeare's Globe Theatre. Partnership continues

to be key, with Oval House, Company of Angels and Cardboard Citizens being recent collaborations. Funding shortages in 2007 saw the department fighting for its life – an extraordinary campaign to save it evidenced the passion and commitment felt for drama at Morley, and garnered support from such luminaries as Kevin Spacey, Steven Berkoff and Ken Loach. The department survived and thrives!

Drama at Morley continues to expand, experiment and deliver first-class teaching and learning through an innovative and thrilling variety of courses, reflecting the exciting and diverse approaches to modern theatre-making, attracting dynamic practitioners who are experts in their field and committed to advancing the learning and goals of their students.

ELAINE ANDREWS

Dance

DANCE AT MORLEY COLLEGE has an extraordinary history. It charts the very patterns, shifts and changes that characterise how dance itself has evolved over the last 100 years. There has been Margaret Morris dance, folk and country dance, ballet, African, Caribbean, and classical Indian dance among other world dance forms, as well as jazz, street dance and contemporary. In addition, there are studies about dance that include aesthetics and criticism, dance and the community, dance notation, historical dance, and also many approaches to health and fitness.

'Students were keen on dancing from the early days – with no TV or radio, it would have formed a large part of their social life', notes Elaine Andrews (Morley College's

Contemporary dance and music improvised performance, 2012

ABOVE LEFT: Barbara
Kane; and a
programme for
the Annual
Demonstration
of Dance, 1934

ABOVE: Scottish
country dancing,
1959

archivist). This palpable enthusiasm for dance was
evident from the 'many and varied Clubs that were also
keen on dances at their regular events', through the
establishment of country dancing which began as a class
in 1912, and also 'national and Greek dancing [that were]
well established by the early 1920s', to various folk dance
forms, including 'sword and Morris', which became very
popular. Morley was well on its way to the unfolding of a
romance with dance that has lasted now for a century
and more.

The handbill for Morley College's annual dance
concert of 1934, showing an illustration of a Grecian-clad
figure resplendent in Bacchic abandon, depicts a kind of
jouissance that is associated with a progressive approach
to dance which flourished with pioneer Isadora Duncan,
with its embrace of the ancient and the primal. It was this
that inspired Barbara Kane's study of Duncan's work,
which she taught at Morley in the late 1980s. Just as the
power of the visionary Duncan was being felt in the West
throughout the early part of the last century, so was the
considerable influence of dance artist Margaret Morris
felt in Britain. Margaret Morris Movement was first established at Morley by dancer and teacher Blanche Ostrehan,
who taught the technique for five years from 1933. At the
same time, teacher Nelly K. Noble was noted for her
direction of the 'Annual Demonstration of Dancing', as
well as for her classes in Gymnastics, Keep Fit, and Greek
and national dancing.

From the 1930s to the 1950s and into the 1960s there
was Scottish country dance with Nancy Owen, ballet with
Tricia Shallcross and Wendy Hilton, national dancing with

Maria Fay and Kate Newman, historical dancing (also
with Wendy Hilton), sword dancing with R. M. Callender,
modern dance with Rosamund Shreeves, modern dance
for the theatre with Robert Harvey, and 'Theatre School'
led by Mary Skeaping. Practical classes in folk dancing
were taught in the early 1930s by Susannah Sharp,
daughter of the great champion of folk arts in this
country, Cecil Sharp.

In the late 1930s, the popularity of ballet at Morley was
triggered by lectures given by Antony Tudor, a figure
recognised for his enormous influence on the development of ballet as a modern dance form by means of his
innovative choreographies created for Marie Rambert's
newly established Ballet Rambert (now Rambert Dance
Company), one of Britain's great dance organisations and
now a neighbour of Morley at London's South Bank.
Dame Peggy Van Praagh, the distinguished dancer of a
number of Tudor's original productions, was also a ballet
teacher at Morley for a period during the Second World
War. Later, opportunities to learn about dance were
enhanced by a series of influential lectures, such as the
development of modern ballet given by the distinguished
dance critic Clement Crisp in the 1960s and 1970s, and
about the legacy of Diaghilev by Philip 'Pip' Dyer. This idea
of legacy in relation to Diaghilev was to impact on Morley
explicitly as, for a time in the 1950s, ballet was taught by
Laura Wilson, who had danced in productions staged by
Diaghilev himself.

Another strand of dance as a modern art form was the
teachings of Rudolf Laban, Kurt Jooss and Sigurd Leeder;
their work had considerable effect in terms of how

modern dance and movement studies would develop throughout Europe in the middle part of the last century. At Morley, Jane Winearls and June Kemp taught classes from 1958 to 1964 and 1966/7. *The Guardian*'s obituary of Winearls in November 2001 remarks that by 'fusing the work of those three men ... [Winearls] forged a modern dance training method that anticipated many of the philosophies and practices now common in European contemporary dance'. The Sigurd Leeder School of Dance was actually based at Morley for a time and the choreographer Kurt Jooss lectured at the College.

Brian Bertscher in Balletmakers, 1963

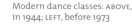

Modern dance classes: ABOVE, in 1944; LEFT, before 1973

BELOW: Tap dance performance 2012

In marking the College's achievement of its 125th year, it is important to communicate a historical view together with a contemporary perspective of dance at Morley. In September 1963, Teresa Early (now artistic director for Theatre Peckham, which provides a range of experiential theatre-based learning provision for young people in South London) and her brother, Fergus Early OBE (artistic director of Green Candle Dance, one of the country's leading proponents of dance for community), brought Balletmakers – dance artists, musicians, composers and scenic artists – to the College. In discussing Teresa's and Fergus's recollections of some 50 years ago, and hearing about their work now, I am struck by the sheer vitality of creative enquiry that characterises their work and that we value as having such importance at Morley. Their intention was to run two evenings and one afternoon a week for cross-discipline experimentation. With this notion of breaking new ground, Teresa and Fergus recall the choreographic experimentation they undertook during that time with Ann Hutchinson Guest, using Laban movement principles. Fergus writes: 'I remember her doing simple choreographic exercises that were really useful, giving you form and structure, but nobody [else] was doing that then.'

Reflecting on the significance of the role that Morley played in providing a base for Balletmakers at a formative stage, Fergus remembers the sheer scale and ambition of their first performance at Morley: 'For the end of the year show ... we had a full forty-strong student orchestra. [Teresa] choreographed to Bartók's *Concerto for Orchestra*' – at this point Teresa observes that it was something 'you would only do if you were 20 odd!' The conductor working with them was Ian Horsbrugh, who went on to become

the principal of the Guildhall School of Music and Drama (1988–2002). Fergus also choreographed for that performance with a musical composition written by composer Richard Hewson and performed by the Morley student orchestra. He remarks fondly that, for that piece alone, there were three future ballerinas of the Royal Ballet involved: Laura Connor, Lesley Collier and Marguerite Porter.

The sheer calibre of performing and choreographic talent that Balletmakers at Morley represented underlines Morley's ongoing role as a venue for creative and educational innovation in dance. Brian Bertscher – a contemporary of Fergus's at the Royal Ballet – currently teaches on the main programme at Morley. His wealth of expertise and insight is invaluable to students seeking to experience, as he puts it, 'the joy of dance'.

Students' appetites for the diversity of dance in all forms continued through the 1970s and into the 1980s. World dance classes introduced African, Bhangra, Bollywood, Indian classical dance, Yugoslav, Polish, Egyptian and Israeli dance. Today there has been a revival of social dancing with salsa, tap, ballroom and Latin American classes, no doubt sparked by the popularity of BBC TV's *Strictly Come Dancing*. Dance-based exercise classes have been popular for years, with Zumba being the latest craze. In 1980, African musician Adesose Wallace, who in the late 1970s had spent time in Lagos,

Nigeria, playing with visiting artists Hugh Masekela and Miriam Makeba, taught African dance and drama workshops. Also at this time Yulisa Amadu Maddy, one of Sierra Leone's greatest writers and playwrights, taught an African dance and drama workshop at the College. This was followed later in that decade by classes in African and contemporary dance taught by Asabi Bakari, Alfonse Gneole, Danny Hamond and Carl Campbell, and Afro-Caribbean dance by Jenny Bynoe. By the late 1980s, Bhangra was being taught by Pamar Bharat, Bharatnatyam by Vali Subbiah

LEFT: Corali Dance Company in performance, 2012

BELOW: Cate Brick in a ballet class

> The first time I encountered Morley College was around 30 years ago – it was before I had done any formal dance training and I wanted to try a ballet class . . . I can't even remember who the teacher was but I do know that I enjoyed it and I got a good foundation in technique . . . As a result I embarked on professional dance training and then eventually became a professional dancer.
>
> Fast forward 30 years and I am now working as a belly dancer and occasionally teaching at Morley, as well as taking regular ballet classes there. And now Morley College has become the new home for my current project 'Company of Dreams', which is a group that fuses contemporary and Middle Eastern dance. I feel that I've come full circle and am so excited that Morley is supporting us in our new artistic venture.

NEW VENTURES

CATE BRICK

and, by the start of the 1990s, Sushma Mehta was introducing students to the classical Indian Kathak.

Jazz dance was developed at Morley as an addition to the other theatre dance forms. Early teachers at Morley were Ellen Miller, who taught many aspects of jazz dance throughout the 1990s, and Evrol Puckerin. In the late 1970s, Puckerin established the company MAAS Movers: a group of artists, as choreographer Emilyn Claid observes, who were instrumental in how black dance artists were perceived at that time, in that they 'set the path, opening up an awareness of black dance politics and the many different emerging black British artists'.

BELOW: Salsa performance, 2012

BELOW RIGHT: Tap dance rehearsal, 2012

What contribution might Morley usefully make as an institution moving forward? Teresa Early believes that 'the benefit of any education is that an institution can develop and pick up on ideas which don't yet exist in the mainstream and can foster and bring those ideas forward'. The benchmark of Morley's success will always be how well it creates opportunities for its students. As Teresa notes: 'There are a lot of grown-ups who are educated enough to want to be educated more. Morley could be a very good place for that to happen.'

TIMOTHY TAYLOR

Languages

Classes in Russian 1944, ABOVE; and in Spanish, 1950s, RIGHT

'ÇA VA?' THIS BEAUTIFULLY succinct greeting, perhaps the commonest phrase in the French language, completely floored me, aged 15 and on my first French exchange. I saw the family's shocked faces: 'She can't speak a word – how will we manage?' Five years of school French and now this – where was the formal greeting to which I had prepared an elaborate reply? Fortunately, matters improved, leading to a lifelong friendship. Ten years later, visiting Russia after an intensive audio-visual course for teachers, I had a much better experience; the correct endings of the highly inflected language came almost automatically. Thus when I took up my post at Morley in 1973, I knew exactly where I stood in the Great Debate raging over methodology: traditional grammar or modern audio-visual?

Morley had a long and distinguished reputation for languages, offering courses in five including, far-sightedly, Russian. Part of my brief was to develop communicative methods and I was asked if I would like to refurbish class-rooms with the latest hardware and software, install a language laboratory and provide individual study booths in the Library. Accustomed to dragging one battered tape recorder along dusty corridors, this was paradise indeed. With all this and the support of media resources, what could go wrong? Alas, the Great Debate was as prevalent at Morley as elsewhere and a small core of traditionalists wanted none of it. Fortunately, I realised that Morley's highly professional band of part-time tutors was a far more important resource than any equipment. Some grammar-based classes attracted large numbers of loyal followers; indeed, it was rumoured that nothing short of a death certificate would excuse absence in one particularly traditional class.

My arrival increased the full-time academic staff from only three to four – the Principal, Vice Principal, Staff Tutor and myself. The heads of Art, Music and Printmaking were all part-time, although such was their commitment and enthusiasm that this was easy to forget. With Barry Till, the Principal, declaring himself (in Latin) as merely 'first among equals', the small staff meetings provided fertile ground for innovative ventures. A number of new ideas for language classes took off.

Over the years we increased the number of languages from five to 20. Intensive courses, offering 50 hours of tuition over two weeks, were oversubscribed, as well as family classes (the latter being the brainchild of the Vice Principal, Raymond Rivers). We worked closely with colleagues to develop cross-curricular study days, celebrating the art, music, literature and food of a particular period in another culture. Links were made with the Bangladeshi community to provide mother-tongue classes for children and we included Bengali in our regular programme. Courses in bilingual skills and community interpreting were introduced to enable the growing number of second-language speakers in London to demonstrate the value of bilingualism, hitherto viewed as a disadvantage. These led to qualifications from the Institute of Linguists – equivalent to degree level – enabling a number of our students to gain work as interpreters, despite coming from disadvantaged educational backgrounds. All this was possible thanks to our hard-working tutors whose students were prepared to try a range of languages from Anglo-Saxon to Urdu, and spoken Latin! Inspections by local authority and HM inspectors earned our department tributes such as 'the jewel in the crown of the ILEA' and 'a national example of good practice in language teaching'. This was heart-warming for the tutors, some of whom were promoted from hourly paid part-timers to associate lecturers in recognition of their commitment to Morley.

The 1970s were heady days for linguists. Britain was becoming less insular as cheaper travel opened up the rest of Europe. Comprehensive schools broadened their curriculum: modern languages (mainly French and German) had hitherto been taught only in private and grammar schools alongside Latin, using the same grammatical methods and regarded as academic and elitist. Before the ending of National Service, courses devised for the army during the Cold War had enabled Russian and Chinese to be taught communicatively, thanks to developments in technology.

In adult education we were able to embrace the new methodology more swiftly than schools, where public examinations tested the old grammar-based skills. When the introduction of the National Curriculum in the 1980s finally made communicative, topic-based language teaching mandatory in schools, many of our students tried the new GCSEs with great success.

FOR FRANÇOISE MARIE-LOUISE KNIGHT

WANDA BARFORD

This poem is for my French literature teacher at Morley who died in 2009.

> A frisson of French floated
> round the pews we, your students, filled.
>
> Your son, then your daughter spoke of you:
> your love of nature, of your work, of Proust.
>
> Then the pallbearers carried in your coffin
> with its white and yellow flowers, and six brass
> handles.
>
> Just then you began to lift up the lid,
> asking: 'What are you all doing here?
>
> Get back to the classroom quickly, we're starting
> the chapter on Tante Léonie today.'
>
> And we'd have followed you, running
> all the way back to college
>
> Through the squelchy grass of the cemetery,
> leaving behind us the ancient stones,
>
> The weathered crosses and inscriptions,
> and back to work, back to life.

We received a generous grant from the ILEA. After we had devised the programme for the following year, the appropriately named inspector, Sidney Heaven, would appear in his rather funereal suit in the Principal's office. Without pausing to remove his bicycle clips, he would agree to the grant before cycling back to County Hall. For such a meticulous man, known for his almost OCD attention to detail, this demonstrated a high degree of trust and lack of bureaucracy that was never misjudged. Those were the days! The ILEA provided excellent resources for languages and another inspector, Walter Morley, gave us inspiring support, holding regular meetings for heads of languages and providing in-service training courses at the beautiful old manor house at Stoke D'Abernon. With its elegant staircase, minstrels' gallery and resident ghost, it would have provided a perfect setting for an Agatha Christie whodunnit,

Friends of Morley
Christmas Fair, 1961

particularly after murderous passions were stirred by the Great Debate. But a truce was always called in the bar in the evenings as Walter accompanied the songs of Georges Brassens on his guitar and the wine flowed.

Goethe recommended finding a lover in the language you wish to learn, and while that may be unattainable, it always impressed me that students fell in love with the culture they studied and how this could unite a class. This was particularly evident at the Christmas Fair, when language groups would vie with each other to create atmospheric cafés. Legends abound of goats being roasted, plates smashed and wild bacchanalian excesses, but they certainly raised much-appreciated funds for the Friends of Morley.

In 1991 came my final opportunity to reflect on the unifying factor of our classes when we held an intensive Spanish course in Andalucía. Students enjoyed learning under the Spanish sun until the last day when Operation Desert Storm was launched in the Gulf. Would we be interned? Our party included an Iraqi woman and the sister of a British soldier in the Gulf, but the group remained mutually supportive. As we flew back, I realised how I would miss the bonding spirit of Morley and the lively band of students and tutors from whom I had learned so much. Had I also said goodbye to arguments about methodology? Not exactly. I am now in the world of psychotherapy where divisions have reigned since the time of Freud. Psychoanalysis or CBT? *Plus ça change* ...
NORMA HIGSON

Complementary Therapies

IT IS SURPRISING HOW health studies have prominently and consistently featured in the curriculum since the College's inception in 1889. It is clear that the College has always provided opportunities for students to learn not only more about their own health, but also how to look after friends, family and, in latter years, their clients.

It all started in 1890 with a lecture by Dr P. H. Carpenter on 'Our Bodies', as well as a course on Wednesday evenings titled 'Elementary Physiology'. (Coincidentally, in 2014, anatomy, physiology and pathology is still taught on Wednesday evenings!)

In many respects, the health-related curriculum is a social history, reflecting the social aspirations, concerns

predicted the decline in demand for exercise teacher training and sought out a worthy replacement. Jenny was keen to ensure that the curriculum offered students what they wanted, when they needed it. Ron Nauth, who has been teaching massage at Morley since 1992, recalled how Jenny 'was constantly researching for new courses and consulting her staff on therapies that she thought would make good subjects to study'. Between 1991 and 1993 the curriculum, which had only featured massage, homeopathy and yoga, was extended to include aromatherapy, reflexology, shiatsu, Alexander Technique, beauty therapy, sports massage, meditation, and advanced anatomy and physiology. Today, there are in excess of 30 different therapies being taught, including subjects not offered at other adult education colleges such as hypnotherapy and neuroskeletal realignment therapy.

Throughout its history Morley has attracted very experienced health professionals as teachers, who come to teach at Morley because they enjoy the diverse range of students and working in a team with like-minded professionals. They help students to develop skills and impart their knowledge so that graduates have the confidence to gain employment. Renée Tanner, chair of the International Federation of Reflexologists, taught reflexology at Morley during 1995–2002 and is still one of the examiners today. Renée originally agreed to teach as interim cover for a teacher who had had to move abroad, but ended up staying much longer:

> I realised Morley classes offered students a social
> function as well as adaptability and flexibility,
> valuing vocational and academic students equally.
> The College has always offered an education that
> was more than about acquiring a practical skill; it
> prepares students for lifelong learning, offers a
> means to earn a living and the grounding to
> progress to further professional development.

The result of this approach is what makes Morley complementary therapists unique; they know why, when and how to apply their skills, which is what should happen but rarely does. One massage student graduating in July 2014 summed up her Morley experience as 'transformational'. Her confidence and self-esteem have developed since the beginning of the course as a result of feedback from her case study clients, who frequently

and fashions of the day; moving from 'new' science in the 1890s, through nursing and first aid in the early 1900s, and then to anatomy and physiology from the 1940s onwards. Even the 1980s' exponential growth of health clubs and personal trainers was mirrored in the vocational courses taught by the PE department (as Health Studies was then known). In fact, physical exercise has also been a constant feature, from gymnastics to netball to swimming and aerobics classes.

Then, in the early 1990s, the head of department, Jenny Thomas, precipitated a change in direction away from an exercise-based curriculum towards what has become the most comprehensive range of complementary health studies courses in adult education. Her vision for the new curriculum was ahead of its time; she comment on the excellence and effectiveness of her treatments. Certainly one of our 2010 graduates Mark Beaton would agree. Mark was the national winner of the Adult Learners' Week Learning Works Award presented by the National Institute for Adult Continuing Education. He won this award because he overcame severe mental health problems to train first in massage, then sports massage and now runs his own successful practice.

The complementary therapy industry has certainly changed since the 1990s, when therapists would work from home, visit their clients in their homes or rent a room in a health club; there were no spas or therapy centres. These days Morley graduates work in many different places: in London at Neal's Yard Therapy Rooms, The Sanctuary, and the local Waterloo Body Station, and across the world. The future for health studies is always difficult to predict – sometimes I wish I had Jenny Thomas to teach me the art of curriculum development! However, what is certain is the importance of continually supporting our students to develop skills that are relevant today. This is why they are given opportunities to work with different groups in a variety of challenging settings, for instance charities such as MENCAP, Kids Company, Ronald McDonald House (King's College Hospital), Terrence Higgins Trust and the Parkinson's Disease Society. In our 125th year there are opportunities to study new courses such as health psychology – as well as old favourites such as anatomy and physiology on a Wednesday evening.

JULIA WOOD

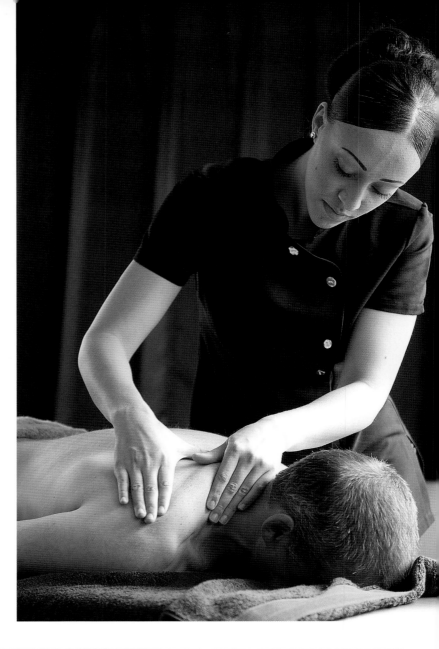

I have been both student and teacher at Morley College and have fond memories of creative times spent there. As a student I studied psychodrama, tried my hand at pottery and relaxed in various yoga classes. But it is my experience as a teacher at a pivotal time in Morley's history that I want to remember.

It was an exciting and challenging time, the birth of holistic massage classes and

BEGINNINGS

CAROLINE SHOLA AREWA

practitioner-training in complementary medicine. In the mid-1980s, I was brought in to help set up the first professional training in massage, anatomy and physiology. At this point massage was still deemed a bit 'nudge nudge,

wink wink' or all-out hippy. We went from cancelling classes, low attendance, to queuing around the block for places in a few short years. Jenny Thomas was head of department and I was the principal tutor. I am proud to have started complementary medicine at the College, developing a recognised, accredited and sought-after training. Morley College has gone on to develop a diverse range of integral health studies.

Fresh Start ...

I FIRST HEARD OF Morley College whilst at a European Union Conference on effective strategies to combat poverty, in 1977. I had presented a paper on an anti-poverty project for young families in Rotherhithe, which employed a self-help approach whereby a team of unqualified local women were recruited to run a Family Centre with 'on the job' training. An important part of the philosophy behind this approach was Paulo Freire's *The Pedagogy of the Oppressed* (1970), which emphasises the educational primacy of the lived experience. It arose in parallel with an American initiative called 'New Careerism', based on *New Careers for the Poor: The Nonprofessional in Human Service* (1966) by Pearl and Reissman, which endorsed the social benefits of prior experience for employment in certain caring and community activist occupations.

I heard from a co-presenter that a place called Morley College, in Waterloo, was recruiting a Director of Social and Community Studies to develop and lead an ILEA-funded community education project in North Lambeth and North Southwark, with a similar ethos to the Rotherhithe scheme. I applied and commenced work in September 1977.

I quickly became aware that my line manager, Principal Barry Till, was atypical of the leadership in adult education in the UK at this time in the sheer breadth and depth of his vision of adult education as a potent instrument for social change. In due course I learnt he was also an adviser

ABOVE AND ABOVE RIGHT: Arts and crafts workshops in the new community building, later renamed the Nancy Seear Building, 1985

RIGHT: Morley community learners visiting the Roots and Shoots garden training scheme in Walnut Tree Walk, 1985

Today's community learning classes are as broad in their reach as ever

LEFT: Learning about computers at the Oval Cricket Ground

ABOVE: 'Keep Fit, Keep Young' at Tomkyns House Sheltered Housing Scheme

OPPOSITE: Participants at Morley Family Fun Days

to the Baring Foundation – at that time a highly entrepreneurial charitable source supporting innovative schemes to combat poverty in the UK – which helped explain his acute awareness of what underpinned good practice in the field. It also became clear that his vision of Morley reconnecting with its origins as a provider of education for local disadvantaged people – 'low achievers' – was not welcomed by everyone. Indeed, it met with stiff resistance from several quarters and was inaccurately perceived as a threat to the 'literary institute' status which Morley College enjoyed at the time.

An important part of my job was to gain support for this project from several key figures on the Academic Board and the Governing Body of the College, as well as a myriad of local agencies. Whilst some local agencies welcomed this Morley initiative unconditionally, others

photos of local buildings, streets and past events from the Coin Street area, and featuring recorded interviews with local people, especially older residents who had lived there all their lives; in effect, they were presenting their own collective case for preserving this unique heritage for all Londoners. This audio-visual aid was employed as a powerful campaigning tool, generating mass support well beyond the local area, and forming a key part of the formal submission of evidence to the ultimately successful public enquiry. The Coin Street area now forms an important, vibrant part of the South Bank community, alongside the College and, of course, the Old Vic.

It was the success of these early off-site and one-off classes and workshops, which resulted within two years in a demand for extended learning programmes by and for local residents whose belief in the benefits of an educational *partnership* had by now been firmly established. Equally, the College Academic Board and Governing Body had acquired increased confidence for making further investment of its resources (tutor hours) towards more innovative programmes within its mainstream programme. Two experimental programmes, of three terms each, were launched as a result: 'Introduction to Social Work' and 'Introduction to Community Work', which were oversubscribed in their first year. These two pilot courses expanded to form the basis of a complete educational package designed to lead towards accessing

were more conditional and often partisan. Some indeed were deeply sceptical that the College could be effective in this endeavour. Both internal and external factors often combined to perform a kaleidoscopic display of changing allegiances and contrasting views and challenges over time, which required considerable diplomatic agility and patience so as to manage them effectively and efficiently – not least from Barry Till. I well remember Baroness Seear (then Chair of the Governing Body) saying to me, after one such political *pas de deux*, 'Barry does tolerate fools, but . . . *never* gladly!'

As the project got under way, the College's local interface changed rapidly. Numerous initiatives unfolded in response to identified needs off-site, ranging from 'How to be an Effective Committee Chair' to 'Teaching Children How to Read'. All initiatives in their different ways contributed to positive change by promoting direct action on the part of local residents, facilitated by a community education tutor working in partnership with the group. The ultimately successful 'Save Coin Street!' campaign was at its height during the formative project period, and support was given by the College (in the form of tutor hours) toward a slide-show presentation, comprising

a tertiary qualification in the Applied Social Sciences. At their peak, these courses enrolled over 100 students per year and ran successfully for more than 20 years.

Morley's 'Fresh Start', as the programme was called at the time, led to the 'Second Chances' programme (see below). But, fundamental to the success of this work was the co-creation of a basic education department at the College which, from its inception (under the leadership of Ela Piotrowska, later College Principal), liaised meticulously with the Fresh Start team in providing necessary literacy, numeracy and study skills backup. Without that fundamentally important component, this second-chance work could not have flourished, nor succeeded in influencing so many similar initiatives elsewhere across the UK. It would have made complete sense to Paolo Freire, had he visited the College during this period, and has absolutely vindicated Barry Till's belief that a 'literary institute' could only flourish further if it were to nourish its own roots.

ROGER FOGGITT

... and Second Chances

W HEN I FIRST started working at Morley in 1976, I was accompanied by my two very young children. They were able to spend a happy and productive morning in the excellent crèche facilities, while I trained volunteer reading helpers to work in ILEA primary schools. The crèche facilities were the first in any Adult Education Institute in London and were a real boon for parents of pre-school children wishing to participate in educational activities. The College then had a largely middle-class and middle-aged student body.

TOP LEFT: Introduction to Sewing class held at Loughborough Children's Centre

ABOVE LEFT: A Skincare and Nail Care class at Streatham Hub Children's Centre

ABOVE: Members of the Tulse Hill Singing Group rehearsing at the Rotunda Community Centre

But things began to change. In the late 1960s and early 1970s there had been a lot of radical education theory with works such as Ivan Illich's *Deschooling Society* that had heightened our awareness of inequalities in education, and reminded us of the power of education to bring about social change. The Department of Education and Science set up the Russell Committee in 1973 to report on participation in education post-15 years. The results were shocking. At a time when only 12 per cent of the population went on to higher education, less than 5 per cent were participating in adult education. The ILEA, which had submitted evidence to the Russell Committee, admitted that it was singularly unsuccessful in attracting manual workers and labourers, the very people who had gained least in the school system.

It was the Russell report that gave birth to the community education projects. Morley's principal, Barry Till, was granted the North Lambeth and North Southwark Community Education Project, which could provide any classes in any suitable venues across the community area requested by local people, who would never have dreamt of attending the College main site. I remember one woman saying: 'I always thought that it was a private music college and not for the likes of us.' True, it was an imposing building and classical music did pour out of the

windows most evenings. My first assignment in the project was to teach Keep Fit to a group of women on the Ethelred Estate. It was what they themselves had requested, but as one of them later commented: 'We soon realised that we needed something more for our brains.'

The Access to Higher Education courses, of which I became the co-ordinator for the next 20 years, grew out of the community education project. The idea had begun in America where it was realised that the best people to train as social workers were people who had experienced poverty or raised a child with a disability; social work in the Costa Rican community was best achieved by trained Costa Ricans. The first Access course at Morley was a social sciences and psychology course for local people who had had substantial life experience and wanted to train in social work, but who lacked conventional qualifications for higher education. Much of the focus was on how to study, and the curriculum was negotiated with the students. The students were wonderful: I learned far more from them than they from me. They came from every ethnic group in North Lambeth and North Southwark, and included recovering addicts, ex-offenders, ex-police officers, a man who had been hidden away by his mother for over 20 years, bored housewives, long-term unemployed and an ex-SAS officer.

Discussion was important in the learning process. There was a lot of mutual support, such as reading each others' essays with my feedback. When individuals received offers from universities, they would tell the whole class and everyone would share in the success. I felt very well supported by the rest of the College in this venture: the librarians and the audio-visual department provided an excellent service. The Access courses grew across all the departments so that by the year 2000, the College offered access to higher education in social sciences, humanities, languages, dance, drama, music and health studies, all accredited by the London Open College Network. The student body had changed, visibly, in 20 years – they were younger and from multi-ethnic backgrounds. Morley College was, in many ways, a microcosm of British society, and the changes that I saw during my years there reflected what was going on in the outside world.

JUDY CRAVEN

More Family Fun days

Community Learning Today

During the 1970s the College turned its focus to its original mission and belief that adult education was a force for good, with an important role in building social and community cohesion. Some of the first childcare provision in adult education was set up to enable women to attend courses at Morley; and the 1973 Russell Report influenced the development of a new range of courses, providing first steps back into learning for some of the most disadvantaged communities in Lambeth and Southwark.

Many of the challenges of discrimination, poor education and social exclusion continue today and Morley's Renaissance, which started in 2008, provides a new chapter for the College's work as a force for good. Today our Community Learning programme works closely with over 50 community, voluntary and statutory organisations and groups. We work with people who are at high risk of social exclusion including the homeless, ex-offenders, sheltered scheme residents, dementia sufferers, those affected by domestic violence and human trafficking, learners with disabilities and/or learning difficulties, and adults with mental health problems. Our community courses are created in response to specific local needs and aspirations, and are driven by our commitment to building community cohesion, developing social, employ-ability and entrepreneurial skills, and contributing to enhanced physical and mental well-being for all our learners, regardless of their individual circumstances.

ELA PIOTROWSKA

Horses for Courses

WHEN STANLEY BALDWIN, leader of the Opposition, declared open the mural paintings by Bawden, Ravilious and Mahoney in February 1930, the Chairman of the College Council quipped that people said that nothing of use was taught at Morley. Baldwin famously rejoined: 'Sir, I thank God there is such a place left!' The Chairman was of course not quite correct. Despite a founding mission to offer subjects 'pursued for themselves alone and the pleasure rather than the pecuniary profit', Morley has always offered subjects that were hardly useless.

Many areas of study from the past may now sound quaint, but reflected their times: elocution and electricity

Microscopy class, 1960s. These classes ran 1957–85, with a variety of tutors

in the 1910s, Esperanto between the wars, wireless science in the 1930s, 'The Financial Pages of the Daily Newspapers' in the midst of the Depression, 'The Nuclear Debate' in the 1960s, practical microscopy (is there any other sort?) in the 1980s. Others turned out to be passing interests: heraldry, 'Getting to Grips with Grasses', Yugoslav folk dancing, bonsai, vintage cars, 'Bamboo Pipe-Making and Playing' . . .

'Sword Dancing (Advanced)' could be pursued at Morley in the 1930s – the introduction of elementary and intermediate classes being added only later, suggesting that due risk assessment needed to be undertaken! 'The Idea of Europe' may seem as relevant now as it did in the 1970s and what a shame that the 'Clear Thinking' class of 1936/7 was not attended by those who oversaw world affairs three years later. At best, Morley's curriculum combines the pleasure of learning for its own sake with areas of interest which, while not necessarily vocational, are of some practical use, as the following particular examples demonstrate.

The courses of lectures on 'The Care of Horses', which ran from 1894 to 1899, were given by Professor Pritchard,

an ex-president of the Royal Veterinary Society. The cost of the course was met by the Royal Society for the Prevention of Cruelty to Animals. The lectures were an instant success and 130 men enrolled, most of them van men, cab-drivers, ostlers and farriers. Quite how the classes were conducted we must be left to wonder at since one of the three questions asked of Mary Sheepshanks at her interview for the post of Vice Principal was whether she could tell 'if a vet was too drunk to take the horse class'. The class made a visit to Ethel Everest's farm at Hever to see her Shetland ponies, cows and sheep in 1896, and several visits to the Royal Stables.

Gardening was introduced in the 1930s, and the tutor, David White, branched out into horticulture and bee-keeping. The hives were kept on the College roof, and it was noted in the syllabus for 1951/2 that 'remarkable yields of honey' had been produced before the war.

The first astronomy lectures took place in 1889/90 under the University Extension Scheme. All 14 students passed, with three gaining a distinction. Astronomy lectures lapsed after 1902, but saw a revival in 1914, reappearing again in 1929 and 1938. After the war, astronomy was revived with Ernest Noon (a singularly inappropriate name for someone who watched the night skies), who taught from 1949 to 1963. He was presented to the Queen Mother when she opened the new building in 1958. Ernest donated a telescope to the College in 1974, and an observatory was set up on the College roof. It is said that someone from Century House (at the time a MI6 building) opposite the College was once obliged to

come over to the College and enquire exactly what was being observed.

The next tutor, Leslie White, was frustrated by the lack of a proper base to teach from and, passing Christ Church Upton Chapel in Kennington Road one day, he saw the tower and enquired if he could use it. In 1967 he purchased a Japanese Goto E5 planetarium and had it installed in the former band practice room in the tower. As far as is known, this is the only planetarium to be installed in a clock tower, and the local press covered the event with great interest. At the Open Day in 1969, visitors were invited to climb the 120 stairs to watch demonstrations. This new apparatus gave Leslie White the opportunity to widen the course in astronomy. He organised weekends in Surrey and Sussex, where he would give lectures and invite guest speakers. From late in Noon's time up to 1989, Eddy and Gwyneth Watson Jones were the social organisers, keeping a unique group of friends together who returned for each year's course. White retired in 1989. Later, Heather Couper gave classes on 'The Violent Universe'. There was also a family astronomy class run by John Dix.

One graduate of the Morley course, Paul England, now runs his own planetarium on the Isle of Wight, opened in 1993. He took a London University extramural course at Morley, and assisted Leslie White by looking after the Goto planetarium, which he eventually took to the Isle of Wight, where it now has pride of place. In 1997, the Morley College Astronomy Group held their reunion at the planetarium.

ELAINE ANDREWS AND NICK RAMPLEY

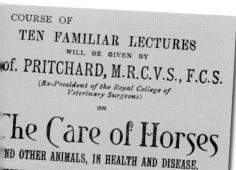

The Queen Mother with Ernest Noon, 1958

5

MORLEY'S
COMMUNITY

> **Many and touching are the proofs which we have of the place our College holds in the life and affections of the students** EMMA CONS

The Community of Morley

'We always try to make [our students] feel that the College is theirs, that it exists for their benefit, and that its success depends mainly on them.'

SO WROTE MORLEY's founder, Emma Cons, in the College's Report of 1893. That ethos has guided a strong democratic tradition ever since, emphasised the collective spirit of learning, and recognised the importance of bringing together social as well as educational activities. 'Morley-ites', as they were often referred to in the College's earlier years, have always played an essential role in supporting and developing this ethos. Interests and activities may have changed over the years, but the essential spirit which inspired groups like the Rambling Club continues to motivate and nurture student life at Morley today. Students have also played their part in supporting the College's development financially through a

LEFT: Relaxing in the refectory

BELOW: The Rambling Club at Cuckmere, 1950s

Dorothy Mead's *The Pianist I*, purchased for the College art collection from funds raised by the Friends of Morley College

whole host of fund-raising ideas and initiatives. At the forefront have been the Friends of Morley, founded in one of the College's times of direst need just after the Second World War and who have helped the College ever since – the latest addition to the College's art collection, Dorothy Mead's *The Pianist I* was only made possible through the Friends' generosity.

And what luck that over the years much of Morley's community has been captured in the pages of the *Morley Magazine*! How many other adult or further education institutions can draw on such a wealth of recollections and reportage? Pages that feature staff as well as students – we are all Morleyites! – and even, on occasion, members of the College's Governing Body, too often hidden from view, perhaps, but Morleyites nonetheless, with (hopefully for the better) a significant influence on the College's future.

Let's leave the last word to Emma: 'Many and touching are the proofs which we have of the place our College holds in the life and affections of the students', who speak 'warmly not only of the means of further study afforded by the classes, but of the society of those like-minded with themselves to be found in the clubs and common room'. For many of today's Morleyites, what was the case in 1892 still holds true.

NICK RAMPLEY

TRASHCATCHERS' BALL

TAMARA GALLOWAY

In summer 2013, Morley teamed up with the Phakama arts organisation for a two-week-long arts project, culminating in the most wonderful party! I spent a fascinating time constructing a costume entirely out of rubbish, for my role as a 'materialist mermaid'. The mermaid's silvery tail was made out of CDs that would have just been thrown away, but glistened with the colours of the rainbow. We also made some very curious musical instruments, out of various bits of junk. The photo shows my mum, Maureen, who was one of the guests, with me as a 'materialist mermaid'!

Morley's Magazine

A word or two is needed from the Editor in committing his child to the tender mercies of the Morley College public. The intention is that it should be another help to bring us all together in that fellowship which lightens all the work of the college. It is hoped that the students will find in it the expression of their aims and hopes, and that each will feel that personal interest in it, which will ensure its success. It is to be essentially the students' paper, its columns are open to all, and the Editor will carefully consider all that is sent to him, and do his best to carry out any wishes or suggestions expressed in letters to him.

Morley College Magazine declared its mission on the first page of the first issue on 1 May 1892, and it has never changed (though its name later changed to *Morley Magazine*). Throughout the years, editors and contributors have done their best to carry out that mission. Editors have always emphasised to students that it is their magazine, and carefully maintained its editorial independence. It is an entirely voluntary magazine, and depends on students sending in their 'news, reviews,

Front covers for *Morley Magazine*, designed by M. Ilin, TOP LEFT, and Eric Ravilious. Ravilious's design was used for several issues from 1932 until 1936

achievements, opinions, poetry, stories, articles, photographs, anything and everything' – and they do, including activities in the community as well as in the College.

The first issue reported that 'The women students of the College (Members of the Gymnasium) gave their first display . . . in the Victoria Hall', and the Morley College Band 'accompanied their fellow-students through all their various exercises' and afterwards played the 'Morley College' Waltz, composed by a student. The Debating Club carried a motion 'That every locality should have power to suppress or control the sale of intoxicating liquors within its boundaries'. There was a Good Friday excursion to Theydon Bois and a visit to the Natural History Museum. The drawing and woodcarving tutors 'report very favourably on the work done in their classes'.

A recent issue of the *Magazine* (Autumn/Winter 2013/14) featured *MADE 2013*, Morley's major annual exhibition of the work of visual arts students, with full colour photographs. There was a review of a concert at the Royal Festival Hall by a community choir led by Morley College, which included Holst's *Planet Suite* and Tippett's *A Child of Our Time*. There were also reports on the Accordion Orchestra's participation in the World Music Festival in Innsbruck, Austria; the Trashcatchers Lunch and Ball with costumes made from recycled material; concerts by the Gospel Choir, the Big Band and the piano classes; an excursion by students of Spanish to Asturias; work by the photography classes; and an article on the College's 'Missing Murals', the work of a wall-painting class in the 1950s, later painted over.

Though the mission has not changed, the size, shape and frequency of the *Magazine* has varied over the years with different editors and different levels of finance. It appeared up to ten times a year at first; now it is twice a year.

Some issues consisted of a single sheet; some of a few typewritten pages stapled together. There were several years of A5 booklets, sometimes with illustrated covers. From 1999, issues included black-and-white photos in increasing numbers, and in 2009, the *Magazine* blossomed into full colour. There is a full collection of the *Magazine* (except for March–July 1905) in the Morley Library with a complete Index and a number of issues on the College website. There are also extensive collections of the *Magazine* in the British Library and Lambeth Archives.

Issues of the *Magazine* provide much interesting information about Morley not found elsewhere, and reflect the changes in the College and society over the last century. For instance, in May 1908, an item about adult suffrage reports that 'Three ladies connected with Morley College have been concerned in recent demonstrations and their consequences. Two have been added to the prison roll, and we understand that the third, though wishful to do so, was released by the magistrate on account of her health.'

'Science Gossip' by Herbert Robson, BSc was a regular item from 1902 until 1910, and offered many small gems of information, such as: 'A United States meteorologist, who has been studying snow-crystals for the last twenty years . . . finds that the largest and finest tubular crystals occur in the west and north west of the American continent, during heavy storms, and that they are scarce in other districts.'

During the First World War, the *Magazine* often makes sad reading, with Rolls of Honour and obituaries of former students, but there were also many bravely cheerful letters from others at the front. In December 1918, shortly after the war ended, there was an advertisement for a free lecture on the League of Nations.

Gustav Holst, Morley's Director of Music, tried to enlist but was rejected as unfit for military service. As the war neared its end, the music section of the education department of the Young Men's Christian Association (YMCA) recruited volunteers to work with British troops awaiting demobilisation. Holst went to Salonika, in Greece, and wrote from there in February 1919 about a concert he organised: 'Never, never have I seen such an audience. They sat on seats, on the ground, on petrol tins, on instrument cases (the double bass one held five men and a dog); they sat among the orchestra, behind the choir, and in the green rooms … so many people had to be refused that we were forced to repeat the concert.'

The economic depression which followed the financial crash in 1929 had its effect on Morley. The November 1931 issue reports that the College will run a course on unemployment: 'The lectures will deal both with the broad problem and also with the various schemes that have been put forward. A subject of such urgent importance should appeal to a large number of students.'

An article entitled 'Crisis' says:

The financiers have received a good deal of prominence, and there is no reason why they should be let off lightly. In recent years large quantities of money have wandered about the world seeking a quick profit with little consideration apparently of the ultimate effects … we shall be subjected to increased taxation, a rise in the cost of necessities and economy in public expenditure, all of which will contribute to lowering our standard of living.

The *Magazine* was not published during the Second World War, as the College was largely destroyed by a bomb in October 1940. Though the College classes struggled on, there were limitations on other activities. The last issue, in January 1940, included reports on public lectures, including one on the 'Psychological Problems of War'. The *Magazine* resumed publication in October 1945, and included articles on 'The New Morley Students' Constitution' and 'Plato and Music'.

In recent years, the *Magazine* has been actively concerned with serious changes in funding of adult education in London after the abolition of the GLC in 1986 and the ILEA in 1990. There was a strong campaign, fully reported in the *Magazine*, by students both at Morley and three other London adult education institutions (City Literary Institute, Mary Ward Centre and Working Men's College), which resulted in them coming under the general supervision of the Secretary of State for Education and receiving funding from national government.

The issue has rumbled on, however, as national government increasingly took the view that only accredited, work-related courses would be funded. The Autumn/Winter 2010/11 *Magazine* reports that a delegation of students and staff from Morley and other London adult education colleges went to Downing Street to present a petition to the prime minister on the subject,

An extract from *Morley Magazine*, June 1916

122   MORLEY COLLEGE MAGAZINE

Tpr. J. H. SEARL, 3317,
6th Company Imperial Camel Corps,
Egyptian Expeditionary Force.
Monday, May 1st, 1916.

I was very glad to receive a copy of the Magazine, for which will you please thank Miss Brennand for me. I also noted that you received my letter, and had it duly printed in the Magazine.

It pleased me to read of the success of the Women's Gymnasium, and I hope that when we live in peace again the men will bring their work to such a high standard.

You will note that I have left the Rough Riders for the Camel Corps. We have formed a company of 150 men from the 8th Mounted Brigade, and many more than were needed volunteered, and I happened to be among the number selected.

We have had two months hard cavalry work on the Egyptian Frontier, and in that time we encountered the enemy several times, and a sergeant in D Squadron and Reggie Smith, one of my troop comrades, have been awarded D.C.Ms. for rescuing men while under heavy fire. My troop suffered much on the 11th of April. We were caught in a mountain pass, and we had some wounded, and my sergeant and a friend of mine were lost and their bodies have since been found. Our poor horses received many bullets, which, by the way, are several times the size of our own Mark vii., and they inflict nasty wounds.

I arrived at the camel camp yesterday, and was given my camel this morning, and I attempted to groom him this afternoon, but I couldn't keep him down for long, and although I tied his head to his near fore he insisted on standing and lopping about on three legs, and it was highly amusing. After trying to talk to him in Arabic and much pulling of his head, I managed to get in about 10 minutes brushing in 45 minutes. I shall be riding in the morning and I shall expect some more fun. We have hundreds of camels here recently arrived from the Sudan.

They are more useful on the desert than our horses, as the water is scarce, and whereas a camel need only be watered once in five days a horse must be watered once a day at least. I have no more to say at present, so I will conclude.

ABOVE: A group of Morley staff and students went to Downing Street in 2010 to present a petition about the funding of adult education

RIGHT: Some recent *Morley Magazine* covers

and stood outside afterwards singing, 'Somewhere over the Rainbow, skies are blue, and the dreams that you dare to dream really do come true'. The petition asked the prime minister to consider that colleges like Morley provide courses 'designed to fit around people's lives and work and which promote personal development, well-being, citizenship and increase employability . . . For people who have benefited least from their initial education and training, or are disadvantaged for reasons such as disability, language or self-confidence, adult learning provides opportunities to transform lives.'

The primary focus of the *Magazine*, however, has always been, and remains, Morley students. It emphasises student achievements in order to help students become aware of their potential and of Morley's ability to help them fulfil it, and it often reports their feelings about what Morley has given them.

In November 1934, James Cross wrote of his first day at Morley, at the New Students' Tea and Social:

> Lone and friendless, I stood there at the Hall portals and looked at the feast within, the Hall bright with life and laughter . . . our Principal . . . spoke. Morley was not stationary, it was ever moving forward . . . we had to do our part, we were Morley and Morley was us. A strange feeling awoke in me, a feeling of comradeship, of being kindred with these others in the Hall . . . I had come a poor shrinking worm of a new student, I left a colossus, a Morley student.

MARGUERITE PERKIN

Molly Bryant's association with Morley lasted for over 60 years. She first enrolled at the suggestion of her mother, who had sung in the choir with Gustav Holst. Not being musical, Molly started with French, and over the years sampled heraldry, Londoner's London, 'Health in Retirement', Italian and cookery. She was a keen ballroom dancer and went to the regular Saturday dances, where she met her husband Walling. Molly was soon drawn onto the Student Executive Committee, and this led to helping with the *Morley Magazine*, eventually becoming the Editor. She had been a Friend of Morley for some time, was 'head-hunted' onto the Committee and became its Secretary. Molly and Walling were stalwart members of the Morley College Rambling Club, and Molly served on its Committee, eventually acting as Chair and General Secretary. She was made an Honorary President in 2011. Molly

MOLLY BRYANT

ELAINE ANDREWS

was present at the Club's centenary lunch in 2012 and cut the cake. Sadly she died a few days later, at the age of 89.

Choose or Lose
I'm distraught
I'm overwrought
You're not my sort
You'll sell me short
Yet against my better judgement
You've become my waking thought.

SUE REARDON SMITH
Morley Magazine:
Autumn/Winter 2004/5

Suky Tomlins (right) and Mary Hawkey were elected student members of the College Governing Body in 2014

The Student Voice

WHEN I TOOK ON THE job of chair of the Student Executive Committee, I had no idea of the long history of student democracy at Morley. Having been a student at Morley for several years, I knew that student views were taken extremely seriously. As an adult educator myself, I also soon realised that student involvement in the College is exceptional in comparison with most other institutions of its type.

The first reference I can find is in the *Morley Magazine* of June 1893, when the College was only four years old. A general meeting of students was held to elect a Consultative Committee (later the Advisory Committee) of students and unpaid teachers whose duties, outlined in the *Magazine* of October 1893, were 'to aid the Council in procuring the assistance of those who may be willing to act as lecturers or as class teachers in the College. The wisest regulations on the part of the Council would fail to make the College a success without the hearty co-operation of both teachers and students. This they have had in the past and hope to have more and more.'

By 1928 there were few unpaid teachers, so the Advisory Committee consisted of students only and was tasked with electing two of its members to the College Council. Ten years later the Class Secretaries (now Class Representatives) Association was set up. This is a forum where representatives of each class meet the Principal to discuss class issues. The Advisory Committee was then renamed the Student Executive Committee. Its members were chosen by the Class Secretaries with the addition of the Editor of the *Morley Magazine* and others. This

structure continues broadly to the present day; the Student Executive Committee has changed its name to the Student Council and continues to be actively involved in the work of the College.

The Class Representatives Association (CRA) gives students a very direct and personal access to the Principal, with termly meetings where individual class representatives can raise matters particular to their group and discuss the minutiae of course planning and resource allocation. The CRA forms a unique and vital part in the student voice at Morley. The Principal receives praise and opprobrium with equal equanimity and responds constructively to whatever brickbats are thrown at her or him. The Student Council, by contrast, focuses on broader issues. It has members who represent the student viewpoint on a range of committees, including Equality and Diversity, and Health and Safety; it has input into writing and revising College policies; and it has discussions with staff members. In addition, there are two student members of the Governing Body, one chosen by the Student Council and one by direct election.

I hope this has given a picture of the importance and value of the student voice at Morley in the last 125 years. Here's to the next 125 years!

SUKY TOMLINS

Morley's Governors

IN 1889 WHEN MORLEY COLLEGE was founded, it was initially governed by the same committee that had been in charge of the educational activities at the Old Vic. The College's constitution did not receive the various statutory approvals until 1891, when the governing body, known as the Council, took control. This consisted of 13 members, three of whom were appointed by the City Parochial Foundation for a six-year period. The Foundation had been created by Parliament to administer the City Parochial Charities Fund, from which an annual grant of £350 was provided for Morley.

Two more members of Morley Council were appointed for six-year terms by the Board of the Old Vic (the College's landlords), and two more on an annual basis to represent the unpaid teachers. The remaining six members of the Council were co-opted, 'at least three' of which were women – a proviso made at the request of

Emma Cons and Caroline Martineau. They also stipulated that 'so far as is practical, two of the co-optative members shall always be present or past students of the College'.

And this is how it stayed for almost 100 years until, with the imminent abolition of the ILEA, the College reconstituted itself in 1990 as a charitable company with a Governing Body, which also acted as a Board of Trustees. This was cemented by the Further and Higher Education Act of 1992 which brought the College, together with the further education (FE) sector, under the funding regime of the Further Education Funding Council. The Act incorporated FE colleges previously under the control of local education authorities. Morley of course was already there, but with it came a further legal soubriquet for the Board, that of 'the Corporation'.

It is interesting to note that these days Morley's Governing Body comprises around 20 members, including two student members, two staff members, the Principal and individuals from a range of different professional backgrounds. In this respect we link back to and uphold the same democratic principles enshrined by Morley's first governing body.

In addition the College also had a Consultative Committee, consisting of teachers and six elected students, whose role was to promote the virtues of the College amongst the working people, to 'co-operate with the Council in all matters tending to promote the welfare of the College', and to make suggestions to the Council on matters both educational and social. Although the roles are more prescriptive, our Student Council and the Class Representatives Committee provide important channels of communication on all matters relating to the student experience at Morley.

Since its inception Morley has continued to attract highly committed and influential individuals from various backgrounds to serve as members of its Governing Board. Amongst the more noteworthy have been Emma Cons herself, Sir William Coldstream, Lord Fulton, Lord Robert Gaveron, Sir Pat Lowery, Harold Nicholson, Countess Dora Russell, Sir Arthur Slater, Baroness Nancy Seear, Mary Sheepshanks, R. H. Tawney, Sir Michael Tippett, Sir Richard Runciman Terry, Lady Walton, Major General Sir Fabian Ware and Mrs Ursula Vaughan Williams. At least six authors in this book have served on the Governing Body either as a staff member (Roger Foggitt, Michael Graubart, Julia Wood), an external nominee (Alan Tuckett), a student member (Suky Tomlins) or in two guises, firstly as a staff member and some years later as *ex officio* Principal (Ela Piotrowska).

Today the role of the Governing Body is given greater prominence by government and its agencies. In 2011 the Department for Business, Innovation and Skills (BIS) published *New Challenges, New Chances: Further Education and Skills Reform Plan*, which places a new emphasis on the importance of good governance in raising standards in a time of change. The reform programme places an increasing responsibility on governors for ensuring that their college is meeting local needs and is able to manage change with appropriate creativity and innovation.

In line with these reforms the Morley Board continues to attract highly committed and experienced governors from education, commerce and the professions: people who have the skills and knowledge to assist the College in ensuring that it continues to fulfil its mission and, through innovation, meets the changing needs of the communities it serves. I know that my fellow governors and I are proud to be part of Morley's illustrious history.

JOHN STEPHENS

John Stephens

Nancy Seear

IN 1969, MISS NANCY SEEAR was appointed Chair of Governors of Morley and continued her strong association with the College until October 1993. Educated at Newnham College, Cambridge, and the London School of Economics (LSE), she started her career as a teacher and lecturer and was Reader in Personnel Management, LSE 1946–78. Her political career started in the early 1950s and she entered Parliament in 1971 as Baroness Seear, where she continued until her death in 1997. She was leader of the Liberal peers, 1984–8, and deputy leader of the Liberal Democrat peers, 1988–9.

Nancy was formidable, hugely energetic and brought to her role at Morley many of the attributes and skills which made her such a powerful advocate for a wide range of campaigns, including women's rights in employment. Although she was never a feminist, she was fiercely active in campaigning for equal pay for work of equal value. She was a woman of her times and represented that generation of British women who prepared the ground for feminism, but did not believe in revolution and was often scathing about positive discrimination. She was slightly chaotic in appearance, an intellectual and 'English bluestocking', maybe sometimes a little cross, or perhaps it was just outspoken, always interested and a wonderful and much-loved speaker. Along with her variety of interests, she also had a great passion for Morley and its role in adult education.

Indeed, during the 1980s, the protection of Morley's role, distinctive character and future funding was highly influenced by Nancy Seear:

Adult education, in its various forms, gives remarkably good value for money ... I should like to illustrate this point by referring to what has been going on at the college of which I have had the honour to be chairman for the last 15 years, Morley College ... Not only is it very economical in the use of resources: adult education is also able to deal with some of the most urgent problems – problems, which we all agree, are extremely urgent in a way that makes it difficult for other forms of education to contribute ... One of the problems in the world of education is to get rapid response to new demands. The adult education system, of which Morley is an example, is peculiarly well suited to being able to adjust swiftly to new demands ... It is a characteristic of adult educational institutions that there is this great mixture of very high quality advanced work on the one hand and basic work on the other. There are open to people doors which they must have thought never existed, let alone thought they would have any opportunity to go through. I beg the Government to think hard before they attempt to cut back any further on adult education; indeed, to put their policy into reverse and to give priority to institutions of this kind.

From Hansard,
debate in the House of Lords, 20 June 1984

Baroness Nancy Seear is remembered as an important champion for Morley and its role in adult education. Morley's addition to its estate in King Edward Walk, the 'yellow building', was named after her as the Nancy Seear Building.

ELA PIOTROWSKA

Nancy Seear

Morley's Clubs

TWO KINDS OF STUDENT CLUB have been part of
Morley life from the College's earliest days, clubs
associated with classes and clubs of a social or recreational character (and some that were both). Already
in the early 1890s there was a Natural History Club
alongside swimming (separate clubs for men and
women), cricket and debating clubs. Later in the decade
there were also archaeological, cycling, dramatic, photographic and scientific clubs, along with several others.

The story of Morley clubs is a story of opposites.
Keeping a club going at a college with a remarkably
diverse student population in an age of multiple
opportunities and distractions is never going to be easy,
but while some clubs struggle to survive, others thrive.
They do so despite the fact that the College's students
are almost all part-timers, coping with the competing
demands of family and work (or the lack of it), many in
poorly paid jobs, drawn from a wide geographical area
and all taking classes lasting a year or less.

There are several long-lived clubs – the Rambling Club
recently celebrated 100 years of continuous existence –
while others have died almost as soon as they were born
and half the present clubs started after the year 2000.
Some, such as Morley Medieval and Sculpture, are closely
aligned with College classes; one, the Ceramic Circle, born
as an offshoot of a class, has outlived its parent class by
many years; and some, such as Chess and Rambling, have
no link with any classes. Some have nearly 100 members,
while others (including some in good health), have only
around 15. How much it costs to be an active member also
varies widely, depending on the nature of the club's

TOP: Photography
Society club outing,
1910

ABOVE LEFT: Scientific
Society, 1890s

ABOVE: Cycling Club
outing to Sutton,
1910

activities, ranging from a very small subscription to as much as £150 a year, always on top of the expense of travelling to meetings and the added cost of any necessary materials, equipment or special clothing.

There have been changes in the kind of club that were active at different periods. In the 1930s, for instance, there were five sporting clubs and three language clubs; now there are none of either sort, unless walking is counted as a sport. The number of clubs has also had its ups and downs. In 1939, for example, there were 25 clubs; at present there are only eight. A constant has been the absence of political or religious clubs, presumably reflecting the College's non-sectarian foundation.

Clubs have contributed to the cultural life of the College out of proportion to their numbers through concerts, competitions, exhibitions, publications, conferences and other special events, both within and outside the College. They continue to receive encouragement and practical support from the College authorities, and with few exceptions were formed by students and are wholly run by students. Membership is open to all students, and to staff, governors and friends of the College, and the College actively supports the formation of new clubs.

In the following sections some of the clubs are celebrated by their champions.

GABRIEL NEWFIELD

Accordions

At the time of writing, there are two accordion clubs, two accordion orchestras and three levels of accordion classes at Morley, and the orchestras are about to take wing as London Accordion Orchestras. In 1998 there were no such opportunities for adults anywhere in central London. I was the one privileged to be able to plant the acorn! I wanted a club in central London with some solid educational content and links to the 'musical establishment'. I knew two wonderful accordionists, Ian Watson and Julie North, with the ideal skills (and academic qualifications) to direct it – and I knew Morley. Ian and Julie agreed to do it, and fortunately Bob Hanson, Morley's Director of Music, was supportive as he wanted to see as many people making as many different kinds of music as possible in the College.

The Club first met in June 1999 and set up monthly meetings for formal learning, playing to each other and ensemble work. We gave our first Morley Tuesday lunchtime concert within a year, which included our first tentative ensemble of nine players. Then for 2001–2, the College asked Julie and Ian to teach a beginners' course. There followed an improvers' course, and then a group of pupils, who had completed the courses, set up another club: the Intermediate Accordion Club (IAC). The IAC gives its members the opportunity to play in small groups and explore different genres of accordion music, and Julie continues to teach IAC sessions. The IAC is also a source of impromptu groups of accordionists, who spring up at events like the Morley Winter Fair.

In the meantime, the original club slowly grew and became the Morley Accordion Orchestra. We gave regular concerts in Morley from 2004, the centenary of Mátyás Seiber, who taught composition at Morley after the war and wrote for the accordion (and accordion orchestras). We featured in the College's celebrations and travelled to Cambridge to perform in a Seiber celebration – our first venture outside London.

In 2011, we moved onto the wider stage, travelling to Navan to play in the Irish competitions. We came second with 92 points in our very first competition! Back in

Morley exhibiting at Brixton synagogue, 1948

London, a year later, we gave a full-scale Saturday evening concert at the LOST Theatre in Wandsworth Road. The 177 seats were packed, and the audience was ecstatic! Navan made us consider the huge Triennial International Accordion Orchestral Competitions in Innsbruck – and so we went in May 2013, following a tremendous fund-raising effort, to perform 'Europa', a brilliant new piece by Jason Carr, commissioned for us by the College. We gave its world premiere at a gala concert in the Emma Cons Hall to a rapturous audience of well over 200, who sent us off with a standing ovation. A week later we were playing to around 700 people in the Congress Centre in Innsbruck in the top 'Art Level' section, where we were marked 'excellent' – the first UK orchestra to compete in Innsbruck for 20 years!

International contacts bring new opportunities, and in 2014, we have given two joint concerts in London with other orchestras – first a lively young Dutch orchestra, and then the Nuremberg Accordion Orchestra, former world champions, in St John's Smith Square. We filled this major classical music venue with 500 enthusiastic patrons – beyond my wildest dreams in 1999. All you need is hard work, amazing musical leaders and a supportive environment!

NEIL SANDERS

LEFT: Small beginnings: just eight members at the fifth meeting in 1999

BELOW: A rehearsal, 2014

ABOVE: Performance in St John's Smith Square, 2014

Ceramic Circle

For 47 years the Ceramic Circle has been the perfect place for enthusiasts to share their enjoyment of pots. It owed its origins to a series of evening classes on the 'History of Pottery and Porcelain' given at the College from 1960 to 1980 in collaboration with the extramural department of London University. The lecturer was John Cushion FRSA, a senior research officer at the V&A, who was well known to collectors and dealers for his expertise in identifying and authenticating many unmarked pieces of British pottery and porcelain, and was later in great demand as a speaker throughout Britain and abroad.

The classes on antique ceramics became so popular that they were oversubscribed and participants returned year after year, with the result that there were few places available for new applicants. This led to the suggestion that a separate club be formed 'to encourage further study of pottery, porcelain and earthenware, especially antique pieces'. The inaugural meeting was held at the College on 17 May 1967 in the presence of 20 members. It was decided to meet on the first Monday of each month and the first lecture was given by Robin Bichard on the subject of blue-and-white porcelain.

In addition to its monthly lectures, the Circle arranged visits to museums and collections, which it continues to

Displays from the Ornamental and Remarkable Ceramic Wares exhibition at Morley, 2012. English pottery and tiles (right) and 18th-century Derby porcelain (above)

do, and it also established an important series of annual seminars which commenced in 1970. The subjects have varied from the pottery and porcelain of particular areas, such as Derbyshire, Staffordshire and London, to the decorative styles and design of ceramics and their origin. Speakers have included Dr Geoffrey Godden, the author of many groundbreaking books on British manufactories, and John Sandon, international director of European Ceramics and Glass at Bonhams, who is better known to the public as an expert on the BBC's *Antiques Roadshow* and who is currently the honorary president of the Circle. The 2012 seminar on the subject of 'Ornamental and Remarkable Ceramic Wares' reintroduced the idea of an accompanying exhibition, which took place in the College foyer and was well received by staff and visitors.

Throughout its existence, the Circle's members have been deeply involved in improving their knowledge of British ceramic history. There are too many to name individually, but their work has included the excavation of factory sites, assisting museums with the cleaning of shards and the identification of wares, and writing groundbreaking works on particular manufacturers or particular shapes. Currently the Circle has formed a working party to study the mysterious Factory 'Z' and intends to publish their results in the near future. Aware of the College's prominent position in the teaching of ceramics, the Circle keeps in touch with the department and offers two free places to students for its annual seminar.

The original name of the club was the Morley College Ceramic Circle, but the College authorities have recently given permission to change the name to the London Ceramic Circle at Morley College. This reflects the geographic membership and follows the example of similar clubs elsewhere, while retaining the very important link with the College.

JIM SEWELL

Folk Dance

Morley College Folk Dance Club was formed in 1927 to encourage folk dancing as a form of social recreation among members of the College. Membership was open to staff and students of the College, with ex-students enrolled as associates. A programme of events was established and tickets were sold in aid of Club funds, Morley College and charitable causes. The Club held monthly meetings and highly successful public dances twice a year. An annual 'Weekend of Dance' began in 1929, a tradition that continues.

During the 1930s, the College Folk Dance Team, all members of the Club, were chosen to perform at the English Folk Dance Society All England Festival at the Royal Albert Hall, and at competitive and non-competitive festivals in London and the Home Counties. They won the Harmsworth Cup 11 times at the Hampstead and Hendon Festival.

The outbreak of war meant that Club meetings were held on Saturday afternoons because of night air raids. When the College became a Rest Centre in 1940, a member found a hall in the London College of Printing for Club use. Morley College was bombed in 1940, but much of our Club property, including our precious photograph albums, was salvaged from the ruins.

Post-war, meetings continued, both in College and out of doors in summer. Members gave demonstrations of country, long sword, rapper sword and morris dancing at Kensington Folk Dance Club. The Spring Party in 1955 was attended by two Club members, Dennis and Dora Erdwin, who had married that day and were invited to lead the dance, *The Wedding*. Dennis still dances today! At another meeting in the grounds of an hotel, the young son of Eric Adie, our current president, was so excited by the dancing of the whirligig that he nearly landed in the goldfish pond.

Membership from the 1960s to date gradually decreased, largely because founder members died, older members retired and moved away from London, and there were changes in College policy as to who was eligible to join Morley clubs. The mainstay of activities in the 1960s and 1970s were regular meetings on Saturdays and also Friday meetings in July. This continued until the demise of the ILEA in 1986, when funding for the College changed, which affected College opening hours and room bookings.

Now we aim to have four meetings a year in College and two summer meetings arranged by a member in her local hall in South London. We usually have excellent live music and rarely use CDs.

TOP ROW:
Left and centre left: Two photos from a Club album of 1938 found in the ruins of the College after the bombing
Centre right: Imogen Holst and other Club members dancing Kemp's Jig at Chichester, 1930
Right: Dancing at the International Co-operative Day, Morden Park, 1960

BOTTOM: Dancing the Circassian Circle, Plaistow, 1938

In the Emma Cons Hall, 2007

Hazel James holding the rapper sword lock at a demonstration dance at Morley, November 2012

To celebrate 90 years of folk dance at Morley, in 2002 the Club published a book *The Dancing Years* by Hazel James and Sally Phillips, a history of the Club and the class which began in 1912. The book was launched at a party in the Emma Cons Hall, and we performed a mummers' play to honour the occasion. In 2012 we gave a demonstration of country dance in the College foyer to mark 100 years of folk dance at Morley. Long may we continue!

HAZEL JAMES

Morley Medieval

Visits to Le Mans Cathedral, 1995 and Istanbul, Palace of the Porphyrogenitus, 1999 (inset)

Art history is a relatively new academic discipline, for it barely existed in the UK before the 1930s, when it was galvanised by the arrival, principally from Nazi Germany, of a number of art historians with established reputations in their

homeland. By the 1970s, much had changed, not least the spelling of 'mediaeval' into 'medieval', and art history had become a major subject.

It was at this time that Morley College engaged the services of a young graduate of Cambridge University and the Courtauld Institute named Barrie Singleton. As a supplement to his art history lectures, he created a new society, Morley Medieval, which, within a very few years, had gained a formidable reputation in academic circles. Its principal activity consisted of Friday evening lectures, held, in the absence of a lecture theatre, in the Holst Room, and given by the most respected art historians in this country and, indeed, on occasion from abroad. They opened the eyes of their audience (literally, since these were slide lectures) to the wonderful heritage of art and architecture which still exists, despite the ravages of the Reformation, iconoclasts of various kinds and countless wars.

The lectures progressed to trips in the UK and abroad, organised by Barrie for the purpose of seeing the originals of the beautiful images displayed on the screen. Usually, these made an accidental profit, of which, for many years, Morley College Library was the beneficiary. The focus of the trip would be art history, but this by no means precluded learning about the history, geography and culture of the places visited. Minds were broadened by the realisation that art was never an exclusively European interest – no one with the slightest knowledge of Byzantium, Egypt and the Middle East could ever have believed that. And what of China, India or the New World of which our medieval forebears were ignorant? The more we learnt, the more we discovered there was to learn.

Barrie retired in 2010, but a number of his former students felt that Morley Medieval was too valuable to be lost – their historical studies left them under no illusion as to how easily this could happen! So the Club continues and, thanks to its reputation, the Friday evening lectures continue to attract speakers of the highest distinction. Inevitably, with the passage of time, much has altered; there are now three lectures per term, the images are shown digitally, and the society is run by a committee of eight people. The overseas trips have been maintained with some difficulty in the current economic climate, and UK visits go from strength to strength. In fact, Morley Medieval has become a cultural icon in its own right!

DAVID CULVER

Rambling

The Morley College Rambling Club was founded in 1912 and has been organising walks ever since, continuing through two world wars. Its dedicated founding secretary (1912–21) was a student called Felix Webster, who later became the College Librarian, retiring in 1945.

The Club began at a time when the countryside could be found just a short tram ride away from the smoke and dirt of Lambeth. Its first title was 'Scientific, Photographic and Rambling Club', and the reports of early walks in the *Morley Magazine* show that the ramblers often found time to study plants and pond life, as well as pose for photographs during their outings. If the weather was bad, they sometimes visited a museum instead.

In any case, the clothes worn by the early ramblers did not make for energetic walking. In the *Morley Magazine* (December 1938), 'F.C.' remembered a lost photograph album which had shown the ramblers of the first decade: the women in cartwheel hats, leg-of-mutton sleeves and flowing skirts; and the men in high starched collars and tight trousers. The Morley ramblers were also unusual among walking clubs of the time in having a large number of women members, and those flowing skirts made it difficult to climb a stile: 'But what we do beg and entreat is that we may be spared the stiles', wrote C. Mary Broderick, after a walk in May 1914.

In the 1920s the clothes became freer and the walks became more ambitious. Longer walks (including, once a year, a walk of 30+ miles in a day), night walks, and walking in all weathers, were all on the programme. As rambling became more popular in the 1930s, Club membership also grew. One long-time member ('F.C.' again) complained, 'We had our share of rowdy individuals, complete with ukeleles'.

With the growth of rambling and rambling clubs, access to the countryside became increasingly important (highlighted by the famous mass trespass on Kinder Scout in 1932). In 1949, legislation was passed that recognised 'rights of way', provided they were surveyed and mapped. The Ramblers' Association (RA) (now The Ramblers) organised this process. The Morley Ramblers Club – as an affiliated club of the RA – took part in the mapping of footpaths from the 1950s on, and later joined in a scheme to 'walk' footpaths and keep them clear.

In 2012, the Morley College Rambling Club celebrated its centenary, with a dinner, costume walk and centenary book, *Morley College Rambling Club: The First One Hundred Years*. It was also a time to celebrate the fact that we are still going strong. We keep up many old traditions of the Club, including a weekly walk through all weathers (about 9–10 miles, at a 'moderate' rate), an annual holiday, a photographic competition and a Christmas Lunch. Rambling and talking go together, and rambling is an excellent way of combining exercise and the making of new friends. Come and join us!

JANET VAUX

Boots by Ann Usborne

Morley's 125th anniversary

125 years to the day, Morley celebrated the formal opening of the 'Morley memorial College for Working Men and Women' with a tea party at which a birthday cake was cut by one of its longest-standing students. An evening reception, attended by guests from across the adult education world, followed that same evening and inaugurated a year-long festival of lectures, concerts, exhibitions and events celebrating the anniversary and culminating in the publication of this book! Here is a taste of some of them.

ABOVE: The 125th anniversary tea party

BELOW: Marian Cooke in conversation with local MP Simon Hughes. Marian, who cut the College's birthday cake, began studying English at the College as a 17-year-old in 1945 and is still a regular today coming along twice a week to take part in singing classes and the College's Can't Sing Choir

ABOVE: 125th anniversary evening celebration

RIGHT: Shami Chakrabati delivering 'On Liberty', one of the 125th Anniversary series of Penny Lectures

FAR RIGHT: Former Principal (1991–2003) Bev Walters (centre) at the anniversary reception

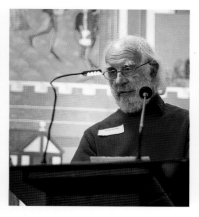

LEFT: Ela Piotrowska, and ABOVE, Richard Bawden, the artist's son, at the opening of 'Edward Bawden: Storyteller'

ABOVE: Morley Tutor Julian Wild's sculpture *Pelham System* at the House of the Flying Wheel exhibition in the Gallery, January 2015. It celebrates the legacy of Samuel Morley through an exploration of industrial heritage and social activism

BELOW: Nick Rampley at the anniversary reception

Two of the prize-winning motifs from the College's competition to design a plate to commemorate its 125th anniversary

ABOVE AND RIGHT: Visitors to 'Edward Bawden: Storyteller'

FAR RIGHT: Andrea Brown conducts the Chamber Choir, accompanied by instrumentalists from the Guildhall School of Music and the Centre for Young Musicians, in a performance of Bach's Christmas Oratorio in celebration of Morley's anniversary

> **Perhaps the greatest achievement has been our ability to grasp Morley's mission and inheritance and combine them with the needs of the present and future** ELA PIOTROWSKA

I N 1999, I LEFT MORLEY COLLEGE never imagining that I would be back as Principal in 2008. I first started working at Morley in January 1981, following the reorganisation of ILEA adult education, which offered Morley the opportunity to take on a wider community brief, extend its curriculum and operate over six 'branches' in addition to Westminster Bridge Road. Over the years, much of the College's early work within the Waterloo community had disappeared and it had evolved into a 'literary institute', with an emphasis on non-vocational adult education and concentrated on largely high-level academic, cultural and creative studies. Although the College had already set up a community education project and a new department for Social and Community Studies in 1977, the reorganisation provided an impetus for further change.

Ela
Piotrowska

So, in 1981 I was seconded by the ILEA to set up a course in 'Basic Education'. It was the time of national literacy campaigns, when refugees arriving in the UK required English language teaching, and the expansion of community education to support initiatives to increase adult participation in education. These initiatives were designed to respond to the 'rediscovery of poverty', the economic requirements of a rapidly changing society, the impact of new technology, mass political migrations and the growing understanding of the urgent need to address the inequalities of poor education. Equal opportunities became the catalyst and further served to reconnect Morley with its founding mission to encourage and provide learning which responded to the needs and demands of the times.

While it was Barry Till's vision in the late 1970s to broaden the range of people and courses and provide a continuum from the most basic to highly specialised classes, it was not an easy journey. For those of us arriving at the College to create new areas of work, we soon learnt that there were many conflicting forces within the College and not everybody shared the vision of opening Morley to its wider communities. During the post-war years, Morley had come to occupy a rather rarefied position in adult education, and debates about the positioning and resourcing of Basic Education and the Community Education programmes alongside courses often associated with the 'high culture' of society were frequent and heated. But the strong liberal traditions of Morley understood the need for a truly comprehensive range of adult education, including positive engagement with people who may have missed out on education the first or even second time around.

Morley's expansion in 1981 to undertake 'more general adult education' heralded significant change for the College. The Principal's introduction to the prospectus at the time announced:

There will no longer be a danger, which has undoubt-edly existed in the past, that potential students will be typecast as 'the sort' who go to Morley or to an Adult Education Institute. Such educational divisive-ness is obviously to be deplored.

In this book, 'Fresh Start ... and Second Chances' provides a sense of some of this work during a period of significant development for Morley. Literacy, numeracy and English as a second language provided the first steps back into learning for a new community of Morley students and a new range of work, including home studies, physical education, women's studies, health- and childcare courses, and languages such as Bengali and Arabic were introduced to meet the needs of the local communities.

Morley's Fresh Start programme, the setting-up of the first Open Learning centre for Basic Skills, research and development of practice to support the literacy needs of refugee communities, and research to identify and assess dyslexia in adults all provided new and exciting develop-ments for Morley and the adult learning sector nationally. While much of this work took place in more than 20 local schools and community centres, it also inspired the design of the Nancy Seear Building. During this period it was known as the Community Education Building and was a significant part of Morley's vision to invigorate the curriculum and make it more responsive to the times. User-friendly, the building provided a welcoming environ-ment for people who had little experience of formal learning, and during the latter part of the 1980s, it was used by numerous local organisations to support a wide range of interest groups, including local campaigns.

However, the political and economic landscape was changing and with it the funding for adult education and Morley. During the late 1980s, the Education Reform Bill and the omission of Morley from any of its provisions, reductions in the ILEA budget and the consequent reductions in the grant made to the College, and the impending abolition of the ILEA with a transfer of respon-sibility for education to the local borough, posed a serious threat for the future of Morley. A tumultuous period of change, restructuring and a growing acceptance that Morley could not survive without a strategy for income generation alongside grant aid, also coincided with Morley's centenary year in 1989. Although the future for the College at this point was in the balance, it was also clear that 100 years of educational service to London was worth campaigning for.

The year 1992 heralded a new period in the history of the post-16 sector, adult education and Morley College. Successful campaigning and the identification of Morley as part of a small elite of adult education colleges, 'the jewels in the crown', led to it being appointed as a Specialist Designated Institute (SDI) under the 1992 Further and Higher Education Act. This privileged position

secured Morley's future through the continuation of a grant, albeit much reduced; income generation through fees and other sources of funding was now an essential component of Morley's survival.

My own role at Morley went through much change over these years and for a short period I left the College for a secondment. Returning during the 1990s, I found Morley much altered from the vibrant, creative and forward-thinking days of Barry Till. The College slowly rebuilt some of the work that had been destroyed by ineffective leadership and cuts in funding, but much of the community education outreach failed to flourish and over the next 18 years the College drew back into itself. All of its local centres and purpose-built childcare facilities were closed, and its connections with Lambeth and Southwark became weaker; indeed its prominence and unique position in London and nationally were diminished.

In 1999, I left the College to take up a post in Ofsted only to return in April 2008 as Principal and, as one of my colleagues remarked, as poacher turned gamekeeper! I had never thought I would be granted the privilege of appointment to such a post. It was a twist of fate but I felt excited by the challenge, although also anxious about the task ahead. There was much to do to restore its heritage, but more importantly to ensure its future. And so began the Morley Renaissance.

There have been many achievements and lessons learnt over the last seven years. Strong partnerships have been formed with Lambeth, Southwark, the Waterloo Quarter Business District, universities and a wide range of cultural bodies, including the South Bank. The College has undergone significant refurbishment and again provides some of the best facilities for the arts in adult education. Some 2,000 new courses have been added to Morley's offer to meet the needs and interests of our growing student body. Once again we provide an unrivalled and inspiring range of concerts, events, exhibitions, celebration of students' achievements, and clubs, and are proud to have strengthened our long-standing democratic traditions.

Perhaps the greatest achievement has been our ability to grasp Morley's mission and inheritance and combine them with the needs of the present and future. Learning needs to have a way of reinventing itself. Today, our provision combines advanced cultural courses with

Reviewing plans for developing the College's main building at the 125th birthday event

access to learning for some of the most disadvantaged communities in London. The language has changed: Basic Skills is now a flourishing Essential Skills programme, Fresh Start, a greatly expanded Access programme. New enterprise courses and a growing programme of vocationally relevant courses provide skills to support economic ambitions. Community Education is now Community Learning and as in the 1970s and 1980s, again occupies a central platform in government thinking about bringing learning to the most disadvantaged communities and promoting social renewal. Things come around if one stays around for long enough!

The sustainability of Morley is dependent on its ability to stay close to its purpose, to hold strong values which inform its work and to understand its history while listening to the times it inhabits. Another factor is the dedication and skills of its staff. Morley has never been afraid to appoint outstanding musicians, artists, writers, dancers, actors, as well as adult educators, to benefit its students. Many of these grow into inspiring teachers who understand the relationship between teaching and learning, and who aspire to excellence in themselves and their students. Today some 14,000 students come to Morley, people from all sections of London's diverse community and beyond. Our tutors' ability to respond to their students' needs and to form equitable relationships which stimulate and challenge while recognising the diversity of cultural and educational backgrounds that often exist within a class remains Morley's great strength. It lies at the heart of the democratic and egalitarian principles which have fuelled Morley's history and which will take it into the future.

Looking ahead is not that difficult. We know that adult education is important. It is a powerful leveller and there are few places you can bring together a refugee from Somalia, who doesn't read music, with a musically literate solicitor from the City to sing Tippett's spirituals from *A Child of Our Time* at the Festival Hall. Of course there are challenges. Once again the College faces cuts in public spending and the need to raise income by increasing fees and diversifying its funding, and this will pose a threat to the inclusivity of the College and its egalitarian spirit. There is also the urgent need to redevelop and modernise parts of the estate. Plans have been drawn up and now require sustained and vigorous fund-raising. Morley will continue to change as it has over the last 125 years. The College must continue to innovate, aspire to the highest of standards and bravely stand up for its role to contribute to the continuum of lifelong learning which is driven largely by needs and interests rather than economic demands. I have every confidence that Morley will flourish for another 125 years as an educational, cultural and social force that enriches life, nourishes the heart, feeds the intellect and brings much joy to people of all backgrounds and where, in Maggi Hambling's words, 'people of all ages from all walks of life are offered a chance to discover the selves they never knew they had'.

ELA PIOTROWSKA

MORLEY'S DEFINING QUALITY

MARY VAN DE WATER

I have been a student at Morley for decades. I have studied widely: music, textiles, jewellery-making, languages, acting. I am privileged.

Casting my mind over all of this I can see a common thread and I think this thread is a defining quality of Morley – it is encouragement. Being encouraged by tutors to inch along to greater knowledge, skill, expression. Being encouraged by fellow students to experiment and develop. Being encouraged by fellow students/friends to join in social moments. Being encouraged by the College's ethos to take risks at the frontiers of my abilities and learning.

This is a very important quality because it supports and enables students from backgrounds with less learning than is required in 'a knowledge economy' to take a step ahead into an improved life. And not just economically.

SOURCES AND ACKNOWLEDGEMENTS

Sources

Much of this book is greatly indebted to the College's archive of Annual Reports, Prospectuses, Course Guides and of the *Morley Magazine*. A further rich source of information has been Denis Richards's history of the College from its inception to the opening of the new building in 1958:

Richards, D. (1958) *Offspring of the Vic: A History of Morley College*. London, Routledge and Kegan Paul.

In addition, the following sources have provided much useful information:

1. Morley's Story

Morley's First 50 Years
Richards, D. (1998) *It Might Have Been Worse: Recollections 1941–1996*. London, Smithson Albright.

Samuel Morley
Hodder, E. (1889) *The Life of Samuel Morley*. 5th ed. London, Hodder and Stoughton.

Morley's Manor
Gibberd, G. (1992) *On Lambeth Marsh: The South Bank and Waterloo*. London, J. Gibberd.
Inwood, S. (1998) *A History of London*. London, Macmillan.
Pember Reeves, M. (1913) *Round About a Pound a Week*. London, G. Bell and many later editions.
Reilly, L. & Marshall, G. (2001) *The Story of Bankside from the River Thames to St George's Circus*. London, London Borough of Southwark.
Reilly, L. (2009) *The Story of The Borough*. London, London Borough of Southwark.
The Streets of London: The Booth Notebooks – South East, (1997) London, Deptford Forum.
eds. Weinreb, B. & Hibbert, C. et al (2010) *The London Encyclopaedia*. London, Pan Macmillan.

Emma Cons
Baylis, L. & Hamilton, C. (1926) *The Old Vic*. London, Jonathan Cape.
Morley Magazine, 'A History of the Royal Victoria Hall and Morley College' (leaflet).

Miss Catherine Webb's unpublished history of the College.

Eva Hubback
Hopkinson, D. (1954) *Family Inheritance: a life of Eva Hubback*. London & New York, Staples Press.

Morley in the Great War
Commonwealth War Graves Commission: http://www.cwgc.org
Ancestry: http://home.ancestry.co.uk/
Royal College of Nursing Archive: http://www.rcn.org.uk/development/library _and_heritage_services/library_collections /rcn_archive

Bombshell!
Anon, (1946) *Lambeth Civil Defence*. Unpublished, Lambeth Archives.
Hook, J. (1997) *Nor the Years Condemn – the Air Raids on the Metropolitan Borough of Lambeth, 1900–1945*. Unpublished, Lambeth Archives.
'Metropolitan Borough of Lambeth bomb incident files, 1940–45'. Unpublished, Lambeth Archives MBL/TC/25.
Newman, J. & York, N. (2005) *What to do when the air raid siren sounds: life in Lambeth during WWII*. London, Lambeth Archives.

Denis Richards
Bev Walters and Molly Bryant (2005) *Morley Magazine* articles.
Richards, D. (1958) *Offspring of the Vic: A History of Morley College*. London, Routledge and Kegan Paul
Richards, D. (1998) *It Might Have Been Worse: Recollections 1941–1996*. London, Smithson Albright.
Obituaries from *The Independent* and *The Guardian*.

Morley's Library
Library Annual Reports

Morley's place in Adult Education
Devereux, W. (1982) *Adult Education in Inner London 1870–1980*. London, Shepheard-Walwyn.

Kelly, T. (1970) *A History of Adult Education in Great Britain*. Liverpool, Liverpool University Press.

2. Morley's Art and Design

Morley's Art Collection and the Artists' International Association
Medley, R. (1983) *Drawn from the Life: A Memoir*. London, Faber & Faber.
Morris, L. & Radford, R. (1983) *A.I.A.: Story of the Artists' International Association, 1933–53*. Museum of Modern Art, Oxford.

3. Morley's Music

Morley's Choirs
Holst, I. (1938) *Gustav Holst*. London, Oxford University Press.
Stuart, C. 'Full Score' *Musical Times*, 1951.

A Harmonica at the Feast: Holst and Thaxted
The Times 12 June 1911.
Gibbs, A. (2001) *Holst Among Friends*. London, Thames Publishing.
Holst, I. (1938) *Gustav Holst*. London, Oxford University Press.
Gustav Holst's letters to W.G. Whittaker, 18 June 1916 and 4 June 1917.
More magazine (1976) 'Dulcie Nutting talks to Roger Lucas about Holst'.
Morley College Annual Report for 1908–09.
Morley Magazines July 1911, September 1916, Sept–Oct 1917, Sept–Oct 1918 and May–June 1976.
Short, M. (1990) *Gustav Holst: The Man and His Music*. Oxford, Clarendon Press.
Undated letters from Jack Putterill to Graham Treacher.

Tippett at Morley
ed. Robinson, S. (2002) *Michael Tippett: Music and Literature*. Aldershot, Ashgate.
ed. Gloag, K. & Jones, N. (2013) *The Cambridge Companion to Michael Tippett*. Cambridge University Press.
Cecily Pile archive (at Lambeth Archives).

Cardew and the Morley Scratch
Cardew, C. (1974) *Stockhausen Serves Imperialism*. London, Latimer New Directions.
Cornelius Cardew Archive.
ed. Prévost, E. (2006) *Cornelius Cardew, A Reader*. Harlow, Copula.
Tilbury, J. (2008) *Cornelius Cardew (1936-1981): A Life Unfinished*. Harlow, Copula.
Private collections

Supporting Young Talent
'Central Tutorial School for Young Musicians' first prospectus (1962).
Sugden, J. (1989) *A History of the Purcell School*. Harrow on the Hill, The Purcell School.

4. Morley's Magic Casements

Introduction
Geddes Poole, A. (2013) *Philanthropy and the Construction of Victorian Women's Citizenship: Lady Frederick Cavendish and Miss Emma Cons*. Toronto, University of Toronto Press.

Drama
Winifred Leigh Theatre Archive.

Dance
Adamson, A. (2001) 'Jane Winearls – Britain's first full-time lecturer in dance'. *The Guardian* (online).

Carr, J. (2010) 'Claiming their space: virtuosity in British jazz dance' from *Dance and Spectacle: Annual Conference of the Society of Dance History Scholars, 8–11 July 2010*, University of Surrey, Guilford, UK.
Claid, E. (2006) *Yes? No! Maybe.... Seductive Ambiguity in Dance*. London, Routledge.

Horses for Courses
Island Planetarium website:
http://www.islandastronomy.co.uk

Acknowledgements

Like any creative project, this book is the product of extensive and fruitful collaboration. The contributions reflect the powerful collective spirit that has characterised Morley over the last 125 years and we are grateful for the commitment and work of everyone involved, whether it is writing for the book or supplying images.

However, special thanks must go to Nick Rampley for his creativity, inspiration and leadership of the project and for his tireless efforts to provide an important archive celebrating Morley's heritage and its role in adult education. Many aspects of this project have also been made possible by the research, commitment and hard work of Elaine Andrews who has supported many of the contributions with her knowledge and love of Morley.

Picture credits

Many of the images featured in this book came from the Morley College archives. Much of the modern photography has been taken by Morley photography students on City and Guilds levels 2 and 3 courses, taught by Paul Kemp. The College's art collection was photographed by Tom Gates and Julia Horbaschk. Images from other sources are listed opposite. Every effort has been made to contact the copyright holder of work used in the book, but in the case of an inadvertent omission, please contact the publisher.

82 © Eve Arnold/Magnum Photos; 45 (M), 53, 62 (L) © The Artist; 27 (R), 54 (TL), 55 (BR), 81 (T) © The Artist's Estate/Bridgeman Images; 100–1 Catherine Ashmore; 75 (T) Erich Auerbach/Getty Images; 58 (L), back cover James Aylwood; 91 (T) Tony Barette/Daily Mail/REX; 50 (TL), 50–1 (T), 51 (TR) © The Estate of Edward Bawden; 75 (TL) David Bendix; 135 (T) Andrea Brown; 57 (R), 98 (TL), 99 (TL) Susan Bryant; 65 (L) Design and manufacture by Patsy Abbott, modeled by Katka Kate Madzin, photo by James Robert Buttenshaw; 92, 93 Michael Chant and Carole Finer; 49 (TR), 108 (B) © City of London; 39 (L) © Condé Nast Archive/Corbis; 50 (L) (BL) Robin Cops and Judy Millett; 45 (T) © James Corbett/Alamy; 141 (T) Jameson Davis; 41, 157 Tina Delaney; 55 (TR) © The Estate of Peter de Francia, courtesy James Hyman Gallery, London; 38 Karen Frost; 75 (R) The John Gardner Estate; 132 (B) Caroline Gervay, courtesy of Project Phakama UK; 107 © GL Portrait/Alamy; 87 (T) Aaron Graubart; 26, 33 (T) Maggi Hambling; 44 (R) Jacqui Hawking; 144 (L), (BL) Ann Hignell; 21 (T) Joseph Hipgrave; 64–5 Costume by Alice Angus for Megan Balabey, photo © John Holmes 2013; 37, 72 (TL) © Hulton-Deutsch Collection/CORBIS; 22 (B), 30–1, 42 (L), 115 (TL), 118 (L) Imperial War Museum; 55 (R) © Jane Joseph. All rights reserved, DACS 2015; 55 (TL) © Fondation Oskar Kokoschka/DACS 2015; 14, 14–15, 15, 21 (B) Lambeth Archives; 39 (B), 40–1, 64 (L), 65 (R), 141 (B) Marine Lecondre; 7, 39 (R), 44 (L), 60 (T) Karen Leo; 63 (T) Marian Lynch; 83 Suzie Maeder/Lebrecht Music & Arts; 114 (M) Ann McBroom; 132 (T) © The Estate of Dorothy Mead; 54 (R) © The Estate of Robert Medley, courtesy James Hyman Gallery, London; front cover, 55 (BL) © Morley College Art Collection; 76 (L) Will O'Brien; 133 (R), 135 (R), 136 Marguerite Perkin; 52–3 © The Piper Estate/DACS 2015; 104–5, 106 (R) William Potter; 8–9, 49 (TL) Private Collection; 145 (R) Elizabeth Reed; 52 (TL) © Bridget Riley 2015. All rights reserved, courtesy Karsten Schubert, London; 103 Deborah Roslund; 109 (BL) © Marco Secchi/Alamy; 141 (L) Helen Simpson; 58 (R) (B) Helen Smith; 57 (BL) Mario Socrates; 137 (TR) Women's International League for Peace and Freedom, Swarthmore College Peace Collection; 131, 145 (T) Geoff Tanner; 89 Nicholas Till; 138 © Topfoto; 4–5, 30 (B), 32, 47, 56–7, 61, 99 (TR), 99 (BR) Andrea Van Der Schyff; 113, 115 (B), 116 (L), 117, inside covers Gosia Wilda; 26–7 Paul Wilson; 45 (BL) John Winter

CONTRIBUTING AUTHORS

Jade Amoli-Jackson completed Morley's Acting Studio course in 2008. *Moving a Country* is her debut collection of poetry and prose telling stories of life growing up in rural Uganda.

Shirley Anderson occupied various administrative positions at Morley during the 1980s and 1990s, including PA to Vice Principal Raymond Rivers. She has organised the College's family concerts for over 30 years and continues to do so.

Elaine Andrews has been the College's librarian since 2006, having joined Morley in 2001.

Caroline Shola Arewa taught massage at Morley 1989–98. She is now a wellness coach, speaker and author.

Wanda Barford is a poet who studied at Morley with Christopher Reid and Maurice Riordan.

Adrian Bartlett is an artist and printmaker who has exhibited regularly at the Royal Academy Summer Exhibition, represented the UK at the Florence International Print Biennale and holds solo exhibitions in Greece and the UK. He taught at Morley 1963–99, establishing the printmaking studio and serving as Head of Department.

Anne Bracht was College Librarian 1980–95.

Cass Breen was the College's Deputy Principal 2008–13, having previously been Head of the Faculty for Arts, Teacher Training and Counselling at the City Lit. She also taught at Morley in the 1980s on the community learning programme.

Natasha Briant taught cello 1994–6 and now practises as a music therapist.

Cate Brick is a dance student, professional dancer and teacher.

Andrea Brown is an award-winning singer, vocal coach and choral conductor. She has been Morley's Director of Music since 2009 and is the former conductor of the Morley Chamber Choir.

Alison Cox is Head of Composition at the Purcell School for Young Musicians and founder of The Commonwealth Resounds! She was awarded the OBE in 2012 for services to music in the community.

Sandra Clapham has been a member of the Morley Chamber Choir since 2011.

Judy Craven taught various social science and study skills courses at Morley between 1976 and 1999, and served as Head of the Fresh Start programme and as Access to HE Co-ordinator at various points during the 1990s.

David Culver is the chair of Morley Medieval.

Katherine Darton has attended the Chamber Music and piano accompaniment class at Morley for some years.

Antonia Del Mar is a musician and Alexander Technique teacher. She has taught violin, viola and string group classes at Morley since 1981.

Margaret Drabble is an acclaimed author of novels, screenplays, plays and short stories, as well as biographies and works of literary criticism. She was awarded the CBE in 1980, made DBE in 2008, and was awarded the Golden PEN Award in 2011. She taught at Morley 1969–80.

Hazel Elam has been a long-standing singing and French student at the College.

Simon Emmerson is a distinguished electro-acoustic composer and performer. After many years as Electroacoustic Music Studio Director at City University, London, he moved to his current post as Research Professor at De Montfort University, Leicester.

Roger Foggit taught many social science courses between 1977 and 1985. He was Director of Social Studies and Community Education at the College in the early 1980s and Head of Social and Community Studies 1988–9.

Hilary Friend is currently on the sound art course at Morley, having taken a number of music courses since 2008.

Tamara Galloway has been a Morley student since 2012, following a wide variety of music courses, as well as trying out Latin and Flamenco.

Celia Gibbs taught English literature and study skills courses at Morley in 1986–98.

Anthony Gilbert is a highly respected composer and was Head of Composition and Contemporary Music at the Royal Northern College of Music. He studied with Mátyás Seiber, Anthony Milner and Alexander Goehr at Morley and was on the music staff of the College 1972–4.

Michael Graubart is a composer and conductor who first taught at Morley in 1966. He was the College's longest-serving Director of Music, from 1969 to 1990, during which time he also served for a period as Head of Science. He continues to teach at the College today.

Maggi Hambling is a renowned artist and sculptor. Her best-known works include the sculpture *Scallop*, a four-metre-high steel sculpture on Aldeburgh beach dedicated to Benjamin Britten, her several works in the National Portrait Gallery and her celebrated series of North Sea paintings. She was the first Artist in Residence at the National Gallery, awarded the Jerwood Painting Prize in 1995 and made CBE in 2010. She has taught at Morley continuously since 1968.

Jane Hartwell has been the College's Gallery Manager since 1990.

Norma Higson was Head of the College's Languages department from 1981 to 1989.

Fay Hoolahan is an artist, filmmaker and lecturer who is Programme Manager for Digital Design, Film and Photography, and has taught at Morley since 1998.

Duncan Hooson is Programme Manager for Ceramics and has taught at Morley since 1986. He also teaches at Central St Martins and is Director of the Clayground Collective. He is author of *The Workshop Guide to Ceramic Techniques*.

Hazel James has been Morley's English Country Dance tutor since 1979 and is Vice-President of Morley College Folk Dance Club.

Cedoux Kadima Tshizanga completed the Art Foundation course with distinction at Morley in 2014, during which he was awarded the Clayground/Project Phakama Bursary to study ceramics. He had previously taken classes in photography and English at the College.

William Leigh Knight has been teaching various classes in vocal studies at the College since 2004.

Marian Lynch is Programme Manager for Textiles and has taught at Morley since 2005. She also teaches at the Interior Design School and runs The Colourhouse, a small hand-printed textiles and wallpaper company.

Gillian Moore is Head of Classical Music at London's South Bank Centre.

Jean Mumford has led the College's fashion section since 1989. Her own practice focuses on costume, and garment production, and she has worked on many significant theatrical and cinematic productions.

Gabriel Newfield is Secretary of the College's Clubs Co-ordination Committee and is a member of the London Ceramic Circle at Morley.

Anne-Marie Newland is the daughter of the late Joan Khachik, former Mayor of Southwark, and inveterate Morleyite.

Jon Newman is Archives Manager at Lambeth Archives and the author of several books on Lambeth's history.

Asako Ogawa is a ballet and Flamenco dance student.

Marguerite Perkin has been editor of the Morley Magazine since 2001.

David-Paul Pertaub has studied filmmaking, street photography and sculpture at Morley over the last two years, as well as Tai chi.

Ela Piotrowska was Head of Basic Skills at Morley from 1981–99 and returned to Morley as Principal of the College in 2008, retiring in 2015. In between she served as an HMI with Ofsted and contributed to the development of inspection practice in both adult and community learning and further education. She was awarded the OBE in the 2014 New Year Honours list.

Alan Powers is a distinguished art historian and writer, former Professor of Architecture and Cultural History at the University of Greenwich, past Chairman of the Twentieth Century Society, and an Honorary Fellow of the Royal Institute of British Architects.

Nick Rampley has been the College's Vice Principal since 2009.

Len Reilly is Archives Manager at Lambeth Archives and has produced several reproduction 19th-century maps for the Ordnance Survey.

Murray Rowlands is an author of novels, short stories and poetry, and a regular contributor on political matters to *Tribune*. He began teaching Humanities and Social Sciences at Morley in 1991 and retired from the College as Director of Languages and Humanities in 2006.

Neil Sanders is past secretary of Accordions at Morley, the Morley Accordion Orchestra.

Helen Santer is Chief Executive of the Waterloo Quarter Business Improvement District.

Jim Sewell is Chair of the London Ceramic Circle at Morley.

Howard Skempton is one of the UK's leading composers. He was a member of Cardew's experimental music class at Morley and was instrumental in founding the Scratch Orchestra.

Helen Smith has led the jewellery section since 2008 and is Programme Manager for Jewellery. She is also Visiting Lecturer at Central St Martins and runs her own jewellery business at Clements Yard studios.

Oliver Soden is a writer, scholar and broadcaster on music and the arts whose work has appeared in publications as diverse as *Gramophone*, *The Art Newspaper*, the BBC Proms Guide, and in peer-reviewed academic books and journals. He is currently writing a book on Tippett's vocal music. He is also an occasional member of the Morley Chamber Choir.

John Stephens has been a Governor of the College since 2006, serving as Chair of the Governing Body, 2012–15. He is Emeritus Professor of the University of the Arts, London, and a former Dean of London College of Communication.

Suzan Swale began teaching painting and drawing at Morley in 1979 and currently leads the Gallery Visits course.

Timothy Taylor is Programme Manager for Dance and has also been teaching acting at Morley since 2005. His own work crosses different genres of performance including dance, straight drama, musical theatre, comedy-sketch and song recital.

Antonia Till has worked in publishing with Penguin, Virago and Bloomsbury, and as a tutor-counsellor and specialist literature tutor for the Open University, and has also been a judge in two literary competitions. She has been involved with Morley since 1962 as student, occasional tutor and wife of Principal Barry Till.

Nicholas Till is Professor of Opera & Music Theatre at the University of Sussex, the author of numerous books and articles on the subject, and editor of *The Cambridge Companion to Opera Studies*. He was Associate Director of the Morley Opera Group 1986–7 and also taught music and drama on the College's community programme.

Suky Tomlins is Chair of the College's Student Council and a member of the College's Governing Body. She was formerly Head of Basic Skills, then Vice Principal at Brent Adult and Community Education Service.

Graham Treacher is a conductor and composer. Between 1962 and 1967, he conducted the Morley Choir, The Morley Symphony Orchestra and the Opera Group, as well as teaching musicianship classes.

Terry Trickett is currently principal clarinet in the Morley Chamber Orchestra and has been a member of Morley orchestras for longer than the College has extant records! In 2012, he was the soloist with the MCO in Weber's 2nd Clarinet Concerto.

Alan Tuckett is President of the International Council for Adult Education and the former Chief Executive of the National Institute of Adult Continuing Education, during which time he was awarded the OBE. 'Seriously Useless Learning', his collected columns for the *Times Education Supplement*, was published in 2014.

Janet Vaux is Secretary of Morley's Rambling Club.

Mary Van de Water has been a long-time student of the College, pursuing jewellery and singing classes, amongst others. She was for many years Chair of the Class Representatives Committee.

Kate Vicic was a student on the College's Textiles Foundation course (2009–11), having taken the City and Guilds Patchwork and Quilting Certificate over the previous two years.

Sheila Vollmer is Programme Manager for Sculpture and has taught at Morley since 1995. She exhibits widely in the UK and abroad, and her work is in several major collections.

Jenny Vuglar teaches Art History at Morley and is Associate Lecturer at the Open University, specialising in post-war British art. She is also a published playwright and poet.

Julia Wood is the Curriculum Area Manager for Access, Dance, Humanities and Health, having first joined the College as a tutor in Complementary Health. She is a complementary therapy practitioner specialising in sports injury rehabilitation.

SUBSCRIBERS

Siji Abiodun
Dayo Adeshina
Marian Avsejs
James Aylward
Fenella Juanita Barker
Astrid Hoang Brown
Ruth Brown
June Buckley
Sara Burgess
Jo Cannings
Norma Nongnute Chan
Michael Chant
In memory of Barbara Christie
Andrew Christos
Circaidy Gregory Press
Sandra Clapham
Joanna Clark
Erin Clarke
Jon Cole
Peter Collyer
Graham Cooper
T. Corvi-Mora
Camilla Cox
Angela Croft
Kate Danziger
Katherine Darton
Antonia Del Mar
Paul Drinkwater
Hazel Elam
Maureen Margaret Mary Galloway
Tamara Eileen Galloway
Carol Garrison
Enid Gayle
Rita Godfrey
Tony Goldman
Michael Gornall
Julie Green
Heather Haig-Prothero
Mary-Elizabeth Hellyer
Stephen Hewitt
Julie Hillary
Joseph Hipgrave
Cliff Hobby
Robin Hood
Cyd Jenkins
Annette Jones
Jane Joseph
Christine Keiffer
Stephen Ketteridge
William Leigh Knight

In memory of Yvonne Lattimore
Lynda Levy
Margaret Lion
Darryll Lunn
Aileen Lutton
Marco Macchitella
Polly MacLean
Richard Martin
John Massey
M. McMenemy
Moira Metcalf
Linda Morrell
Helena O'Donnell
OCN London
Sara Osman
Penelope Peacock
Marguerite Perkin
Ela Piotrowska
Hugo Plowden
Michelle Punt
Diane and Derek Purcell
Nick Rampley
Camilo Salazar
Neil Sanders and Viv Aylmer
Anne Scott
Brian R. Sewell
J. R. Sewell OBE
Hardip Sidhu
Pawel Siwczak
Helen Smith
Jane Smith
Rory Hyde Smith
Tansy Spinks
Alison Sproston
Philip R. Stanesby
Suzan Swale
Wendy Taylor
Jeanette Locke Thomson
Stephen Thorpe
Alison Tomlin
Chris and Suky Tomlins
Tontxi Vazquez
Heather Walker
Mary van de Water
Ann Watkins
Marcel Weidner
Billy Weston
Katherine Louise Wilkin
Jim Williams
Julia Wood

INDEX

Principal coverage is denoted in **bold**; illustrations are in *italics*